BATTLEGROUNDS
EUROPE

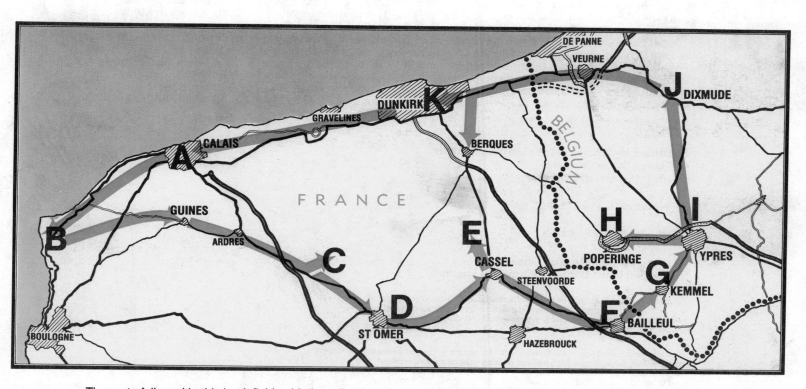

The route followed in this battlefield guide is outlined on the map above, special features being indicated by a letter of the alphabet (see contents page). The total distance is approximately 250 miles, although certain features may be easily omitted according to the reader's interests.

NIGEL CAVE

Additional research
JON COOKSEY

Wharncliffe Publishing Limited

With the twentieth century barely begun the world became embroiled in a war that was to set the scene for a new violent age. Although the Great War of 1914—1918 was truly a global affair, it was France and Flanders that became the main killing ground when the nations marched out to assert their sovereignties. The institutions of the day encouraged the waves of patriotism and nationalism swilling over the people and the slaughter began. Just over twenty years later and the Great Powers once again opened hostilities, and once again it was Europe that became the main area over which the battles raged.

Since the end of the Second World War two opposing blocs of nations have sat on the alert, ready once again to engage in conflict should either side feel that a need had arisen. Without a doubt, especially since 1914, this particular area has been the world's arena — the battleground of mankind.

This guide is one man's look at locations, incidents and features of the nations' conflicts, especially where indications of conflict still remain to be seen, usually in durable concrete.

Beginning with the busy port of Calais, Nigel Cave enters the arena and looks at the town itself, which saw a desperate rearguard action fought by 30th Infantry Brigade in May, 1940. The guide then takes us along a short section of Hitler's Atlantic Wall defences to the museum at Audinghen, near the small seaside resort at Wissant. From there we are directed inland to a site that heralded the space age — the V2 German rocket base at Eperleques. A short diversion is made to the site of the massacre of some Royal Warwickshire men by the SS in May 1940. Now we move into an area heavily contested in World War One: first the area around Kemmel where some famous personalities served and then on to the notorious Ypres Salient. From the rebuilt town of Ypres we are directed to where selected actions are described on the ground and in some cases something remains to be seen and examined. Northwards out of the Salient area we are directed to visit the Trench of Death, a preserved trench system on the banks of the Yser River, and get at this point an intriguing look at an ignored German bunker still with its armour plated weapon slits. Finally, the guide travels the coastline back to Calais via Dunkirk, where the British Expeditionary Force escaped to fight another day.

Nigel Cave's selection of sites and incidents of the two world wars is a personal one and this should be kept in mind should any be tempted to enquire why such and such an action has been omitted.

We have tried to keep this guide simple and easy to follow by illustrating the area as we find it today. Where possible we include pictures of what it must have been like for men of the warring sides, thus aiding the student of history to get the feeling of being there on the battleground of Europe during the conflicts of our century.

The Publishers

Published by Wharncliffe Publishing Limited
47 Church Street, Barnsley
South Yorkshire. S70 2AS

© Wharncliffe Publishing Limited, 1990

ISBN 1 871647 02 9

Printed by Yorkshire Web Offset
(A Division of the Barnsley Chronicle Limited)

Front cover: Painting by Terence Cuneo of The Rifle Brigade's last stand at Bastion 1, Calais, May 1940. *Reproduced by kind permission of the Managing Trustees of The Royal Green Jackets.*

Below: Advance Dressing Station, Feuchy Chapel, near Tilloy, April 1917.

TAYLOR LIBRARY

Contents

Introduction

When wandering the flat, rather uninspiring ground of Flanders fields it is well to bear in mind why the British seemed to be almost permanently fighting her wars here: there was nothing haphazard about it.

In 1914 it was not just some sentimental idea that called on the Government to defend poor little Belgium; no 'scrap of paper', as the Kaiser might remark. British trading interests would find it completely unacceptable to have the major trade entry route at the control of her industrial adversary, Germany. The British have, therefore, found it in their interest for hundreds of years to intervene actively in the affairs of Flanders: whether it be the establishment of the long-lived English outpost of Calais by Edward III, of Boulogne by Henry VIII or of Dunkirk by Oliver Cromwell. The British intervened to guarantee Belgian territory after its war of independence from the Dutch (1830), and went to war to preserve that neutrality in 1914.

Much of what has happened in the past has disappeared — but often there are remnants of the past which excite interest and curiosity — even if it is only the name of the place. For me often standing on the place where some event of great importance took place is enough to excite enthusiasm; but frequently there is far more. In this account of Flanders I have engaged on a personal enthusiasm — missing much out that may be seen, either because there is a lot already written or because of the dictates of space. So there is no attempt to be comprehensive — rather to be as informative as possible on the places that I have selected. It is now twenty years since I first went to Ypres as a young boy: it continues to hold its fascination. The route that I have taken starts from Calais, follows the coastline to the west a short distance before striking inland, passing through Henry VIII's fortified outpost of Guines, the site of a V2 Flying Bomb position at Eperlecques, on to the stately Cathedral city of St. Omer and then strike east towards Bailleul and towards the Belgian border. Just towards the north west (still in France) is the great vantage point of Cassel, which is immortalised in the nursery rhyme about the Grand Old Duke of York. Entry to this part of Belgium brings us to the Heuvelland, the hill country, which reaches its highest point at Kemmel. From here can be seen Messines ridge which literally had much of its top blown off by British mines in June 1917, a prelude to Passchendaele: for slightly to the north east is to be observed the saucer shaped low ridge surrounding the city of Ypres (Ieper): here armies fought and bled for four years.

Much of this guide concerns itself with the men and places of the Ypres Salient.

The trip includes some of the battles of 1940 and the rearguard actions that were to lead to the Dunkirk evacuation, a port which had also been owned by the British before, when Cromwell's armies helped to capture it from the Spanish and Charles II decided to sell it to the French.

Flanders is by no means an outstandingly beautiful part of the continent; the inspiration and source of wonder to us lies in the deeds that have taken place there over history. By actually seeing an area that appears so often in our history we should be better able to appreciate our involvement here. The stark reminder of the cost of policy decisions lies in the hundreds of British cemeteries that scatter the landscape; the coldness of death is lifted by the beauty and care that characterises them.

Besides, history is not all death and gloom — there is much to find amusing here as well, whilst the visitor should make the most of the local traditions (not to mention the beer) that bring, especially the Belgians, to holiday in this part of the world.

Dedication

To Lieutenant Colonel A. C. H. (Robbie) Robinson DSO,
TD, Bronze Star (USA), a survivor of the horrors of
Passchendaele, who died on his way home after a
memorable Armistice Tour with the WFA to Ypres in 1984.
May he, and all who fought in that conflict, rest in peace.

(A) CALAIS

To the majority of Britons who first go to the continent by ship, their first view of France will be Calais. They are following ancient precedents, for ever since the town was captured by Edward III in August 1347 it has been a favoured entry to France, with the relatively short crossing (a Godsend given the notorious storms and discomforts of Channel crossings) and its reasonably good access to Paris. In fact it is the major passenger port of France. The vast increase in this traffic has helped to underline the split into two (north and south, old and new) of the town.

As the car driver emerges from the ferry or hovercraft he or she is normally too concerned with ensuring that the correct side of the road is being used, that the passports have been found, and with a bit of luck that the control points will not ask too many questions in French, to take much notice of immediate surroundings. If things are taken slowly, however, both at the Ferry Port and at the Hoverport there exist the remnants of huge bunkers to be viewed that formed part of the Atlantic Wall that the Germans erected during their years of occupation. The drunken appearance of those near the car ferry is due to demolition work in progress.

They are situated behind a more ancient part of the fortifications, well over two hundred years older, part of the outer redoubt and moat of the town. Feeling that the north French coast was the most vulnerable to an allied invasion this is where the German command fortified most, and kept their reserves most accessible.

Although close in proximity to the English coast, the Germans seemed to have ignored certain historical lessons - that this area has rarely been used as an invasion route, not least because of the treachery of the coasts here. It is a point worth noting that there are very few large natural harbours on the French coast before one gets to Brest.

1940 — A desperate defence

For the interested visitor, the desperate defence of Calais by Nicholson's 30 Brigade can provide an interesting and enlightening tour. There is still a good deal to see, and, if the imagination is allowed a little freedom, it is possible to stand at various points in the town and reflect on what it must have been like for the men involved in that siege. This is particularly true in the case of what was once known as the Old Town of Calais-Nord. Although some 95% of Calais-Nord, which is now most famous for its role as a car ferry terminal, was destroyed, it is still possible to explore certain fortifications and features which were of particular significance to both the British and French defenders and their German assailants.

Above left: The peculiar shaped Harbour Master's Office which approximates the site of Bastion 1. Bastion 1 was the first of twelve strongpoints which once surrounded the city of Calais. It was on the grass covered mound behind the office building where men of The Rifle Brigade made their last stand against the German infantry on Sunday afternoon, 26 May, 1940 (see front cover).
Above: Burghers of Calais, the famous sculpture by Rodin and behind is the Town Hall (Hotel de Ville) the tower of which was used effectively by German snipers during the fighting in 1940.

Below: The Rifle Brigade memorial close by the Harbour Master's Office.

Right: A Panzer Division on the move through France in May 1940.

On 4 June 1940, Winston Churchill stood at the despatch box in the House of Commons and delivered one of the most memorable speeches ever to have been heard in that great chamber. In that speech, which came to epitomise the weary but unbroken spirit of the British in those uncertain days of WW2, Churchill spoke of a 'British Brigadier' who had led a stubborn resistance in the face of overwhelming German forces. He went on to say: "We shall fight on the beaches . . . we shall fight . . . in the streets. We shall never surrender." Indeed, the British Brigadier of whom Churchill spoke had refused to surrender the town of Calais to a German Panzer Division. Brigadier Claude Nicholson, and his brigade of fine troops, consisting of 2

Battalion the King's Royal Rifle Corps (60th Rifles), 1 Battalion the Rifle Brigade and 3 Royal Tank Regiment, (all regular troops) along with the Queen Victoria's Rifles, a well respected Territorial unit, had fought in the streets and on the beaches side by side with 800 French soldiers and sailors. After four days the town was finally taken and those who had survived the German onslaught were taken prisoner, but they had fought, in many instances, to the last bullet.

It had been a long and bloody struggle; a fight to the finish which raged from barricade to barricade and from house to house. It produced four days and three nights of taut nerves, of uncertainty, of heat, dust, raging thirst and hand to hand fighting in the narrow streets of this channel port.

After all the elements of his force had been landed and placed under his command on 23 May, Brigadier Nicholson was faced with a barrage of conflicting orders. At first he was ordered to aid the garrison at Boulogne to the west. There was then a proposal to send his brigade to St. Omer to join up with the British Expeditionary Force (BEF) main body under Lord Gort, VC, and finally he was ordered to send a sizeable portion of his brigade to accompany 350,000 rations to the developing beachhead at Dunkirk. All these ideas were, however, abandoned, and the offensive nature of the brigade was transformed into a defensive one as the Wehrmacht continued its scything sweep through France. Nicholson's political masters — Prime Minister Churchill and his Secretary of State of War Anthony Eden, determined not to evacuate the Brigade to freedom, but rather instructed its commanding officer to hold on at all costs. The reasons for this were twofold. The French insisted that the Channel ports be held,

Map labels:

Ostend • Bruges
DUNKIRK
CALAIS
Furnes
Bergues • **Dunkirk Perimeter**
Guines
Wormoudt
• Cassel
Ypres
R. Lys
Ghent
BOULOGNE
1 Pz
Hazebrouck
1st French Army
German Sixth Army
Pz 2
• Lillers Bethune
Lille
Pz 6
• Lens
Mons
Pz 8
Pz 3
Pz 10
Pz 4
Pz 7
Pz 5
St Valery
Abbeville
XIX Panzer Corps
R. Somme
German Infantry Divisions
FRENCH ATTACKS
Amiens
ALLIED LINE
0 10 20 30
Miles

SITUATION 22 to 29 MAY

although the British felt that Calais itself had no strategic value; still it was considered vital to hold Calais for the sake of allied solidarity. The second factor was that a hard fought defence of Calais by well trained regular and territorial troops side by side with the French defenders could well delay a large force of German troops which might otherwise have raced for Dunkirk. It was hoped that this delaying action would ensure a more successful evacuation for the huge numbers of Allied troops gathering there.

Sailing into the modern ferry port today, designed as it is to get the maximum number of people on and off the waiting ferries as quickly and as safely as possible, it is difficult to imagine the chaos and confusion on the quaysides which must have characterised those fraught days of late May 1940. The troops of Brigadier Nicholson's 30 Brigade had been so hastily dispatched to Calais that most of the units were pitched straight into a situation which was more akin to a farce had it not been so serious. Set against a backdrop of Luftwaffe bombing raids, the troops who landed in Calais were hampered by an annoying mixture of adherance to army regulations and inept organisation compounded by a lack of vital equipment. When 3 Royal Tank Regiment under Lt. Col. Reginald Keller landed at 1.15 p.m. on Thursday 23 May it had to wait until 4 p.m. for the arrival of its vehicle ship. With the threat of a Heinkel raid ever present the vehicles then had to be unloaded. All guns, including machine guns, were packed in thick mineral jelly, a nightmare to clean off. The tanks were at the bottom of the ship with light vehicles above, and all the petrol for them, 7,000 gallons of it, was packed on deck in four gallon cans. To make matters worse, no one seemed to know whether the ammunition for the guns and machine guns was on the vehicle ship or not.

As for 1 Battalion, Queen Victoria's Rifles, which had been trained in its role as a motor cycle reconnaissance battalion, it sailed for Calais on Wednesday 22 May without any means of transport whatsoever. Out of the 238 vehicles it had possessed in mid-May it had arrived in France without so much as a staff car. One third of its number — 556 officers and men — had not been issued with rifles since they were classed as cavalry and thus carried only revolvers. By Wednesday, 22 May the officers were still unarmed, they had not even been issued with revolvers!

To make matters worse as Nicholson's troops were arriving, many of the town's inhabitants and civilians from the outlying villages were intent on leaving via the docks. In spite of the best efforts of the soldiers who were guarding all roads into Calais many locals were converging on the town in order to make their escape ahead of the German advance. One of

Left: Leutnant-General Heinz Guderian, commander of XIX Panzer Corps, ordered one of his three panzer divisions, the 10th, to take Calais. They were kept busy for three vital days as the defenders fought until overwhelmed.

IMPERIAL WAR MUSEUM

the local families attempting to join that exodus was that of Mr. William John 'Taffy' Davies; the Welsh born father of Mr. David Davies who now owns the Hotel Normandy in Wissant and runs the Atlantic Wall Museum just off the D940 at Audinghen, Cap Gris-Nez.

'Taffy' Davies was born at Truddyn, North Wales and at the outbreak of World War One had joined the Royal Welch Fusiliers with whom he fought throughout that conflict. Then after

Below: British trucks leaving the Citadel's East Gate. A matter of days later German infantry stormed across this bridge to capture Brigadier Nicholson in his HQ.

Above: British Army transports in Calais Nord just prior to the attack.

demobilisation he had returned to France and married his French sweetheart whose father owned the Hotel Normandy a few miles west of Calais. He stayed in France and gradually took over his father-in-law's hotel, combining this with operating a transport business during the slack winter months. He was one of the first to organise charabanc excursions to the old World War One battlefields during the early 1920's.

David Davies was nine years old when the German Army pushed patrols up the coast to the west of Calais on Thursday, May 23, 1940. Hearing that the Germans were close at hand his father made plans to escape to the South of France but after an abortive attempt to get away the family returned to Wissant to contemplate their next move. In the middle of the night the Davies family were awoken by a sharp rap at the shutters. It was a neighbour with an urgent message, "Taffy, the Germans are at Cap Gris-Nez. Get out quickly." It was Friday, 24 May. David Davies takes up the story.

"My father went for my grandfather from the grocery shop next door while my Aunt dressed the two youngest children. My mother grabbed what she could; just two suitcases and seven kids and rushed us to the car. While my mother was preparing to leave my father saw the advance guards of Germans in the square outside the Hotel and went out to talk to them. The Germans asked if there were any British troops in the area, and, although the RAF had been stationed at St. Inglevert, my father said there were no troops around at all. The Germans failed to discern his Celtic origins and told him to go back to bed, but

we took the car and drove towards Calais. The Germans saw the car but they didn't fire."

All along the road from Wissant to Calais British Military Policemen (MP) and other troops were trying to prevent all civilian traffic from causing congestion and preventing the movement of the troops. Every time the Davies car was stopped Taffy would pull out his old British passport, tell the soldiers he had seven children and that he must get through, and each time he was allowed to pass.

Arriving in Calais the Davies family made its way towards the Pont Vetillard, the swing bridge near the present day ferry terminal. Here the children were taken across by British soldiers and led to a large building which was filled with hundreds of people awaiting evacuation. Inside the MP were filtering out those who were bound for England and those who would not be allowed to leave. David Davies again:

"My father said he wanted to talk to the British Vice Consul, a Mr. Carter who was a family friend. The particular MP said we would have to take our turn like everybody else. My father was ready to fight and voices rose. The British Vice Consul came over and said 'What's the matter Taffy?' and my father said, 'This silly bugger won't let me through and I've got seven kids with me.' The gangway was cleared and we were allowed to pass. We finally got through to Mr. Carter's desk and my father's passport was stamped 'O.K. for U.K.' It was the only stamp which allowed people to land in England. I think we left on one of the last fishing boats which left Calais."

Meanwhile other residents were on the move in the opposite direction. M. Henri Hidoine who is now the curator of the Calais War Museum (which is housed in a great concrete bunker built as a communciations centre by the Germans in the Parc St. Pierre, opposite the Hotel de Ville) recalls that there was an exodus of people to the countryside around Calais. He maintains that the people of Calais began to leave in large numbers from Friday, May 24 to escape the aerial attacks of the Luftwaffe. One of those on the move was M. Georges Fauquet, now a prominent member of the Calais Historical Society.

"I was not yet 16 but I had to leave Calais a few days before the main German attack. We left our house in the Rue du Havre and went out into the country 16 miles from Calais. As I was a schoolboy I continued to go to school in Calais St. Pierre from the country after the Germans had taken the town. Our house had been in the Old Town of Calais-Nord, and the fighting had been so bad that 95% of Calais-Nord had been

Below: A German 37mm anti-tank gun crew seen here speeding through the French countryside during the race for the Channel ports. Produced in quantity during the 30's and used in the Spanish Civil War, this weapon proved to be inadequate against the heavily armoured French and British tanks. Its failure to penetrate armour plating eventually earned for it the name 'Doorknocker'.

THE TANK MUSEUM

destroyed: The entire street on which we lived had completely disappeared. We lost everything — we had to start again."

So began the incredible suffering of the civilian inhabitants of Calais. Driven from their homes by the ruthless destruction of modern warfare, they were yet to be subjected to an almost total breakdown of their way of life. They were to suffer further hardships in the shape of food shortages, deportations and the continued fear of air attack for four more years until the Canadians came to liberate them. Only then could the rebuilding begin.

The situation Brigadier Nicholson found himself in when he arrived in Calais on Thursday 23 May was not an enviable one. After his first reconnaissance mission he decided that his small force could not possibly be used in an offensive capacity. What he decided he would have to try to do was to hold a heart-shaped outer perimeter of approximately seven miles which was formed by a continuous sytem of bastions, ramparts and ditches, and which surrounded not only the old town of Calais-Nord but the whole of the southern industrial suburb of Calais-St. Pierre.

At dawn on Friday 24 May a rain of heavy mortar shells on the QVR positions to the south west of the outer perimeter signalled the onset of the German 10 Panzer Divison attack. By that time the QVR's had acquired rifles and some Bren guns from some of the troops who had been disembarking. For the defenders of the western and southern ramparts Friday was to be a day of fierce fighting. On the western defences B and C Companies of 60th Rifles were subjected to the most terrific fire from dawn until 8 p.m., especially around the Pont Jourdan railway bridge where the Boulevard Leon Gambetta crossed the rail track.

By late afternoon the position on the west and south west perimeter had become critical and it became clear that the defensive line in that particular area could not be held for another day. Towards late afternoon a decision was made to withdraw to a line of posts which stretched across the centre of Calais-St. Pierre and Lt. Col. Miller, commanding 60th Rifles, ordered the three bridges over the canal to the south of Calais-Nord to be held. Those three bridges — Pont Freycinet, Pont Georges V and Pont Faidherbe — were to witness some of the bitterest street fighting of the entire battle. Explosives to blow the vital bridges into Calais-Nord had been landed but without the correct primers. It had been agreed that the blowing of the canal bridges should be a French responsibility but when the appropriate time came, for whatever reasons, the vital task was not carried out. The defenders had to resort to barricades — thus their fate was sealed. Later that evening Brigadier Nicholson moved his HQ from the clinic on the Boulevard Leon Gambetta

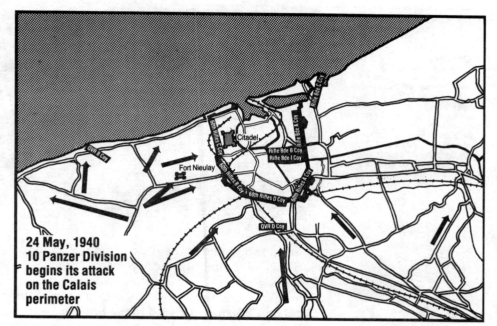

24 May, 1940 10 Panzer Division begins its attack on the Calais perimeter

to the Gare Maritime near the present day ferry terminal.

From 8 p.m. onward the ominious rattle of German tank tracks could be heard moving up through the streets of south west St. Pierre as the British withdrew to their next line of defence.

With the withdrawal to the inner perimeter the defence of Calais took on an ever more desperate air. The Germans were intent on 'squeezing the heart' of Calais and forcing the defenders onto the 'island' of Calais-Nord, surrounded as it was by waterways to the west, south and east and by the sea to the north. With their backs to the sea many of the defenders still believed that evacuation was a possibility but alas, that was not to be.

At 7 a.m. on Saturday 25 tentative patrols of 1 Battalion, The Rifle Brigade, now holding a precarious salient bounded by the Canal de Calais, the Canal de Marck and the Eastern ramparts from Bastion 2 to Bastion 4, saw armed German motor cyclists in the Boulevard Leon Gambetta and outside the Hotel de Ville. An

Above: Junkers 87 divebombers helped to overwhelm the defenders and reduce Old Calais to rubble.
Below: A German medium tank, Panzer MkIII, devoid of supporting infantry rattles through narrow streets flanked by burning buildings.

THE TANK MUSEUM

Right: Outside the walls of the Citadel today. The Citadel was an important feature for the defending troops — it was the key to the defence of Calais Nord. Both General Schaal, commanding the 10 Panzer Division and Brigadier Nicholson in command of 30 Brigade, knew that if the Citadel fell the old town and harbour could not be held for long. The Citadel was also of great pyschological value and Nicholson, fearing that the defenders would be the first to crack under the relentless artillery bombardment and bombing from the air, moved his HQ there at 6 am on Saturday 25 May. There he joined the French Commandant Le Tellier, the commanding officer of the French troops in Calais, to make a joint stand.

Below: Hotel de Ville situated close by the vital bridges into Calais Nord, provided an excellent sniper's platform for the Germans; it managed to escape damage during the battle. Note the German motorcycle combination in the foreground.

BUNDESARCHIV FREIBURG

hour later the men of the Rifle Brigade and those of 60th Rifles holding the waterfront from Pont Freycinet to Pont Faidherbe, groaned as the Swastika inched its way up the flag pole of the Hotel de Ville and fluttered in the breeze.

From the Hotel de Ville today it is a short walk to the centre bridge, the Pont Georges V, which was then being held by elements of D Coy of 60th Rifles under Lord Cromwell. At each of the three bridges road blocks were constructed using every abandoned vehicle which became available, and barricades were set up across the streets leading from the canals. Almost every house overlooking the waterfront along the Quai de L'Escaut and the Quai de la Tamise was turned into a defensive position. This was no easy task as the houses had to be first broken into and then cleared of all civilians and unarmed French and Belgian troops sheltering within. Throughout, the defenders faced the ever present dangers of Fifth Columnists; German snipers who had succeeded in infiltrating Calais-Nord and now fired on the British from behind. It was claimed that one of them had taken up a position atop the roof of the Church of Notre Dame with a sub machine gun. Other German snipers took up positions in the clock tower of the Hotel de Ville and made all movements around the bridge area and along the waterfront extremely hazardous.

At 11 a.m. men of D Coy of 60th Rifles saw an armoured vehicle approach the southern end of Pont Georges V carrying a white flag. General Schaal, commanding 10 Panzer Division, was about to launch an all out attack on the inner perimeter and the Citadel with every available gun and with dive bomber support. Before that however, he first tried to save lives and win some time. At the Hotel de Ville the Mayor of Calais, Andre Gershell, had been taken whilst he sat at his desk, and the Germans decided to send him to see Brigadier Nicholson to ask for the formal surrender of the defending forces. Gershell was taken to Brigadier Nicholson who had by now moved his HQ to the North East Bastion of the Citadel to be with the French army commander, Commandant Le Tellier. Brigadier Nicholson's reply to the German request was resolute. "If the Germans want Calais" he said, "they will have to fight for it." Andre Gershell and his interpreter were not permitted to return and were locked in the Post Office in the Place Richelieu until Calais finally fell. Nicholson's refusal to surrender was the signal for an incredibly ferocious bombardment of the Citadel and Fort Risban.

The bombardment was as heavy as any Nicholson's troops had suffered so far. From the Citadel to Fort Risban the shells screamed down on the defenders. At the roadblocks and in the houses along the waterfront machine gun bullets thudded into the furniture and vehicle barricades and whined crazily off the walls and pavements. At the Pont Mollien, mortar bombs set fire to the bridge and Stuka dive bombers terrorised the Rifle Brigade in their salient behind the Canal de Marck.

At 2 p.m. Nicholson received a message from Eden which told him that "The defence of Calais to the utmost is of the highest importance . . . The eyes of the Empire are upon the defence of Calais." At around 3 o'clock Schaal once more attempted to force Nicholson into surrender and sent Lieutnant Hoffman of 2 Battalion, 69 Rifle Regiment across Pont Georges V. There was an ominous lull in the battle as Schaal awaited Nicholson's reply. Hoffman demanded the immediate surrender of the Citadel otherwise, he promised, the whole of Calais-Nord was to be razed to the ground. In characteristic fashion Nicholson refused. Hoffman recrossed the bridge at 4.35 p.m. and the battle resumed.

Slowly, relentlessly the Germans applied more pressure to the British units defending Calais-Nord, particularly the Rifle Brigade and the units of the QVR which had withdrawn from their outlying positions by then. With 60th Rifles still fighting hard along the line of the canal the Rifle Brigade and the QVR retired along the Quai de la Loire and the southern shore of the Bassin des Chasses de l'Est towards the narrow neck of land which now houses the railway station and the car ferry terminal. It would be on that strip of land with their backs to the sea, that the Rifle Brigade and the QVR would make their final stand.

BUNDESARCHIV FREIBURG

At 3.30 in the afternoon of Saturday 25, just before he received a fatal wound from a shell splinter, Lt. Col. Chandos Hoskyns leading the Rifle Brigade agreed that a counter attack should be made along the Quai de la Loire by elements of I Coy under the already wounded Major Brush. Some 17 men moved forward past a British road block but intense fire stopped them in their tracks. Out of the swarm of bullets a truck raced towards them driven by a man in Belgian uniform. Sitting beside him with a pistol to the man's head was Corporal Lane of the Rifle Brigade. Lane had arrested the man as a suspected Fifth Columnist and had seen to it that the truck was loaded with wounded before forcing the captured man to drive back towards the British lines. When the driver was hit and the truck slewed to a halt 2 Lt Edward Bird ran forward and tried to restart it. At this point he was struck in the head and Major Brush and his men raced across to the truck, pulled the wounded from the blazing vehicle and dragged them back to the British position. 2 Lt. Bird managed to stagger back with them, but died half an hour later.

By 4.30 p.m. the Citadel appeared to those observers who could see it to be enveloped by a great wall of flame and from 6.30 p.m. another terrific artillery bombardment pounded the British positions. At 7 o'clock the bombardment suddenly ceased and the rumble of tracks heralded the appearance of German tanks at those three vital bridges which crossed the waterway separating Calais-St. Pierre from Calais-Nord. At Pont Faidherbe on the left of the 60th front three tanks followed by a saloon car

began to force the British road block but were repulsed when two of the tanks and the car were hit. At the centre bridge, Pont Georges V, the first tank across triggered a mine and the attack faltered. The situation was most critical at Pont Freycinet. Under cover of a heavy mortar barrage one tank forced the road block and was followed by German infantry. Although a valiant counter attack forced the tank to retire it was not enough to dislodge the German infantrymen who had now taken up firing positions in houses near the Citadel. As it began to grow dark the flames leaping from the burning buildings cast an eerie orange glow over the streets and barricades. The Germans had breached the inner perimeter and were preparing to finish the job.

Above: Smashed British barricade made up of army trucks on the Calais Nord side of the bridge — Pont Faidherbe. Note the shattered houses, these were used as cover by the British defenders as they tried to stop the Germans crossing into old Calais.

Below: General Ferdinand Schaal, commander 10 Panzer Division; he twice called for the British to surrender. Brigadier Claude Nicholson, commanding 30 Brigade replied to the demand: 'The answer is no, as it is the British Army's duty to fight as well as it is the Germans.' Hopelessly outnumbered the defenders fought on.

By kind permission HQ 16/5 Lancers

BUNDESARCHIV KOBLENZ

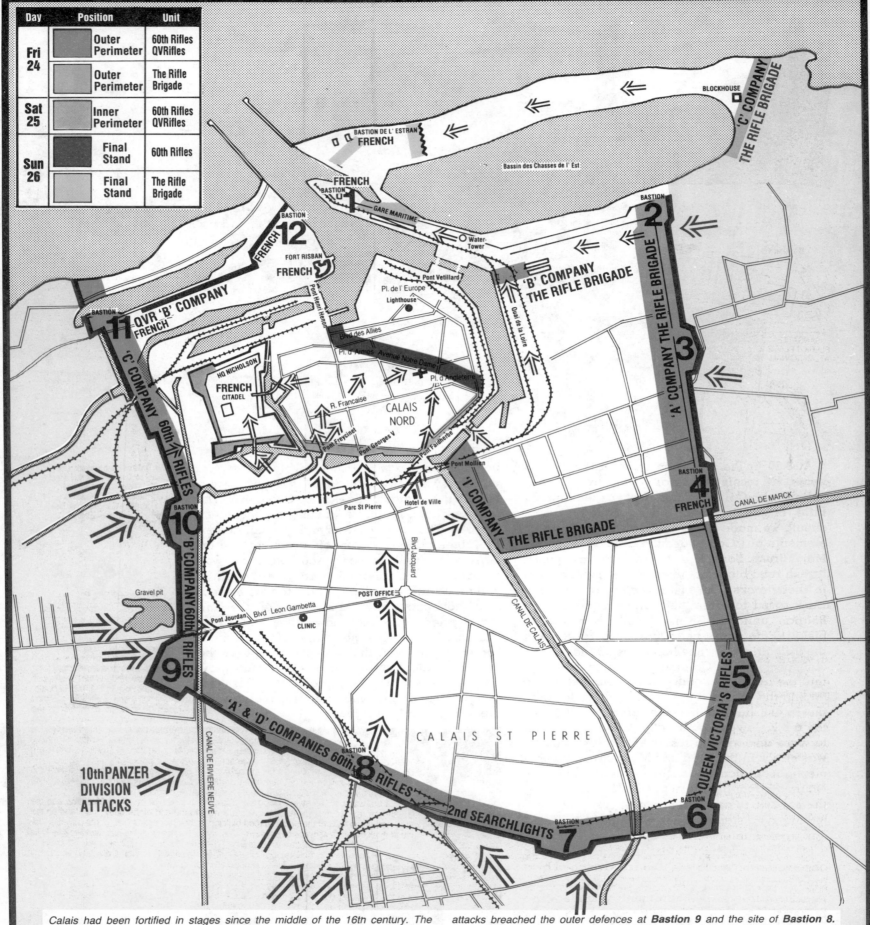

Day	Position	Unit
Fri 24	Outer Perimeter	60th Rifles QVRifles
	Outer Perimeter	The Rifle Brigade
Sat 25	Inner Perimeter	60th Rifles QVRifles
Sun 26	Final Stand	60th Rifles
	Final Stand	The Rifle Brigade

BLOCKHOUSE

'C' COMPANY THE RIFLE BRIGADE

BASTION DE L' ESTRAN
FRENCH

Bassin des Chasses de l' Est

FRENCH
BASTION 1

GARE MARITIME

BASTION 2

Water-Tower

'B' COMPANY THE RIFLE BRIGADE

'A' COMPANY THE RIFLE BRIGADE

BASTION 12
FRENCH

FORT RISBAN
FRENCH

Pont Vetillard

Pl. de l' Europe
Lighthouse

Blvd des Allies

BASTION 3

QVR 'B' COMPANY
FRENCH

BASTION 11

'C' COMPANY 60th RIFLES

HQ NICHOLSON

FRENCH CITADEL

Pl. d Armes Avenue Notre Dame

Pl. d Angleterre

R. Francaise

CALAIS NORD

Quai de la Loire

BASTION 4
FRENCH

CANAL DE MARCK

Pont Henri Henon

Pont Freycinet

Pont Georges V

Pont Faidherbe

Pont Mollien

'I' COMPANY

THE RIFLE BRIGADE

BASTION 10

'B' COMPANY 60th RIFLES

Parc St Pierre

Hotel de Ville

Blvd Jacquard

CANAL DE CALAIS

Gravel pit

Pont Jourdan Blvd Leon Gambetta

POST OFFICE

CLINIC

QUEEN VICTORIA'S RIFLES

BASTION 5

RIFLES

BASTION 9

'A' & 'D' COMPANIES 60th RIFLES

CALAIS ST PIERRE

CANAL DE RIVIERE NEUVE

10th PANZER DIVISION ATTACKS

BASTION 8

2nd SEARCHLIGHTS

BASTION 7

BASTION 6

Calais had been fortified in stages since the middle of the 16th century. The system of fortifications which Brigadier Claude Nicholson inherited, comprised of twelve bastions linked by ramparts and earthworks constructed between 1880 and 1900. On the eastern or Dunkirk side of Calais defences the ramparts and bastions were more or less intact. It was in that area that 1 Battalion Rifle Brigade under Lt Colonel Chandos Hoskyns took up positions upon their arrival. The western side of the defence perimeter was also strong. However the southern defences were weakened by the intrusion of railway lines; **Bastion 7** had been partially demolished and **Bastion 8** had disappeared completely. Those weak sectors were exploited by General Leutnant Ferdinand Schaal, commander of 10 Panzer Division. Nicholson's plan was to withdraw and take up an inner defence line behind the canals surrounding **Calais Nord**, should the outer perimeter become untenable. The defence of that inner perimeter hinged on the ancient **Citadel**, which was begun in 1560, rebuilt by Cardinal Richelieu in 1636 and enlarged by the military architect Vauban in 1680. On the evening of Friday 24 May German

attacks breached the outer defences at **Bastion 9** and the site of **Bastion 8**. Nicholson, who's HQ had been at the **Clinic** on **Boulevard Leon Gambetta,** had withdrawn and later established his HQ in the **Citadel.** By 8 am Saturday 25 May the swastika was flying above the **Hotel de Ville.** By that evening panzers were threatening the bridges which crossed into old Calais; also heavy attacks supported by Stuka dive bombers had forced 1 Battalion Rifle Brigade to pull back from the eastern perimeter towards **Bastion 1.** Throughout Sunday morning, 26 May, heavy fighting took place around all the bridges and the barricades on them were forced 3 pm. The defenders retired through the burning streets to take up their final positions. At 3.30 the Rifle Brigade were overwhelmed close to **Bastion 1.** In the **Citadel** Nicholson and his staff were taken at 4 pm. By 5 pm panzers had penetrated as far as the **Lighthouse** and fought the remaining defenders to a standstill. Isolated pockets battled on until their ammunition was used up. Nicholson had twice refused to surrender, declaring that if the Germans wanted Calais then they would have to fight for it.

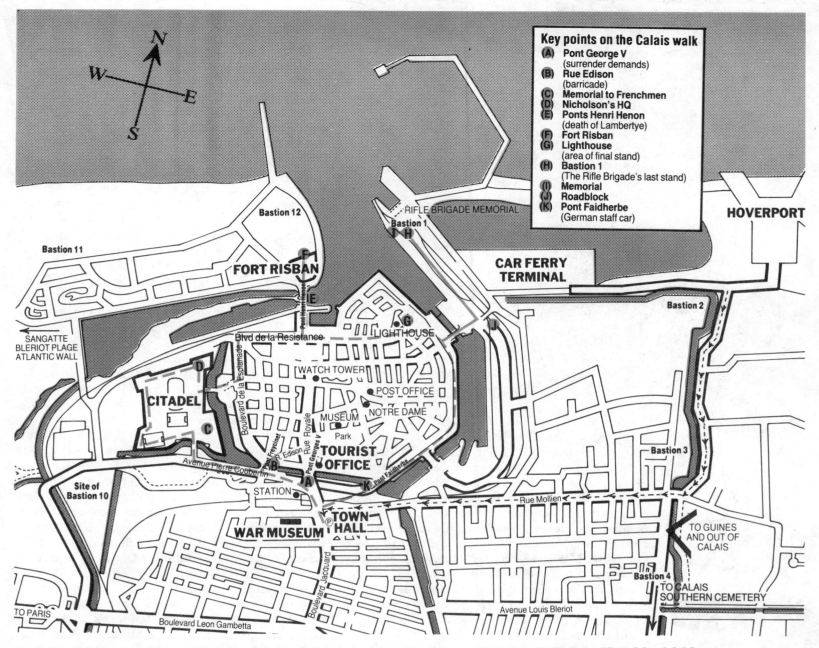

A walk around some of the key points which featured in the defence of Calais Nord in 1940

I suggest that visitors drive from the ferry terminal and head towards the **Hotel de Ville** (Town Hall) where ample parking is available. Note here the clock tower of the Hotel de Ville (see photo page 5) which provided an excellent platform for German observers and snipers in May 1940. From that vantage point marksmen and artillery observers could overlook Calais Nord, including the vital bridges, Freycinet, Georges V and Faidherbe where the British had blocked them with vehicles.

Proceeding into the **Parc St Pierre** (the park close by the statue of the Burghers of Calais) visit the **War Museum** which is housed in a concrete blockhouse within the park. The ferro concrete constuction was built by the Germans during the occupation and was used throughout the war as a communications centre by the German navy. The museum is open from 10 am to 5 pm and houses exhibits from the occupation. One room is dedicated to the Green Jackets, who hoplessly out-gunned and out-numbered, fought alongside some French units to the bitter end.

From the museum walk north past the railway station to **Pont Georges V (A)** the centre of the three bridges held by 60th Rifles. This bridge has undergone extensive reconstruction since 1940. It was at this point at 11 am on Saturday 25 May that Andre Gershell, the Mayor of Calais, arrived in a German armoured car with surrender demands for Brigadier Nicholson. Here also, four hours later at 3 pm on the same day, Leutnant Hoffman of the German 69th Rifle Regiment arrived on the same errand. Both requests were refused point blank by Nicholson (see page 10).

Walk west along **Avenue Pierre Coubertin** and the bridge **Pont Freycinet** then cross over towards the corner of **Rue Edison (B)**. It was across the end of this street (nearest the bridge) that the British had a barricade (see photo on page 16). It was here that Private Matthews, 60th Rifles, won the DCM when he backed up a truck in the street to help recover some of the wounded under heavy machine gun fire (see page 15).

Recross the bridge, which appears much as it did in 1940, and walk further west towards the **Citadel** entering by the South Gate. You will be following in the tracks of German infantrymen who forced their way into the stronghold on the afternoon of Sunday, 26 May. Note the memorial plaque on the wall of the inner gate. Once inside, and to the right, there is a memorial stone **(C)** to five young Frenchmen who were shot on that spot at dawn 3 September, 1944. They had been imprisoned in the Citadel for attempting an act of sabotage in the factory where they worked. A walk around the ramparts of the Citadel will reveal its great strength, although it is overgrown today. Imagine what it must have been like those 50 years ago, with Stuka dive bombers screaming down through the smoke-filled skies to drop their deadly loads on the desperate defenders. In the north east corner of the Citadel Brigadier Nicholson had his HQ **(D)** during the last two days of the battle (see photo on page 10). He was taken prisoner there at 4 pm on the Sunday afternoon; note the brick built entrances leading to tunnels. From the top of the ramparts at this point you can look out eastwards towards the harbour and another fort.

Leave the Citadel by the East Gate and turn left, heading north along the **Rue Jaques**

Vendroux and then east along **Blvd de la Resistance** towards the two bridges **Ponts Henri Henon (E)**. As you cross recall that it was at some point on one of the bridges that the French naval commander, Carlos de Lambertye, suffered a heart attack and died in the heat of battle. He had been returning to the Citadel after bolstering up some French marines who were getting nervous at the ferocity of the German onslaught. **Fort Risban (F)** is at the other side of the bridge and in 1940 was held by French troops. A walk round the earth ramparts and you will be able to see the grass covered depressions caused by the German bombardment. Note also the series of tunnels and entrances at ground level, also the remains of a chapel built at the time of Vauban in the 17th century. The concrete emplacements on top of the ramparts were constructed by the Germans during the occupation.

Recross the Ponts Henri Henon turning left and walk east along **Blvd des Allies** towards the area around the **Lighthouse (G)**. It was in that district during Sunday afternoon, 26 May, 1940 that panzers and supporting German infantry hunted out the remaining British soldiers.

Cross the water at the **swing bridge** and follow the signs for the **Gare Maritime** and the **Captainiere** (the harbour masters office). Walk right to the end of the quay and stand on the grassy mound in front of the oddly shaped building of the Captainiere (see photo page 5). The mound is all that now remains of **Bastion 1 (H)** and is the scene of the last stand of The Rifle Brigade. Close by is the **Memorial (I)** to The Rifle Brigade on the quayside with its cross of sacrifice marking the site of the final struggle (see photo page 5). A tunnel which housed many of the wounded during the battle, has disappeared in recent times.

Return towards the swing bridge, but before recrossing pause and consider that at that point and to the left was the site of a road block and barricade **(J)** of The Rifle Brigade. It was from there that a force under the command of Major Brush launched a counter attack at 3.30 pm on the Saturday. Here also Corporal Lane arrived in a truck from the direction of the advancing Germans with a gun pressed at the head of the driver, who was a German 'fifth columnist' (see page 11).

Recross the bridge by means of the pedestrian path, and walk south along the waterfront towards **Pont Faidherbe (K)**. At 1 am on Sunday 26, May, Corporal Humby and Rifleman Ewings, 60th Rifles, crawled across the bridge to search a German staff car which had attempted to cross with tanks the previous evening. Their journey across and back again took two hours (see page 15).

Note the houses along the **Quay de la Tamise** these have been completely rebuilt along with 95% of the rest of Calais Nord. It was from the original buildings running opposite the bridges that elements of 60th Rifles fired on the advancing Germans, as they forced the British road blocks (see pages 10 and 15).

Cross the canal at Pont Faidherbe (see photo page 11) and return to the Hotel de Ville. Allow a day if you intend to complete the whole walk.

13

Above: German artillery and the Luftwaffe reduced Calais Nord to rubble.

Above: German infantrymen pause to rest from the fighting.
Right: Remains of a British roadblock at the end of Rue des Thermes and the corner of Place d'Armes.

THE TANK MUSEUM

BUNDESARCHIV KOBLENZ

The final act of Saturday 25 May was the dive bombing of the few troops who remained to defend Bastion 2, but General Schaal, convinced now that the British would fight for every inch, decided to call a halt to the attack at 9.45 p.m. During the night the last British troops withdrew to their final positions. Messages received by Dover from Major Alexander Allen, second in command of the Rifle Brigade, near the Gare Maritime on that Saturday evening conveyed the gravity of the situation:

"Citadel a shambles stop Brigadier's fate unknown stop Rifle Brigade casualties unknown stop Being heavily shelled and flanked but attempting counter-attack stop Am attempting contact with 60th fighting in the town stop Are you sending ships stop

Quay intact in spite of very severe bombardment."

On the Western side of the battle front the Citadel was still being protected by a small mixed force of 60th Rifles under Captain Radcliff and French soldiers and sailors under the command of Capitaine de la Blanchardiere in Bastion 11.

This bastion has now disappeared and the only reminders of it on the sea side of the D940 out towards Bleriot Plage are the new apartment blocks which rise from a knoll due west of Fort Risban. The French soldiers and sailors inside Bastion 11 were in one sense volunteers as they had responded to a call by the French Naval commander in Calais, Carlos de Lambertye. Men like de Lambertye and Capitaine de la Blanchardiere have a special place in the hearts of the French since they, along with some 800 other French volunteers, fought to the last alongside the British forces.

At the beginning of the battle French naval gunners in some of the coastal batteries had used up their ammunition and were then ordered to spike their guns prior to evacuation. Carlos de Lambertye knew that if all the defences on the seafront were abandoned simultaneously then the way to the Citadel would be left wide open. In defiance of French naval orders de Lambertye appealed to the sailors who had left their positions, for volunteers to go back and defend the bastions. Capitaine Michel de la Blanchardiere, a staff officer of 21 French Infantry Division, was the first man to step forward followed by others who are remembered today as the 'Volunteers of Calais'. Instead of sailing away, these men stayed to hold the coastal defences. Carlos de Lambertye had his HQ at Fort Risban which had come under an incredible bombardment along with the Citadel and Bastion 12. This bastion is

now a caravan and camp site just north of Fort Risban on the western side of the harbour entrance and can be seen clearly from the ferry as it enters port.

Carlos de Lambertye, an old and sick man, was later to die of a heart attack as he made his way across the Ponts Henri Henon towards Fort Risban after a visit to his men in the trenches on the west side of the harbour. He had heard that a white flag had been shown and he had made a personal visit to allay their fears.

At 3 a.m. in the early hours of Sunday 26, the small force in Bastion 11 was attacked, and four hours later De la Blanchardiere had been badly wounded. By 1 o'clock that Sunday afternoon, after a stand of some ten hours, the Germans finally took Bastion 11. Of the French contingent only 17 were left alive and just 30 out of the 80 riflemen of the 60th were unwounded. The way to the Citadel was now open from the west.

On the waterfront there had been high drama at Pont Faidherbe during the early hours of Sunday. At 1 a.m. Lance Corporal Humby and Rifleman Ewings of 60th Rifles had risked their lives to cross the bridge to search the German saloon car which had attempted to follow the German tank across on the previous evening. The car was only 100 yards from a German post and from under the noses of the Germans the riflemen took papers from the pockets of a dead German pioneer officer and recrossed the bridge safely. The entire journey across the bridge and back, a distance of some 60 to 70 yards, had taken two hours.

At 5 a.m. the whole of XIX German Army Corps artillery opened up on 60th Rifles holding the waterfront, the Citadel and on Bastion 11 which by then had been under attack for two hours. The shelling increased in intensity from 7 o'clock, and from 9.30 a.m. wave after wave of Stuka dive bombers lashed Calais Nord with high explosives and incendiary bombs, turning what little was left of the old town into a raging furnace.

At 9.15 two German infantry companies attacked the lock near the Quai de la Volga under cover of a mortar barrage and at the same time another German infantry company had turned north and were fighting seaward along the Quai de la Loire, squeezing the Rifle Brigade ever deeper on to the narrow neck of land upon which the Gare Maritime and the remains of Bastion 1 now sit.

One hour later a vicious struggle developed at Pont Freycinet and Pont Georges V. From behind the burned out trucks at the road blocks and from behind piles of smouldering rubble which had once been elegant residences along the Quai de L'Escaut and the Quai de la Tamise, the men of 60th Rifles fired at the oncoming Germans. At the barricade on the corner of Rue Edison Captain Claude Bower of D Coy of the 60th fell wounded under a continuous stream of

machine gun fire. Concentrating all their fire on the barricade the Germans were intent on pushing through and the intense fusilade made it impossible for stretcher bearers to rush across the street to rescue Captain Bower. Amid the torrent of bullets Rifleman Matthews suddenly careered across the open street in a truck and backed it up to where the officer lay. Jumping out Matthews found Captain Bower to be already dead, but he removed several other badly wounded men and then made his escape unscathed. For this feat of heroism Rifleman Matthews was awarded the DCM.

It was now the turn of the 60th to be squeezed north eastward in the face of the German advance. After the death of Bower at the corner of Rue Edison, the barricades became unten-

Left: Fort Risban, photograph taken by the attackers shortly after its capture.
Below: Fort Risban today still showing signs of damage from the battle in 1940.

BUNDESARCHIV FREIBURG

Below: Germany infantrymen taking cover during an attack in the French campaign, May 1940.

THE TANK MUSEUM

BUNDESARCHIV KOBLENZ

Above: A hot spot of the battle for Calais Nord, the corner of Rue Edison, and the same spot now.

THE TANK MUSEUM

Right: British dead at a barricade in old Calais, believed to be Place d'Armes.

able. German tanks now pushed across Pont Freycinet and fired point blank at the defenders in the ruined houses. German infantry which followed the tanks were already swarming into the Rue Jean de Vienne and the Rue Francaise and were firing on the right flank of Lord Cromwell's D Coy, on their way to the Citadel. Lt. Col. Miller decided to withdraw his remaining troops in stages to make his last stand along a line of posts in the north east corner of Calais-Nord; from the Boulevard des Allies near Ponts Henry Henon up along what was then known as the Avenue de Notre Dame towards the Place d'Angleterre. C Coy withdrew from their positions along the sea front north of the Citadel to take up a line from Fort Risban to the north east corner of the Place d'Armes.

By 3.30 p.m. the Rifle Brigade had used up all their ammunition and reserves and had bitten deeply into the 20,000 rounds landed by the Royal Navy a few days earlier. The situation was now critical and they had been forced back to the mound on top of Bastion 1 which today is the site of the Capitainiere, the harbour masters HQ. In the regimental aid post in the tunnel beneath Bastion 1 lay the wounded, packed like sardines into the dark and filthy casemates, while the battle raged around them. The end was not long in coming. A little later the Germans, having forced Major Brush out of his trenches near the Bastion de L'Estran, had surrounded the remnants of the Rifle Brigade on top of Bastion 1. The excited voices of the German troops entering the tunnel and the

BUNDESARCHIV KOBLENZ

Left: View across Ponts Henri Henon, looking south east; the church of Notre Dame is on the left. All the buildings have been reduced to burnt out shells.

Left: Looking east from Quai de la Colnne. Smoke is coming from the burning oil depot on Rue de la Loire. Notice the white water tower on the left and compare with front cover painting.

clatter of weapons dropping to the floor signalled the end.

The coup de grace was delivered an hour later at the Citadel. With the crossing of Pont Freycinet and the infiltration of the streets surrounding Nicolson's HQ the Germans were beginning to take the upper hand. Panzers had surrounded the Citadel by 3 o'clock and half an hour later the German infantry had battered down the south gate and were fighting hard along the ramparts. Within 30 minutes the shelling suddenly stopped and a German Feldwebel charged across the inner courtyard towards Nicholson's HQ. It was 4.30 p.m. and the Citadel had finally fallen. Nicholson and the rest of the surviving defenders were taken prisoner. A short while later Fort Risban was overwhelmed and what was left of the units of 60th Rifles and QVR were fought to a standstill in the Place d'Angleterre and the Place de l'Europe opposite the Pont Vetillard swing bridge. By 5 p.m. the heroic defence of Calais had finally come to an end, apart from a few isolated pockets which continued to fight the Germans until they too ran out of ammunition and were overwhelmed.

As the daylight faded on the remains of Calais that Sunday evening an eerie silence reigned. At the barricades of Pont Freycinet, Pont Georges V and Pont Faidherbe; on the street corners near Rue Edison and the Place Norvege the British and German dead lay slumped among the smoking wreckage. Along the ramparts and in the bastions British and French defenders lay side by side where they had fallen during the desperate resistance. Those left alive were taken prisoner and were marched off to spend long years in captivity. Some of them, Brigadier Nicholson included, would not survive that ordeal.

Due almost entirely to the fact that all the survivors of the defending force who were left alive were taken prisoner, it is difficult to ascertain the exact number of casualties sustained in the fighting. It is estimated, however, that some 204 men of 60 Rifles, the Rifle Brigade and the QVR were killed in action and a further 100 were lost from The 3 Royal Tank Regiment and the Anti Aircraft, Anti Tank and Searchlights units involved. That left a little under 3000 men who were taken prisoner.

After the war with the benefit of several years of hindsight, Churchill was to write, "Calais was the crux. Many other causes might have prevented the deliverance of Dunkirk, but it is certain the three days gained by the defence of Calais enabled the Gravelines waterline to be held, and that without this . . . all would have been cut off and lost."

Below: British prisoners from 30 Brigade and some French prisoners awaiting transport away from Calais. An abandoned British Cruiser tank MkIII, seen here along with other abandoned vehicles on the Gare Maritime.

Above: Abandoned British trucks on approaches to the quayside.
Right: Entrances to Nicholson's HQ in the Citadel. He used tunnels under the ramparts in the closing phases of the battle.

Right: Fort Nieulay situated on the western approaches to Calais, still bearing the scars of the attack in 1940.

For further reading: 'The Flames of Calais' by Airey Neave, soldier and politician, who was one of the defenders in 1940. Publishers Hodder & Stoughton Ltd.

Fort Nieulay is an impressive testimonial to the genius of that great French military architect Vauban. Situated on the N1 to Boulogne about a mile west of the Pont Jourdan railway bridge and some three and a half miles from the ferry port, it was the scene of fierce fighting on Friday 24 May 1940 during the defence of Calais.

On Friday 24 May, Captain A.N.L. Munby with 50 men of the QVR and three from 1 Searchlight Regiment joined the French garrison at Fort Nieulay which consisted of Captain Herreman and some 40 French troops. Their objective was to delay the advance of the Germans from the direction of Boulogne. The attacks on the small force inside Fort Nieulay began at dawn on Friday 24 when shells started to fall around the position and German infantry emerged from woodland to the north of Coquelles. The attacks went on all day with a very heavy bombardment at 2 o'clock in the afternoon. By half past three the artillery fire had reached a crescendo and mortar shells were beginning to fall inside the fort itself. Under cover of this barrage the Germans advanced to within 100 yards of the walls and at that time Captain Herreman had

come to the decision that the small force could no longer hold out in the face of such overwhelming numbers and the fort was surrendered. By 4.30 p.m. the Swastika had been run up the flagpole signalling the capture of Nieulay to the German commanders.

Today the Fort is undergoing extensive and some would say loving renovation funded by the local authorities of Calais. The restoration work is being carried out sensitively and the Calais authorities have invited the Calais Historical Society to put forward its views as to how best the restoration should be tackled. Much excavation is now in progess and long buried features of the fort are being uncovered almost every week. It is hoped that the Fort will be fully restored and that eventually the walls will be illuminated in order to capitalise on the increased tourist traffic generated by the proximity of the French Channel Tunnel terminal near Sangatte. It should be noted that although the renovation is a large scale enterprise it has been decided not to repair the damage to the walls which was the work of the German guns.

Mediaeval Calais — The English Occupation 1347-1558

Due to persistent military activities —whether from the French recapture of the town in 1558, or the development of its fortifications in the seventeenth century, or the bombing and destruction of the two World Wars — most of the evidence of mediaeval Calais, and consequently its English occupation, have disappeared. Calais North — ie Old Calais — is a relatively small part of the present town, which expanded greatly through the nineteenth century as industry (in particular lace and textiles) grew in the suburb of Saint Pierre, now fully incorporated (1885) into Calais.

There are remnants of English influence — most notably in the Church of Our Lady (Notre Dame). During the fifteenth century the English occupants added to the thirteenth century original, and so there is a church with the English architectural styles of Decorated and Tudor on continental Europe.

A Watch Tower predated the English occupation by about a hundred years; it seems to have been located in the area of the old market place, and until the last century dominated the skyline of the town. The northern-most end of the citadel was originally part of the strongest element of the defences, containing the Keep.

Fort Risban now is the location of a not particulary distinguished camp site. In the time of the English there was a tower positioned here to protect the harbour entrance.

The memory that most of the British have of Calais as far as its connection with England goes centres on its capture by Edward III after a prolonged siege in 1347. After he had decisively defeated the French in August 1346, at Crecy, Edward proceeded to Calais. He had landed in Nor- mandy, and now he needed a port from which he could return to England, and which would provide him with a much closer harbour to Dover (already a very strongly fortified port).

The Calais garrison, under its strong, resolute and gifted commander, Jean de Vienne, put up a spirited — and lengthy — resistance. Unfortunately his King did not show the same sort of performance. Philip VI did put in an appearance almost a year after the siege had begun, but after a small skirmish at Sangatte and a glance at the English fortifications he decided that discretion would be the better part of valour, and left the people of Calais to their fate. Obligation to Philip satisfied, de Vienne surrendered the town of Calais, handing over the Burghers of the Town for Edward to do with as he pleased in return for sparing the rest of the people. The rest of the story is well known: the intercession for the chained Burghers by Edward's Queen, Philippa of Hainault, resulted in their freedom. The well known French sculptor, Rodin spent some years in producing his famous work, now placed in front of the easily identifiable — if somewhat outlandish — Town Hall (Hotel de Ville).

Calais was to play a vitally important part in both the economic and military history of England over the next centuries. The Calais Staple was the group of merchants that managed the sale of wool to the Low Countries, and thus exerted an enormous economic and political influence on the Crown, as well as being a most valuable source of loans. Calais itself, naturally, had to be garrisoned. It provided the biggest royal garrison in the realm, and the office of Lord Lieutenant there was a vital one. During the Wars of the Roses control of the town was considered essential by both sides — both for the troops there and because it was a gateway for potential supporters or opponents from the continent. When the town finally fell to the French in 1558 with it went most of England's gunpowder, munitions and artillery.

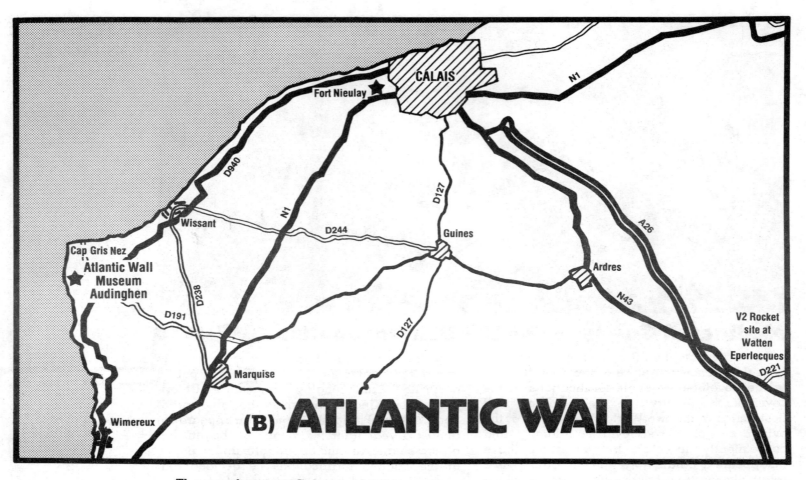

(B) ATLANTIC WALL

Below: Part of the Atlantic Wall defences at Wimereux, September 1943; German artillery observers keep a watch for Channel shipping.

The area between Calais and Boulogne – and to a lesser extent between Calais and Dunkirk – is an outstanding example of remaining coastal defences. To follow that on the Boulogne side, follow D940, which is signposted off the ferry road into Calais. By keeping on the coast road it is possible to see a large number of bunkers on the beaches and larger communications and control bunkers a little further inland.

A huge battery was situated at Sangatte (during the English occupation Sandgate) – the so-called Lindemann Battery – whose 406 mm guns could reach Dover and Folkestone. The position has now gone, largely a victim to the

Channel Tunnel, whose outlet comes out in the vicinity. The most interesting route to follow is to head out through Old Calais and then drive through Bleriot Plage. Along the road on the beach side may be seen a large number of fortified positions. The first place where access is relatively easy is at Cap Blanc Nez. Here there is a memorial to the Dover Patrol. The original was unveiled by Marshal Foch, and designed to commemorate the co-operation between the two nations, besides the tremendously successful work that the Royal Navy had in convoying British troops across to France during the Great War. During the Second War the Germans blew up the memorial - not because they disapproved of its sentiments particularly, but because the British were using it as a ranging indicator for their own batteries at Dover.

All around the memorial are the remnants of the German garrison that was stationed here, with strongpoints, gun positions and observation points. It is an exhilerating spot, with tremendous views on a clear day—and a graphic indicator of just how difficult an invasion in this vicinty was likely to have been.

There is a great drop from here down to the seaside resort of Wissant. It is a small place (just within the old English Pale of Calais), but boasts comfortable (and very reasonable)

hotels. When the weather is good it has a beautiful beach, sandy and well sheltered.

The proprietor of the Hotel Normandie, David Davies, is the son of a Briton who settled here after the Great War and ran the family hotel.

Above: German propaganda picture depicting one of the Channel guns aimed at the coast of England.
Below: Master of Hitler's war construction schemes, Dr Fritz Todt. The gun Batterie at Audinghen was named after him.

21

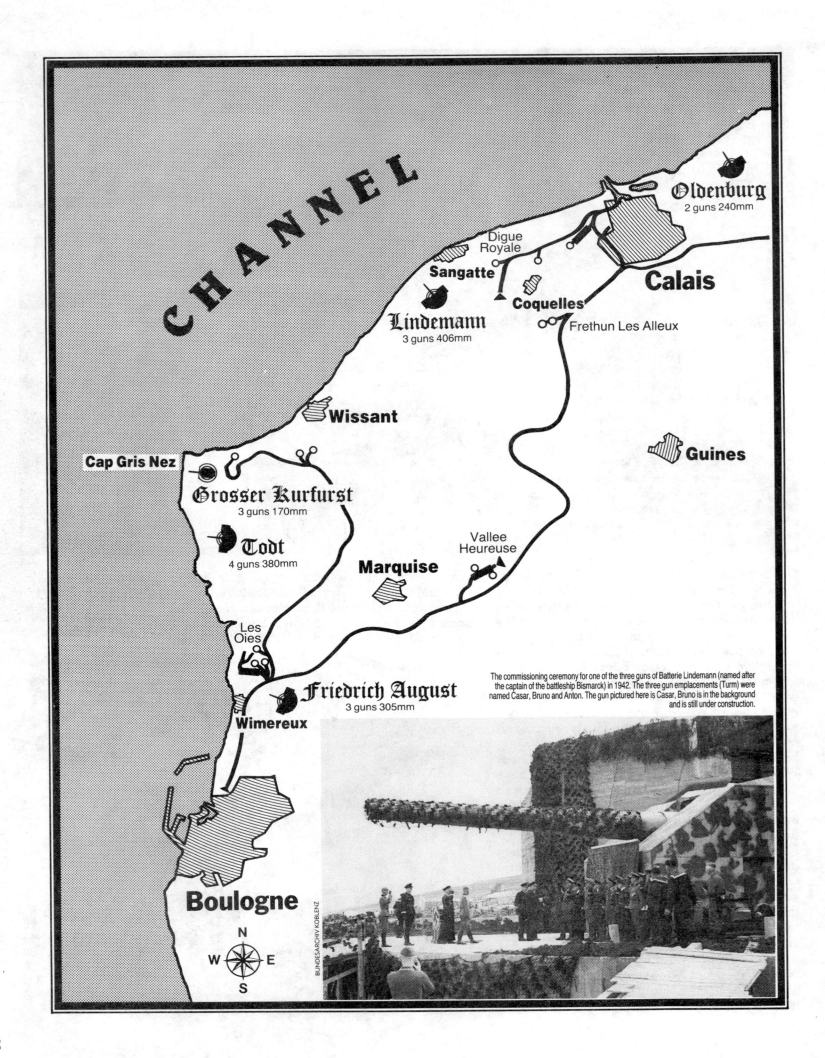

CHANNEL

Oldenburg
2 guns 240mm

Calais

Digue
Royale

Sangatte

Coquelles

Lindemann
3 guns 406mm

Frethun Les Alleux

Wissant

Guines

Cap Gris Nez

Grosser Kurfurst
3 guns 170mm

Vallee
Heureuse

Todt
4 guns 380mm

Marquise

Les
Oies

The commissioning ceremony for one of the three guns of Batterie Lindemann (named after the captain of the battleship Bismarck) in 1942. The three gun emplacements (Turm) were named Casar, Bruno and Anton. The gun pictured here is Casar, Bruno is in the background and is still under construction.

Friedrich August
3 guns 305mm

Wimereux

BUNDESARCHIV KOBLENZ

Boulogne

N
W   E
S

He now also runs the Atlantic Wall Museum a few miles further on at Cap Griz Nez. This is centred on the position which was known as Battery Todt, which once housed a huge 380mm gun. There is a large display of equipment, uniforms and other memorabilia from the war. Also on display at the museum is a British Cruiser tank raised from the beach near Dunkirk in 1978. A visit to Batterie Todt, Atlantic Wall museum is recommended.

Cap Griz Nez's fall in September 1944 ensured that there would no longer be any more German shells falling on southern England - a wave of shelling in the last few days were an indication of the desperation that the Garrison was feeling. The fight was relatively short - the defences were obviously, for the most part, facing the wrong way. The Canadian 7th Brigade captured some 1600 prisoners along with the position.

Top: Turm 1 of Batterie Todt as it appears today compared with a war time photograph. The lettering has long since disappeared along with the chimney.

Below: This diagram of Turm 1, Batterie Todt, illustrates the amount of room taken up underground. In the case of Turm 1, Todt, the underground store rooms and chambers now house the Atlantic Wall Museum.

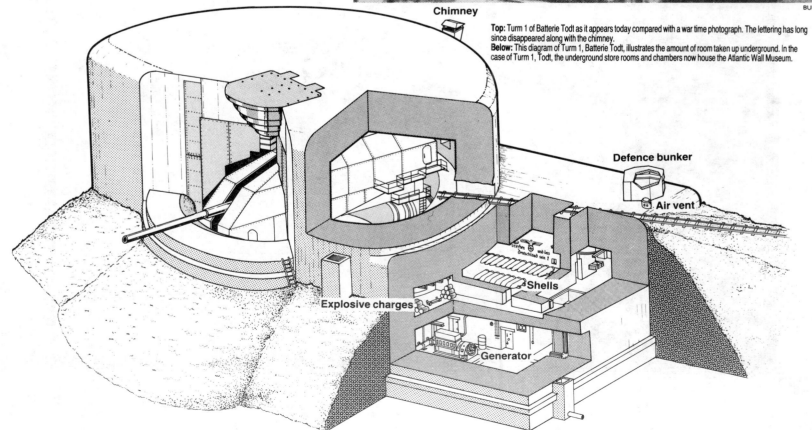

Chimney

Defence bunker

Air vent

Explosive charges

Shells

Generator

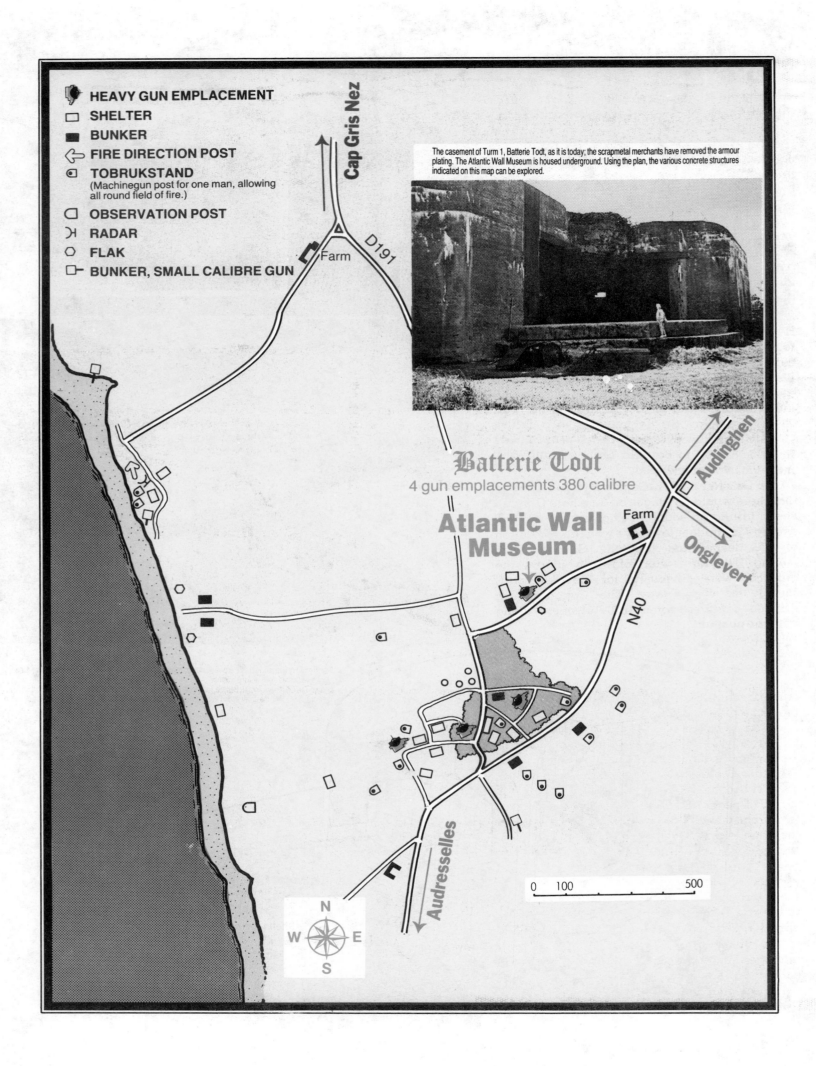

LEGEND

- **HEAVY GUN EMPLACEMENT**
- **SHELTER**
- **BUNKER**
- **FIRE DIRECTION POST**
- **TOBRUKSTAND**
  (Machinegun post for one man, allowing all round field of fire.)
- **OBSERVATION POST**
- **RADAR**
- **FLAK**
- **BUNKER, SMALL CALIBRE GUN**

Cap Gris Nez

D191

Farm

The casement of Turm 1, Batterie Todt, as it is today; the scrapmetal merchants have removed the armour plating. The Atlantic Wall Museum is housed underground. Using the plan, the various concrete structures indicated on this map can be explored.

Batterie Todt
4 gun emplacements 380 calibre

Atlantic Wall Museum

Farm

Audinghen

Onglevert

N40

Audresselles

0 100   500

N
W E
S

The Calais Pale — Guines

When the English held Calais they felt that the town of Calais itself was too vulnerable unless they extended the territory that they controlled. Thus they extended outwards to form a Pale (a barricade of stakes) which may be directly compared to the safe area around Dublin known as the English or Dublin Pale. From this derives the expression 'beyond the pale.'

One of the outer limits of this area was Guines, situated on relatively high ground, and captured in 1352. Although the older part of the town at least appears somewhat run-down now, there is something to be seen, and it makes a pleasant early halt after the scramble to extract oneself from Calais. It will also provide a welcome opportunity to escape those GB number plates. The streets are narrow and cobbled in places and there are a couple of squares with cafes and restaurants available. The old part of the town may be rapidly explored on foot: there is a mound, now surmounted by a clock tower, the clock of which probably ceased to tell the time years ago; there are some remnants of the town walls; and a memorial to Francois de Guise, who liberated both Guines and Calais from the English in 1558. Among Mary Tudor's reported last words were that if her heart was opened there would be carved the name of Calais. She might have got some consolation from the fact that her husband, Philip II of Spain, recaptured Calais in 1596 (and thus made it Spanish) and that the liberator Francois of Guise was assassinated by a French Protestant in 1563 towards the opening of the long drawn out French Wars of Religion. His niece was Mary Queen of Scots.

One other point of interest in the town is to be found on the outside wall of the church - a crucifix in the 'heretical' style of Jansenism, with the arms of the crucified Christ almost vertical above the body. This 'heresy' had its foundations in the mid seventeenth century, and was particularly common in this area.

Guines became best known in English history when it became the base for Henry VIII during a series of negotiations between himself and the two great monarchs of western Christendom of the time, Francis I and Charles V, the Holy Roman Emperor. At a rather crucial period of power politics, England found herself in the position of exerting considerable influence on the international stage, a fact which appealed to the vanity of Henry whilst allowing his chief minister, Cardinal Wolsey, to exercise his skills to the utmost. In fact, for a while, he even managed to get the powers to keep to a form of collective security pact signed in 1518.

The selected site for the meeting with Francis I was on a field midway between the outposts of England and France, Guines and Ardres.

Left: Memorial to Francois de Guise, in the centre of the old town of Guise.

Below: A Jansenist's crucifix on the wall of the Parish Church depicticting Christ with his arms almost directly above his head. The Jansenist movement, which was at odds with the Roman Catholic Church, was branded a heresy in the 17th Century.

Taking the road from Guines, it is the field on the right, just before the turning to Campagne-les-Guines. In 1520 the two monarchs met, each with a vast army of followers, each seeking to out-impress the other.

Literally thousands of men were used to convert the castle at Guines and to create a tented camp, but the masterpiece was an

Left: A 'Poilu' (French equivalent of the British 'Tommy') stands guard over the Guines war memorial in the town cemetery.

25

enchanted summer palace of brick and wood, complete with a banqueting hall. The halfway point happened to be known as the Val d'Or (Valley of Gold), a happy coincidence; whilst to ensure that neither side felt snubbed the neighbouring surrounding hills were made into a uniform size and width. Henry's arrival in Calais must have witnessed scenes of pandemonium as everyone who was anyone from England joined in the jamboree, the harbour chock-a-block with shipping, thousands of local people drawn in to take the benefit of free wine.

Meanwhile a great jousting and tournament area had been created near the meeting point. Both monarchs met and embraced at a place identified by a spear in the ground. It is hard to imagine a Hollywood director going more over the top! There was a fortnight of festivities only slightly marred by the fact that Henry was thrown whilst wrestling with the equally young and dashing Francis I. There were numerous meetings, dinner parties and entertainments, and if nothing else it reopened contacts on a grand scale between the English and French aristocracies, closed for so long by the Hundred Years' War.

Soon after this meeting Henry met up with Charles V (himself only twenty years old) in yet another specially created palace in Calais itself. By the middle of July the negotiations were over and Henry could return to another of his favourite pursuits, hunting. The palaces and camps were soon affected by the winds and nothing now remains of them.

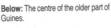
Below: The centre of the older part of Guines.

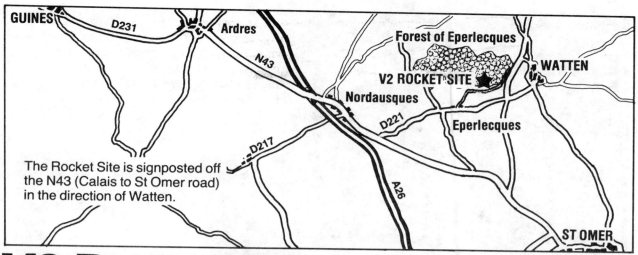

The Rocket Site is signposted off the N43 (Calais to St Omer road) in the direction of Watten.

V2 Rocket Site

(C) War by Terror — Eperlecques

Hitler was an enthusiastic supporter of innovations which might help to end the war, and perhaps the most awe inspiring of the results was the "V" series of bombs and rockets. Due to problems of range, and the need to be able to cover most of southern England, in particular London, it was essential that the base for the launches of V1s, V2s and ultimately V3s be in this area of northern France. Belgium was generally too flat, and provided inadequate security for the huge complexes that would be vulnerable to saturation heavy bombing, at which the RAF was getting more and more adept. Thus the Germans looked for suitable terrain that would make the construction of underground installations possible. This part of

Below: V2 Rocket ready for launching at Peenemunde, on the Baltic coast, 1943. The rocket bunker at Eperlecques was originally designed as a rocket launching site, but because of constant heavy bombing the use of the building changed to one of liquid oxygen manufacture to fuel the rockets.

BUNDESARCHIV KOBLENZ

Right: Guarding the gate to the block house at Eperlecques is a German 88mm gun mounted for the anti-tank role.
Inset: Memorial to the French and Belgian forced labourers who died or were killed during construction work.

France is covered with gullies, quarries and underground workings, often well hidden between deep ridges which run right up to the coast.

Dr Todt, Hitler's armaments and munitions minister in the early days of the war, had already shown what could be achieved in the way of huge ferro concrete constructions as erected along the Atlantic Wall — in fact the Todt Organisation was created to do nothing else.

At the end of 1942 a practicable site was required for the launching of the V2 rocket; although this was still in the stage of development, the launch site would require so much protection from air raids that it was essential that the work be begun as soon as possible. The actual building project was disguised by describing it as a power station. By March 1943 the enormous number of workers required — thirty thousand Belgian and French forced labourers — had arrived at the chosen point, Eperlecques, to clear the forest from the site and commence to build branch lines off the main railway system. Workers were drawn from all sources — over 400 Spanish Republican prisoners (captured during the Spanish Civil War of 1936) refused to take part in the work and were removed to the death camp at Mauthausen.

Pressure to complete this very complex building was enormous — Hitler wanted all to be ready by 1 December 1943, so that launches could be made in time for a German Christmas present to the British. Fortunately a series of raids by RAF Bomber Command on installations at Peenemunde and Friedrichshafen not only destroyed stocks of rockets, but in the human carnage that also resulted, killed key technical operatives and administrative experts. Some six months had been bought.

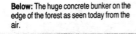

Below: The huge concrete bunker on the edge of the forest as seen today from the air.

Left: Bombers of the US Eighth Air Force first attacked the site whilst construction was underway, in the Summer of 1943. The building was completed in the Spring of the following year and became a target for the RAF.

In August 1943 the bunker at Eperlecques itself was attacked. Despite an attempt to prevent casualties amongst the work force, timings went wrong, and there were horrendous casualties in an air raid that did not last much longer than ten minutes — at least five hundred were killed. Air raids went on and on and on — relentless, using the latest concrete smashing bombs. Squadrons such as Leonard Cheshire's 617 Squadron, using bombs weighing twelve thousand pounds, continued the attack right up to the end of August 1944, when liberation was in sight. It was overrun by the Canadians in November, 1944.

This huge bunker — claimed to be the largest in the world — never became operational. In the event no V2 was launched from here; the rockets were usually launched from relatively mobile

Left: Earthquake bombs called Tallboys and Grand Slams were dropped by the famous 617 Squadron, but failed to penetrate the 16ft thick roof, or to bring the walls down with near misses (causing an earthquake effect). Today the effect of intensive bombing by the largest bombs of the day can be examined by the visitor. In the flooded chambers nothing more dangerous than goldfish now lurk.

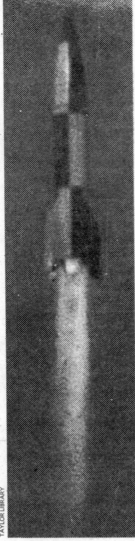

Above: There was no defense against the V2 Rocket and with the abandoning of static launch sites, such as the one at Eperlecques, in favour of mobile sites, the terror weapon was virtually unstoppable.

Far right: In one area of the bunker complex where the roof is much thinner, penetration by a high explosive bomb can be seen.

Right: Damage to the block house roof edge was caused by a direct hit from a Tallboy bomb, dropped by 617 Squadron — it failed to penetrate the 16ft thick roof.

launch sites. The advantage of proximity to the English coast of the static launch site at Eperlecques (and thus putting the rockets well within range of London) was outweighed by the growing expertise in precision bombing of the RAF and the USAF, combined with the growing inability of the Luftwaffe to defend the skies.

Yet there was to be another scare: for the German Ardennes offensive by von Rundstedt in November 1944 caused considerable alarm, and Churchill and his staff decided that huge installations created by the Germans close to the coast, such as that at Eperlecques and at Mimoyecques, had to be destroyed in case of German reoccupation. An attempt to destroy the bunker was made by the RAF using ten ton Tallboy bombs — the results of their handiwork may be seen as relatively minor indentations on the bunker.

A small detour to visit the bunker is certainly recommended. It is vast — 100 metres long by 50 wide about 20 metres above ground level and another 60 odd below. Some 120,000 tons of concrete and 30 thousand of steel and iron were used to build it, and the allies used five thousand tons of bombs to try and destroy it.

The site may be visited 'during the season' — this tends to mean Easter to Remembrance Day, and is usually closed for lunch. It is very much a small village endeavor, the local people themselves have opened it — and so it has its limitations. There is a useful guide book in English (of a sort) and it is possible to wander around the site by yourself, and to shun the guided tour. There is a film shown within the bunker itself. The site is well sign posted, and if you keep within hearing distance of the guided parties, the various son et lumiere parts of the tour help to bring the place alive. Although the facilities are rudimentary, these

continue to improve as income is generated. A little discomfort and disorganization is a price well worth paying to see the lengths to which men are prepared to go in their grim intent to wage war.

30

(D) Headquarters — St Omer

The N43 brings you in through the suburbs of St. Omer; it is here that the mysteries of priority from the right will first make themselves felt to the unwary British motorist. The centre of the town and parking facilities are well signposted. The best thing is to get rid of your vehicle and then proceed on foot.

The dominant building is the great Cathedral: it is said to be the finest in the region. It is dominated by its fifteenth century towers; whilst there is a chilling portrayal in stone of the Last Judgement on the south side entrance. The Cathedral was the scene of the last sermon of Father Willy Doyle, a famous chaplain in 16 (Irish) Division, in July 1917. Into this great church (it ceased to be a Cathedral in 1801) came two thousand Irish soldiers of 16 Division before they were launched into the horrendous fighting of Paschendaele. The Irish connection was highlighted in the sermon by reference to the presence of Daniel O'Connell, the great Irish nationalist, at the English College in St Omer in 1791.

By leaving the Cathedral from the south side it is a short walk to the site of the former Bishop's Palace, a rather fine seventeenth century building, which is now the Palace of Justice. Eventually, off to the right, is the Rue St. Bertin. The architecture ranges from the historically interesting to the modern and occasionally souless.

Number 37 was where Sir John French and Douglas Haig had their quarters, for until 1916 St. Omer was the GHQ (General Head Quarters)

Above: The Place de Marechal Foch, formerly the Grand Place. The funeral ceremonies of Field Marshal Lord Roberts began here before ending with his burial at St Paul's Cathedral in London.
Below: The looming tower of the Cathedral in St Omer where British troops held services during the Great War.

31

Above: A pre Great War photographer evidently captured the attention of citizens of St Omer.

Right: Lord Roberts was one of the great Victorian soldiers: he had entered Sandhurst at the age of fourteen in 1847 — giving a total of sixty seven years in the Army. He won his VC during the Indian Mutiny, and it was in India that he made his name, notably in a number of effective campaigns in Afghanistan. He became tremendously popular within the Indian Army, and introduced training reforms that transformed the musketry and artillery capacity of his command: by the time he left India in 1893 he had created the best trained army in the Empire. In late 1899 he was sent to South Africa to retrieve the fortunes of the British troops there against the Boers. It was a sad arrival for him, as his son had recently been killed — a son who had also managed to win the Victoria Cross. Along with his chief of staff, Kitchener, he rapidly restored the situation. On his return he became the Commander in Chief of the British Army, the last man to hold this job, as the post was abolished and replaced by an Army Council in 1904. On his retirement in 1905 he spent much time arguing the case for conscription to enable the British to be better able to face the dangers from the great continental powers. His statue now stands on Horse Guards parade in London.

of the BEF. Soon afterwards it became the headquarters of the Royal Flying Corps, and on its formation on 1st April 1918, the Royal Air Force.

Further down the road is a very impressive building with its chequered history inscribed high on the wall: originally it was the site of a College founded by the English Jesuits in 1592. Due to persecution here, and improving circumstances in England, the College was transferred to near Blackburn in Lancashire. Stonyhurst, as it was now called, provided the first army officer VCs of both the First and Second World Wars.

On a parallel road, the Avenue Carnot, is the house where Field Marshal Roberts died in November 1914. There used to be a plaque on the wall marking this event: unfortunately it seems to be one of the few houses on this street to be undergoing major structural improvements and it seems possible that this memorial might have been a casualty.

As the casualties in the early months of the war rose, the British government decided to use Indian troops, and an Indian Army Corps was sent to France. Roberts was appointed its Colonel-in-Chief; feeling that he ought to be with his men he arrived in France on the 11th November, promptly caught pneumonia and died on the 14th. Before his burial in St. Paul's there was an impressive service in the Grand Place, now called the Place du Marechal Foch. His death was symbolic: this war was going to be a far cry from 'Queen Victoria's little wars' in which Roberts had served with such distinction.

There was a certain amount of fighting in the St. Omer area in 1940, but as the town was on the west side of the canal line, the Germans captured it relatively easily.

St. Omer is a good place to stop to stock up with French delicacies if one is not in too much of a hurry and wants something a little more varied than a supermarket. One shop in particular boasted some of the most enormous rounds of cheese that I have ever seen.

On leaving the town, follow the signs to Arques: near the church here, on the right, is a most impressive looking chateau. The road soon branches — to the left (the D933) goes on to Cassel, the N42 to Hazebrouck. Much of the area around St Omer was flooded as a precaution against German advances in the Spring of 1918.

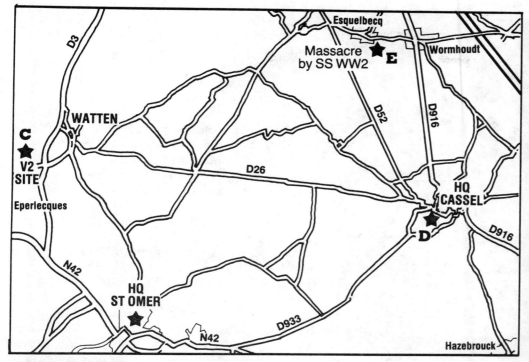

Headquarters — Cassel

Cassel is thought to be immortalised in English folklore by the nursery song about the Grand Old Duke of York. The hill which is the central feature of the rhyme is the most prominent piece of high ground south of the Channel thus far, and when the mist lifts (which is a rare event!) it offers panoramic views across Flanders. Historically it has always been regarded as a vital strategic spot; yet it is no place to keep an army. Its chief function has been as an observation point.

The town itself is charming, with small cobbled streets, a huge Grand Place, cobbled with varying levels, little passages leading up to the citadel, a number of very ancient houses and an interesting museum. For those who like a good meal (and are prepared to pay for it) Cassel offers some of the finest eating in the

Above: Marshal Foch, commander of French forces in the northern part of the line, 1914 and 1915, destined to become the Allied military supremo in 1918.

Below: The cobbled Grande Place of Cassel as it appears today.

FATIGUES OF THE CAMPAIGN IN FLANDERS.

Above: The Duke of York had to suffer the harsh caricatures of British satirists of the 18th Century, who were no respecters of rank or birth.

Below: The Grande Place, Cassel, as it appeared before 1914.

Courtesy of the Director, National Army Museum, London

the political wranglings between the allies who seemed incapable of taking seriously the military capacity of the revolutionary French armies and of coming to united decisions. The consequence was order, counter order and disorder, for which the Duke received much of the blame in popular caricature. Suffice it to say that he did not come out of things too badly, and was to be a relatively popular commander-in-chief, holding that office at the time of Waterloo. Amongst all George III's children he was the one appointed to look after him in his last years, a task he appears to have carried out with great patience and love. Like Nelson, he has been rewarded with a column in London, just off the Mall.

There are many reminders in this beautiful, ancient town, of one of its most famous twentieth century inhabitants, the well known French commander, Marshal Foch. After his successful service on the Marne in 1914 and the Somme in 1916, he was appointed general-issimo of the Allied forces in March 1918. When the German advances, which began in that month, were checked, he went on to lead the Allies to final victory.

In the Autumn of 1914, once the outflanking operations had come to a halt, French armies in the North were commanded by Foch, who took as his headquarters the town of Cassel. Foch had managed to progress in the army despite his fervent Catholicism; not a conviction to hold in secularist France, which only a few years before had thrown most of the Roman Catholic religious orders out of the country. Whilst at Cassel he gained a reputation for spending fixed periods of time in meditation in the Gothic Church. He lived at the Hotel Schoebecque, which stands at number 32 in the street which now bears his name — Rue de Marechal Foch. Whether by accident or design Foch chose a building blessed with an imposing 17th century facade in which to site his office. In keeping with his role as a defender of French freedom, Foch set up his headquarters in what was once known as the Hotel de la Noble Cour on the southern side of the Grand Place. As its name suggested this building was once the home of the noble court of Cassel; a civil and criminal tribunal which was the only one in the Pays Bas (Low Countries) to take on the title of 'court'. There, in a panelled upstairs room, General Foch planned the defence of Flanders in the face of the German invaders.

Today the visitor can wander into the same room and sit in the very chair, behind the very desk at which Foch took some of the momemtous decisions upon which his country's freedom depended. On the desk are the original writing implements and reading lamp. Photographs of Foch adorn the walls. On the ground floor can be viewed an interesting collection of World War One exhibits neatly displayed. These

area. I must admit that this is not from personal experience — the bank balance has never stretched to haute cuisine.

Frederick Augustus, Duke of York was one of the more likeable of George III's many children. He commanded the British troops in the Flanders campaign of 1793-1795 which was something of a disaster. This was mainly due to the incompetence of his military advisers and to

Above: General Plumer, known affectionately as 'Daddy' or 'Old Plum and Apple' to the British and Empire troops, used Cassel as his headquarters for a time.

Left: The office of Marshal Foch carefully restored at 32 Rue de Marechal Foch, where the war museum is housed.

include the usual weaponry, display cases and smiling uniformed mannequins. The rest of the museum could best be described as eclectic, drawing artefacts from the civil, military and religious history of this part of French Flanders.

Marshal Foch moved on from Cassel in 1915, and the next significant occupant was General Plumer, known affectionately to the troops as 'Daddy'. In photographs he looks like the cartoonists portrayal of Colonel Blimp come to life, with his short, stocky figure, large bushy moustache, and a complexion that suggested an excess of port and indulgence. In fact he was a considerate man, meticulous in his planning, as was best shown in the offensive launched at Messines Ridge in June 1917, which was an outstanding success. In fact later in the war, the Australians suffering (so they felt) under Gough

Below: Among some of the items on display at the museum in Cassel are German weapons of WW1 such as a machine gun, mortars and a field artillery piece.

commanding the Fifth Army, had a song in which they demanded to be taken back to Daddy Plumer's Army. A steady hand in a crisis, he was chosen to command the British troops that were dispatched to Italy after that country almost collapsed following the disaster of the Battle of Caporetto in 1917.

Cassel also witnessed fighting in 1940: its position as a vantage point meant that the British had to hold on to it as long as was possible to prevent units of the army being cut off in the retreat towards Dunkirk. The British line ran from here to Hazebrouck. The Germans managed to get a footing on the western edge of Cassel, and thus sheltered by the steep rise of the hill, were able to bring effective fire on the summit. They then attempted to capture the town from the south and south east, but were

repulsed. Due, however, to indecision and poor communications (the universal explanation for military setbacks) most of the British defenders became casualties, the exception being a small group of 2 Gloucesters led by Second Lieutenant Frane who managed to disengage and make a hair-raising dash for Dunkirk, evading German troops on the way. They were picked up by one of the last boats to get away from the beaches.

At the very top of Mont Cassel, in the grounds of the old chateau (long since gone) is a restored eighteenth century windmill. It was from this vantage point that Marshal Foch and other allied commanders looked east over the plain of Flanders towards the cauldron of the Ypres Salient. Today the observation point is marked by a blackened stone slab incised with arrows which point out to significant locations. This is in front of a fine equestrian statue of Foch. If the statue looks vaguely familiar, it could be because you are a commuter to Victoria Station — a replica sits outside it. Also in the grounds there still remains a concrete bunker, under which were offices.

From the summit it is said that one can see five kingdoms: France, Belgium, the Netherlands, England and above the clouds, Heaven. I might be shortsighted, but the weather has never allowed me to see much further than a few miles on the dozen or so occasions that I have been there!

The early days of World War Two were fought — at least on the Western Front — in a quiet and leisurely way. Both sides sat tight in their defences and effectively did nothing. This idyllic life style for most of the soldiers was shattered by the Blitzkrieg offensive of May 1940. Mingled with the German infantry and armour (the Wehrmacht) were a number of SS Divisions.

(E) Royal Warwickshires Massacre at Wormhoudt

It was men from those SS divisions who were responsible for a number of atrocities, and the incident that took place here is one of the more famous. The irony was that public opinion, having been seduced by blatantly exaggerated propaganda in World War One, was disinclined to believe stories of atrocities supposedly committed by the Germans in the latest conflict. It took literally years for people to believe in the concentration and death camps — for many not until these were liberated at the end of the war — and so stories of massacres of remnants of British regiments received little attention. They did, however, happen.

This particular massacre, which took place on the 28th May 1940, achieved notoriety in the spring and summer of 1988 when public pressure arose to put on trial the man alleged to have ordered the execution of 80 members of the Royal Warwickshire Regiment. Wilhelm Mohnke (1989) lives in retirement near Hamburg; despite the passage of time, so great was the outcry that the British government re-opened the case against him, going so far as to advertise

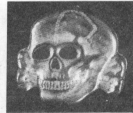

in the Communal Cem. is executed Coldstream Guardsman PHILLIPS

Wormhoudt is 18 kilometres north of Cassel on the D916 (Dunkirk Road). Esquelbecq is on a minor road; turn left in the centre of Wormhout.

in some national newspapers appealing for witnesses.

The massacre took place as British and French troops were being evacuated from the beacheads of Dunkirk. A number of units were left to hold up the encircling German armies, and their desperate efforts served to infuriate Germans eager to complete their rout of the enemy. Facing the Warwicks was the 2 Battalion of the SS Leibstandarte Adolf Hitler Division. The Germans were held off until the afternoon of 28 May, but by five pm the prisoners had been gathered together. It has been alleged that Mohnke was furious that prisoners had been taken, and instructed that they should be removed and shot (this evidence from a German SS NCO). The men were removed and led away towards the neighbouring hamlet of Esquelbecq; their likely

Left: Elements of the 2 Battalion, SS Leibstandarte Adolf Hitler, hot on the heels of the retreating British Army in May 1940.

Above: Hated and feared cap badge of the SS.

Above: Believed to be a photograph of British prisoners murdered by the SS.

Below: The barn where 80 to 100 British prisoners were herded and grenades thrown among them. The farm marked with a cross served as the SS Battalion HQ at the time of the massacre.

fate was made apparent by the execution of a number of members of the Cheshire Regiment that they witnessed en route.

The Warwicks were led into a barn into which the Germans threw grenades. The Germans then went around and shot any prisoners who looked as if they might have survived. A number — some seven or eight — in fact had, and managed to escape immediate German notice. Some of these were caught in subsequent days — but were taken by regular German soldiers, and thus they were hospitalised and then imprisoned.

When one of the wounded,— Private Bert Evans — was returned in a swop of severely wounded and incapacitated prisoners in 1943, the authorities showed little inclination to listen; this was an attitude that was to confront Pte Pooley of the Norfolks who had suffered in a similar massacre at the ill-named village of Paradis (Paradise). For various complicated post war political reasons, Mohnke had

survived the dredge for trial of war criminals; it remains to be seen whether the evidence will be strong enough to bring him to trial now.

And what remains of this gruesome event? There is a memorial; there is the eloquent witness of 36 of the victims buried in the military cemetery at Esquelbecq; and there is a tree to which has been nailed numbers of small wooden crosses — it stands close to the site of the barn. There also remain the tortured lives of the survivors of this nightmarish incident.

There is a footnote to the affair, and it involves the Cheshires, a regiment fighting alongside the Warwicks. Whilst investigating the Wormhoudt matter, I mentioned the story to the campsite proprietor of a site near Arras with whom I stay on Battlefield tours. It turned out that he was a witness to the events at Esquelbecq. He tells how a French unit took its place in the line but did little to camouflage its guns; how he and his father cut down branches and undergrowth in order to conceal them; and

how when it was clear that the neighbouring British troops had been surrounded, the French officer refused to intervene. As a point of explanation he suggested that the French were exhausted and felt betrayed by the decision, which if not openly stated had become obvious, of the British to abandon France.

He recalled harrowing sights — of two young women being beaten to death in a barn, and of members of the Cheshire Regiment being bayoneted or kicked to death. After the skirmish was over he went out and buried three of these soldiers, and after the war was over received a letter from the parents of one of them, thanking him for his care of their son.

Peaceful, quiet and placid Esquelbecq conceals just below its surface the extent and degree to which man is prepared to be inhuman towards man. Its rural solitude makes it an altogether fitting place to see how nature can recover — but man's spirit remains indelibly affected.

Above left: The pond where two men hid, a short distance from the site of the barn. They were sought out and shot; an officer, captain Lynn-Allen was killed, but Private Albert Evans survived.

Left: Site of the massacre barn. The tree on the left bears memorial crosses.

Above: Wilhelm Mohnke accused of ordering the mass murder.

For further reading: Republished in 1988 by Thorsons Publishing Group Ltd in the light of the reawakened interest in the atrocity.

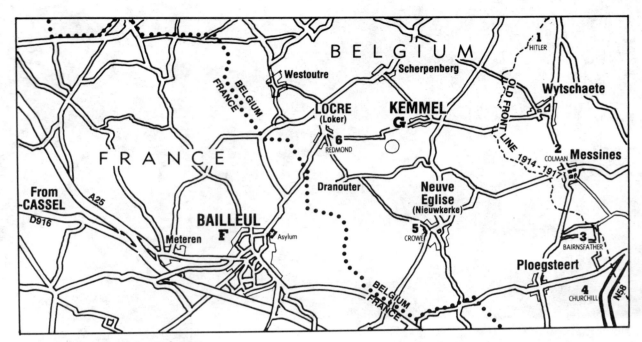

(F) Behind the Front
Bailleul

This town was in the rear of the British and French lines apart from a few months in 1918. It was close to the lines, and thus frequented by many in the armies as the nearest big town in the area that was relatively free from shelling — a fate that it largely escaped until 1918.

There are two points of interest that figure prominently in accounts of the war that remain to be seen. The first is the great Commonwealth War Graves Commission (CWGC) cemetery which is to be found in the communal cemetery on the Belgian frontier side of the town. In the civilian part of the cemetery are a large number of graves of British troops killed in the desperate fighting of 1914, when situations that were saved by Brigades in the later part of the war were saved by skillfully hand' d companies then. A lot of these graves hold more than one man. The Extension to the cemetery is vast.

One of the problems with the war cemeteries is that they can appear as large, almost anonymous things. To the casual observer they are rather beautifully cared for, with endless white stones in symetrical progression. It is always worth while to stop and look — to examine the register, to see some of the information that adds detail to a gaunt stone; then to look at these memorials — the age, the rank, the regimental crest, and often the final words of a relative carved at the bottom. Without a close examination of these graves we lose something of their sacrifice: obviously it is facile to say that they all died heroes, or bravely, or determined to fight their own crusade. But die they did, and we owe it to them to take a real memory away with us.

Below: The town of Bailleul prior to the outbreak of war in 1914, and after it was bombarded by German artillery in April, 1918.

Left: The lunatic asylum on the outskirts of Bailleul. Van Gogh was resident for a while and during the Great War it was used as a forward hospital. It was destroyed when the Germans occupied the town in April, 1918.

Nowadays there is a great resurgence of literature from the First World War. One of the most impresive books to emerge is the diary of Billy Congreve VC, DSO, MC. He was the son of General Congreve VC who was to become a Corps Commander in the war. He writes of one of those killed — a great friend, who was first seriously wounded, and who now lies buried in the cemetery.

"10th Feb 1915. Later — have just got a wire from Dads: Maurice very seriously wounded, doctor says no hope.

12th Feb. Wyatt told me that when hit, he was helping to build up the parapet at a place that he had been warned of as being watched by a certain sniper. The bullet went in at the top of the head and, besides breaking a bit of his skull away, seriously injured his brain...

13th Feb. Everyone still thinks there is no hope, but somehow I believe there is.

25th Feb. The Padre (Neville Talbot, whose name will appear later in this guide) tells me that Maurice died quite peacefully at 12.30. I knew this before I saw him. I feel I don't much care what happens now.

27th Feb. I went down to Bailleul this morning and met Dads and Tom Grenville at the hospital.

We buried Maurice in the cemetery. The coffin was carried in a motor ambulance and we walked behind. The funeral made little or no impression on me, which is either because I have lately learned to understand or else forgotten how to."
His father was to comment:
"Neville Talbot took the service — a simple one. We laid him to rest in the French cemetery beside many other soldiers, French and English. Billy was splendid and quite collected. I felt like a baby."

The dead officer was Lieutenant Maurice Osborne; one of his relations was to achieve fame as the British Minister to the Vatican during World War II.

Returning on the road out of Bailleul towards the Belgian frontier (the crossing point is at Locre), on the outskirts of the town on the right hand side may be observed the asylum. Van Gogh was a temporary resident here. The asylum was used at times as a forward Hospital and as such was well known by the troops. It was destroyed in the fighting which resulted in the German occupation of the town in April 1918. The reconstruction, at least of that part viewed from the road, appears very similar to its appearance in 1914.

Gerald Burgoyne, in 'The Burgoyne Diaries' writes of a visit to the asylum:

"5 March 1915. Just returned from a topping bath at the Bailleul lunatic asylum. Officers are allowed to bathe there on Fridays. Four baths in a room, and a huge bath sheet free gratis. The door of the bathrooms (there are two) are invariably left open as some fellow enters or leaves, and the old nun who hands out the towels toddles past quite unconcerned, and I didn't notice even a downward cast or a pretence of a blush. However, as we all said, if she didn't mind, we didn't."

Below: Reconstruction of the asylum followed a similiar style to the original building.

(G) Base for Famous Personalities

On a clear day there is perhaps no better place from which to view the sweep of the Ypres Salient than Mont Kemmel. Apart from this attraction, the village of Kemmel itself can be used by the curious visitor as a base for further exploration of this part of the Flanders battlefield. From the village several locations of military significance are easily reached.

In a sleepy settlement to the west there lie the remains of William Redmond, MP and Irish nationalist who worked hard for the formation of a Southern Irish Division in Britain's hour of need and was to die in her service. To the east at Messines stands a memorial to the London Scottish, the first infantry unit of Britain's part time army, the Territorials, to engage the Germans in World War One. That same monument also marked the beginning of an illustrious career in cinema for one of the 'Jocks' wounded in that action. Private Ronald Colman, unable to advance further due to a fractured ankle, dragged himself out of the fighting and into Holywood history.

Within a few miles from Kemmel one of the sites of the historic Christmas truce of 1914 can be easily located. It was in this area where the famous war cartoonist, Bruce Bairnsfather first dreamt up his images of 'Old Bill'. It was also in the Ploegsteert part of the Front where Winston Churchill commanded a battalion of the Royal Scots Fusiliers after the failure of the Dardanelles campaign. At other sites close to Kemmel it is possible to walk the ground upon which deeds of courage were peformed by two young men of Britain and Germany. At Neuve Eglise Captain John Crowe, of the Worcesters, was the British officer who led his men against German machine guns and won the Victoria Cross. The young German going to the aid of a wounded superior near Cronaert Wood earned for himself the Iron Cross Second Class — his name was Adolf Hitler.

KEMMEL

CRONAERT WOOD 1914
Adolf Hitler

LOCRE 1917
William Redmond, MP

MESSINES 1914
Ronald Colman

NEUVE EGLISE 1918
John Crowe, VC

PLOEGSTEERT 1916
Winston Churchill

PLOEGSTEERT WOOD 1914
Bruce Bairnsfather

Kemmel

Kemmel is the centre of the Heuvelland (the Hill Country) and boasts some basic hotel accommodation, a tourist information office, and the camp site in the area — this is large, with a shop, restaurant, showers etc, and is also geared for caravans.

Kemmel during the Great War was heavily fought over in 1914 and in 1918; but for the greater part of the war it was three thousand yards behind the Front Line.

A couple of recently published books have served to make this town a place of interest to the British visitor: the *Burgoyne Diaries* and the *Journal of Private Fraser* (a member of the Canadian Expeditionary Force). Their accounts cover the period 1914 to 1916 with a gap of a few months in 1915. The best thing to do is to park your car near the church, and then walk around the various points of interest, many of which are highlighted in these two books.

Inside the churchyard there is a plot of mainly 1914 burials, including a number who were engaged in disastrous attack by the Gordons at the end of the year. In the rear part of the churchyard there lies the body of Kendall, a football international from before the war.

Burgoyne noted that the church was very fine, but that the curate had disappeared to Bailleul, and asked their chaplain (Fr J Gill, SJ) to say mass for him.

Spies were a major preoccupation of the troops in the area, and many of the troops, rightly or wrongly, felt that a lot of the local inhabitants were more sympathetic towards the Germans than towards them.

Private Fraser comments on spies and snipers behind the lines:

> "Notices were posted up in various places and orders were continually being issued warning us to be very careful in our conversation, especially in relation to movement of troops and expected happenings."

He notes that a Canadian was hit by one of these snipers and that 'Lt Martin had shot quite a youngster who was sniping at night from a tree.' Private Fraser gives an excellent description of Kemmel in early 1916.

On the gable of a near-by house to the Church is the hunting horn symbol used by many continental countries to indicate postal services This is the site of the old post office which was run by an old man, his wife and daughter. *'They likewise ran an eating house, and under war-time conditions, put up very creditable meals.'* He goes on to comment that these were the last civilians to leave Kemmel a few months later. He describes Kemmel as being in peacetime one of the loveliest spots in Belgium.

Going into the village of Kemmel proper is as good a way as any to get a feel of pre-war

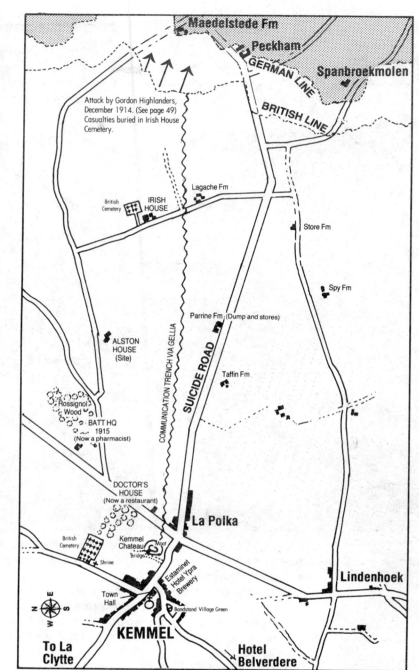

Belgium, as it has been restored to quite a degree. Up the street is the square, on which is situated a bandstand. Here German troops played in October 1914 when they occupied the village.

Coming out of the square, is the Brewery which, according to Fraser, 'seemed to be the outstanding industrial establishment, though at this time it had ceased activities'. This was the site of one of the two guardroom outposts that were maintained. Below this was the Ypres Hotel 'of doubtful repute' (still so indicated in letters of stone at the top of the building, and which now houses, amongst other things, the local tourist office). Another hotel was called the Maison Communale where it was observed, 'a rather prepossessing girl of about fifteen was dispensing drinks to both soldiers and civilians,' Fraser observed.

On the same side as the Ypres Hotel, at the T

Above: In early 1915 Kemmel remained relatively undamaged despite its closeness to the front line.

Below: The guardroom was situated in the cellars of the Brewery in Kemmel — this a recent photograph.

Junction with the La Clytte road still exists an Estaminet on the site of one about which Fraser was very complimentary:

"During these unpleasant nights there was one bright spot, an estaminet below the Ypres Hotel. There were still in Kemmel a few Belgian civilians who figured that the soldiers were a godsend to them and they could not withstand the temptation of braving shells for the sake of enriching their coffers. This estaminet was a perfect haven to us. It was barricaded in front with sandbags and inside, in a corner, were their stock in trade, a few tin goods of dubious age and other odds and ends and the usual Belgian beer and wines. About this time we discovered that red wine and grenadine made a passable drink.

"To get out of the rain and cold, yes and out of fatigue too, we used to slink in here, getting rooted out only to slink back again. Many were the rushes in and out of this half-way house from which much fun and banter issued."

It is probably worth mentioning at this point that the Canadians, like the other Dominion troops, were considerably better paid than their British counterparts, often a sore point. No wonder the Canadians were so popular in Kemmel!

The Guard Rooms at Kemmel (and their duties) are also described by Fraser:

"The Guard Room at Kemmel is in the Basement of the Brewery. There are two posts, one in the square in the front of the Ypres Hotel and the Maison Communale, and the other a considerable distance away in front of the Kemmel Chateau. There are the usual duties, halting everyone at night and seeing that the vehicles are a considerable distance apart. Kemmel is in the shell zone, and for protection parties are supposed to be

strung out and wagons should be at about twenty five yards interval.

"Guards are provided with a whistle which they have to blow as soon as they notice a plane coming towards the village."

Kemmel Chateau — or at least the site of it — may still be viewed. The entrance up a small drive is quite easy to miss: on the entrance post there is a plaque indicating some educational establishment. Walking up the drive, on the right hand side, is the bridge that went over the moat to the chateau proper, which has now completely gone. This was a battalion and sometimes a brigade headquarters. The entrance to the communication trench came through the chateau grounds.

According to Fraser the chateau had belonged to a member of the Hennessy family (as in brandy).

"The Chateau seemed to experience marvellous luck. The building was practically untouched whilst all around was in ruins . . ."

This was the scene of one of Germany's 'atrocious crimes.'

"When the Germans passed through the district, they shot the doctor in front of his two daughters, whilst he was standing on his doorstep. Then his daughters were afterwards outraged and killed."

It is just to the east of this house, almost parallel to the Kemmel-Wytschaete road (known as Suicide Road), that the communication trench ran up to the front line — the trench being known as the Via Gellia (Frozen Road).

Returning to Kemmel, on the right hand side is a sign to Kemmel Chateau cemetery. Just before this is a shrine, which Fraser describes:

"At the western edge of the grounds (of the Chateau) bordering the road was a beautiful little edifice built in the shape of a grotto of stones of all sizes and shapes. It was a shrine and contained all the emblems of Catholicism, candelabra, case of beads and a lovely statuette of the Virgin Mary."

The cemetery itself is in a beautiful situation, and the atmosphere of a park remains. Both Burgoyne and Fraser comment on a number of those who are now buried there: at the time of Burgoyne it was a small cemetery.

"At 8 am a telephone message came down to say that Pigot-Moodie (a Lieutenant of the Rifle Brigade and attached to us) was badly wounded and half an hour later another message told us he was dead. He was in H3, our dangerous trench, and the bullet entered his neck and came down through his nose and he only lived seven minutes after he was hit. Poor fellow — a real good sort — brother in the Scots Greys. He was probably supervising the repairs of his trench. So silly, poor fellow, to expose himself in open day."

That was on January 13th 1915; on January 14th:

"We buried Pigot-Moodie in the military cemetery, set apart at Kemmel. There are already several graves there. Found a French cross to put on top of him."

He went on to comment a couple of weeks later:

"Took some photographs of the tiny military cemetery here: only some twenty five graves there yet. Lt Pigot-Moodie's

Below: Kemmel Hill with ruins of Kemmel Chateau in the foreground. By 1918 the area had been fought over and devastated.

IMPERIAL WAR MUSEUM

grave is the one with the palings around it, just to the left of the tree.

"Lieutenant Tyndall, Dublin Fusiliers attached to us was killed yesterday morning early. He stood up and fired some say two, others four, flares from the same spot and one after another. Either he was spotted by a sharpshooter or it was a stray bullet, but he was hit in the face, the bullet shattering his spinal cord in the neck. A very nice fellow, he only joined us a week ago. We buried him last night on our return from the trenches, together with an officer's servant, who had been sent into Kemmel to buy bread. He was killed by a stray bullet in the wood of Kemmel Chateau."

The soldier-servant is buried directly behind Tyndall.

Burgoyne went on to mention, on the same day, an incident that took place in the dressing station of the Wiltshire Regiment.

"While the Wilts' medical officer was bending down dressing a man's wound, a shrapnel (shell) burst outside in the street, and a piece entered the room, killed the doctor at once.

"Heard over the telephone from Brigade Headquarters that Colonel Du Maurier of the Royal Fusiliers was killed by a shell which blew up Alston House (named after Major Alston, of the Battalion, who was killed on April 15th), the old farm which is always used as Battalion Head Quarters when the Battalion is in the trenches."

He was the author of 'An Englishman's Home', the brother of Gerald du Maurier (an actor, later knighted, and uncle of Daphne, the author) and the son of an artist. Later, on the 11th March, he had more details:

"I hear Colonel Du Maurier was the only man killed in the house; he had just ordered everyone out and into dug-outs outside and was waiting in the house for his sergeant-major to report that everyone was in safety before he took cover himself."

By the time that Fraser arrived at Kemmel some nine months later the cemetery had filled. He commented on November 4th 1915:

"The older graves are well kept, some being planted with roses, ever-green bushes and box hedge. Each battalion has a distinctive cross. The Canadian crosses could have been improved upon. Four or five men were asked to volunteer for a

Below: Sandbag shelters in an old support line in front of Kemmel, 10 June 1917.

IMPERIAL WAR MUSEUM

Above: Kemmel Chateau Cemetery, before its obliteration by artillery fire.

burial party, the inducement being 'no fatigues tonight'. Needless to say, the burial party was more inviting than the fatigue and it clinched the matter. It turned out the dead man was Sergeant Kemp. He was wrapt up in a blanket, which was tied with signalling wire. We carried him to the cemetery on a stretcher. The minister officiating said a few words. The grave was a double one, the other fellow had already been buried, that is a few inches of earth was thrown over him. This had to suffice until Kemp was interred, when the grave would be filled in. When we arrived the grave contained several inches of water, coloured red by blood. Kemp was buried in this mess.

"We found out later that we were a bit previous in volunteering as no one went on fatigue that night."

Before he left the area, Fraser noticed that the previously undisturbed cemetery had been hit by three shells, and noted that:

"As this vicinity was the scene of hot fighting two and a half years afterwards, and fell into the possession of the Germans

BCPL

Left: Burials such as this were a rare event. Many men were buried hastily and under fire, there was not much time for traditional niceties.

this cemetery must now be unrecogniz-
able."

Thus the horror of war.

The camp site in Kemmel is out on the La
Clytte road; a rather insignificant sign post to
the left on the outskirts of Kemmel indicates the
site. Continuing along this road, at a junction
with another, is the approximate site of Kemmel
shelters, which often figures in the accounts of
soldiers who were in the area during the war.

Before departing from Kemmel it is worth
going up to the summit. The Tower at the top is a
reconstruction (though not a replica) of the one
from which British Generals and artillery
observers viewed the flatlands below them: the
good weather when this might be a useful
exercise is not all that common. Continuing
along the summit a memorial to the French who
defended this Hill so bravely but unsuccessfully
may be seen: Fraser noted that there would no
doubt be a memorial to them. Going down the
steeply cobbled road (and noting the disturbed
earth on all sides), one is greeted by a small plot
of ground with a French flag flying over it: this is
the site of an ossuary, one of two in the Ypres
area. The French often collected their dead in,
for want of a better term, boneyards: it is

horrifying to think that in this small area there
are some five thousand plus French soldiers, of
whom only about eighty are known. From this
point there is an excellent view across towards
the Lys, to Locre and to France, showing the
dominance of Kemmel to the west as well as to
the east.

It is worth quoting Fraser's description of
Kemmel in March 1916:

*"Kemmel is fast disappearing. The
village pump is smashed (then in the
square). The Bandstand in the square is
wrecked. Shell holes are in the streets. The
houses and stores are being levelled. Our
engineers and artillery are helping in the
destruction by removing the brickwork
from the buildings for their own use. The
Engineers' dump is gone — Kemmel has
become a dead and deserted village."*

The road to Wytschaete (Whitesheet to the
troops) was known as Suicide Road, and its
exposure to German artillery fire can be readily
appreciated as the Messines Ridge appears.
The Via Gellia, a communications trench to the
left of the road, ran up to Parraine Farm, which
was the forward dump for all the equipment
vital to maintain the trenches in some sort of

Above: The grave of Sergeant A J Kemp, in
the old grounds of Kemmel Chateau.

Right: Remnants of Hotel Belvedere on the
summit of Mount Kemmel.

even vaguely habitable and usable condition. This farm was hidden from German view immediately to the front.

A few hundred yards further up the road there is a turning to the left which is signposted to Irish House Cemetery.

Burgoyne talks much of Irish House — he had two of his platoons based there in support to the front line troops in the H trenches; continuing on this road and going to the left is the site of Alston House, the battalion headquarters when serving in the Front line here. Irish House cemetery is tucked away behind the farmhouse — in fact it is quite easy to sail straight past it, as it is set off well from the road. The cemetery is in its origins a battlefield cemetery — i.e. it was established to bury those killed in a particular engagement, or day to day casualties in that sector, normally by a Divisional Burial Officer. In this case, though, there are some unusual interments — the mass graves of a number of Gordons, all unknown. Fraser's and Burgoyne's diaries both explain why — and recall that the accounts are written almost a year apart.

The attack by the Gordons was part of a concerted operation against Maedelstade Farm (amongst other points) launched in the early hours of December 16th 1914. Burgoyne states that they lost seven officers and two hundred and fifty men. On the 28th December he writes:

"A man tells me he found among the Gordons dead in front of the Hs (the trench system) one man sitting up in a most lifelike attitude in the act of bandaging a wounded comrade. Both men were dead, and I suppose occasionally a bullet strikes some vital spot which destroys life and does not relax the muscles.

"Neither officers nor men knew the positions of their objective . . . the whole affair was apparently very badly organized; never thought out at all . . . after a time we dreaded the idea of making attacks knowing it would mean heavy casualties and a failure. We dug into several corpses yesterday filling sandbags; took the hand off one, came on the feet of another, and the body I believe of another, while cutting a trench. We covered over one poor unburied Gordon. . . we couldn't do more, there are so many

about here and the only thing is quick lime. Impossible to ask a man to search for their identity discs now.

In November 1915 Fraser was to write on the same area:

"I went over the parapet to see what was the matter. It was a dead Gordon Highlander and they (some of our men) were going through his clothes gingerly. A few yards away were some more dead. We found out later that there was a fairly even line of dead three or four hundred yards long principally Gordon Highlanders, though there were a few evidently belonging to an English battalion. Most of the bodies were skeletons or partly mummified, and fell to pieces when moved. Some were half-buried. One

Above: Highlanders killed in action. The Gordon Highlanders were thrown into action in December 1914 against Maedelstade Farm and suffered heavy casualties.

Left: Reconstruction of Hotel Belvedere on the site of the original building. From the vantage point in the original tower British officers were able to observe the actions taking place in the Ypres Salient and Messines Ridge. It now serves as a house and cafe and, is a good spot to orient your map with the terrain — over a cup of coffee.

Highlander was fairly intact. On two of them we found paybooks, a watch and some money."

This is the tragic story behind a headstone that simply records: 'Thirty Unknown Gordon Highlanders of the Great War'.

It is interesting to note that Fraser rescued one of the Gordon's rifles, gave it to a comrade who cleaned it and was able, within half an hour to use it as a functioning weapon — after eleven months in the open without any care. Fraser said how serviceable the British rifle was — a contrast to the Canadian Ross rifle which was universally detested by the Canadian soldiers. It had been foisted on them by General Sam Hughes, their War Minister, and eventually thrown away in disgust by the great majority who picked up British Lee Enfields on the battlefield. The Gordon Highlander's final objective was the northern half of Wytschaete, but first came Petit Bois, the wood to the west of the village. Strong points such as Maedelstede Farm, with their excellent fields of fire, proved to be insuperable obstacles to the bravery of the

Highlanders, provided with a totally inadequate artillery protection and detailed planning. From their start point from the trenches forward of Irish House, the Gordons had to cross some three hundred yards of No Man's Land, exposed and with little cover. The wire in front of them was uncut. Most of them never reached it. The attack of the 14th December should never have taken place. It was a typical example of one ally (the British) being pushed by another (the French) into an attack in which they did not believe in, and therefore was carried out half-heartedly at the expense of the soldiers on the ground. It might not have been an important attack in the history books, but the cost and consequences struck home to those who followed the Gordons in the trenches. And what of Maedelstade Farm?

This strong point remained in German hands right up to the great offensive of June 1917; and then it was the target of the second largest of the mines that went off on that day — some ninety four thousand pounds of explosive. A large crater, filled with water, indicates the spot.

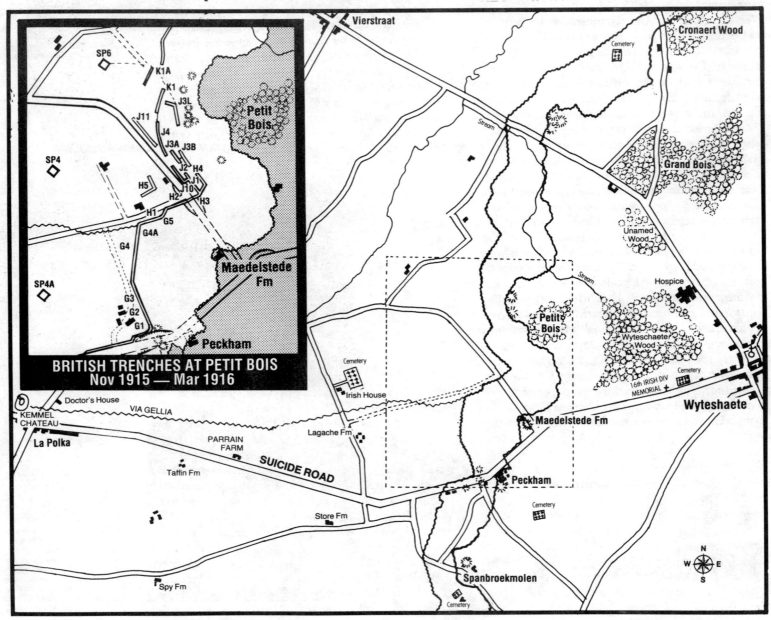

BRITISH TRENCHES AT PETIT BOIS
Nov 1915 — Mar 1916

Hitler was born an Austrian subject, but had lived in Munich for a number of years, scraping a living as an artist. In early 1914 he had been summoned back to Austria to do his military service, but was found to be unfit — even for auxiliary duties. On the outbreak of war, however, he got special dispensation (needed because he was an alien) from the King of Bavaria to join his forces, and he joined the 1st Bavarian Regiment, shortly thereafter being permanently posted to 16 Bavarian Reserve Infantry Regiment.

1. Adolf Hitler's Iron Cross

The British are often criticised for sending undertrained troops to fight on the Somme — but most of them had been in the army for almost two years when they took part in that attack. Hitler's regiment went off to the Front after he had had only two months of basic training. They were sent to join 6 Bavarian Reserve Division, and thrown into the crucial conflict at Ypres. They just failed to meet the sadly depleted British army, men of 4 Cavalry Brigade, who were in the vicinity of Wytschaete. The events took place in early November, 1914.

Men of 32 Division (French troops) then held the line. Hitler described his experiences:

"Now the first shrapnel hisses over us and explodes at the edge of the forest, splintering trees as if they were straw... None of us is afraid. Everyone is waiting impatiently for the command, 'Forward!' We crawl on our stomachs to the edge of the forest. Above us are howls and hisses, splintered branches and trees surround us. Then again shells explode at the edge of the forest and hurl clouds of stones, earth and sand into the air, tear the heaviest trees out of their roots, and choke everything in a yellow-green, terribly stinking stream. Four times we advance and have to go back; from my whole batch only one remains beside me, finally he also falls. A shot tears off my right coat sleeve, but like a miracle I remain safe and alive."

The Germans gradually worked their way forward and occupied the outer edge of the wood and the nearby farms. Hitler, a regimental dispatch carrier (what the British would term a runner) helped to rescue a wounded senior regimental officer from the road near Cronaert Chapel; this was a brave thing to do — it was an exposed position under continuous rifle fire from the French on the slopes below. His work was in vain, for the officer subsequently died. He went on to help save the life of the regimental commander a couple of days later by pushing him into a ditch when machine gun fire opened up on them as they were going forward to try and observe the enemy. The new commander, Lieutenant Colonel Engelhardt, intended recommending him for the Iron Cross, but the following day a shell exploded in regimental headquarters seriously wounding Englehardt and killing three others. As a regimental runner Hitler had been present a short time before, but had been required to leave to make room for four company commanders; they were all either seriously wounded or killed. Hitler had so many close shaves with death — and his accounts of the war were not exaggerated — it is hardly surprising that he felt that destiny had great things in store for him. The Battle in this area petered out in the early days of November.

Left: Adolf Hitler poses for the camera in his brown-shirt uniform circa 1927. He is wearing a wound badge and the Iron Cross First Class, which he was awarded in 1918. He won the Iron Cross Second Class (only the ribbon was worn on the tunic) for his part in rescuing an officer under fire at Cronaert Wood in 1914. Inset: A photograph of Hitler taken shortly before the Great War ended.

IMPERIAL WAR MUSEUM

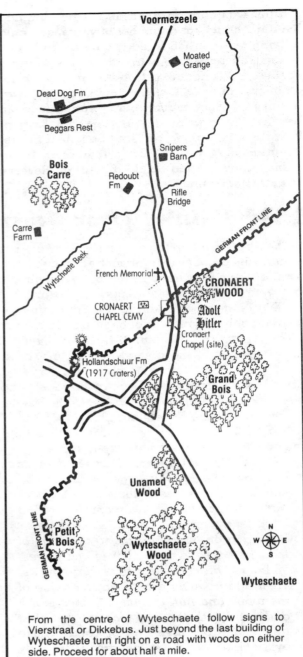

From the centre of Wyteschaete follow signs to Vierstraat or Dikkebus. Just beyond the last building of Wyteschaete turn right on a road with woods on either side. Proceed for about half a mile.

TAYLOR LIBRARY

Above: German soldiers outside a dugout near the ruins of Messines Church. Hitler served in this trench system as a regimental runner from 1914 until the summer of 1916 and regularly took shelter in the church crypt.

Hitler was to serve some considerable time in this sector; regimental headquarters was in the relatively safe town of Messines, and Hitler often took shelter in the crypt of the church there. His bravery in the early days of the war had not gone unnoticed, and he was awarded the Iron cross Second Class — he only failed to gain the First Class because as a member of regimental headquarters his name would have been towards the end of the recommendations — presumably the quota for First Class Iron Crosses had been used up!

Hitler was delighted with the award and wrote to a friend:

"It was the happiest day of my life. Unfortunately, my comrades who also earned it are mostly all dead."

A comrade was to describe 'Adi' Hitler's appearance during that period:

"He seemed too slight even to carry a full field pack, but as he slouched around, rifle in hand, helmet askew, moustache drooping, a lively glow in his eyes, he was the picture of a front line fighter."

It would seem that the other runners respected him for his apparent fearlessness. He was generally liked for his reliability in a crisis. He never abandoned a wounded comrade or pretended to be sick when it came time for a dangerous assignment. Although he had a reputation as a bit of a prude, he would lecture his comrades on the evils of drinking and smoking, he also drew cartoons depicting amusing incidents affecting their lives at the front — thus Hitler attained some popularity with his fellow soldiers.

Whilst at Messines Hitler took the chance to use his talents to paint canvases — one of these

was of Cronaert Chapel, a shelled ruin close by Cronaert Wood (Bois Quarante). He collected a little terrier dog which appeared to have come over from the British lines and they became inseperable; he was deeply distressed when 'Fuchsl' was stolen from him in August 1917. It is worth considering that whilst Hitler wintered in 1915 at Messines, a few miles away to the south his great future foreign opponent, Winston Churchill, was battling with the winter near Ploegsteert (Plugstreet).

Hitler's regiment stayed in the Ypres sector until the summer of 1916; then they were moved to the Fromelles sector, about 15 miles south of Amentieres. He was subsequently wounded in the thigh in October 1916. Whilst recuperating on leave, Hitler the fierce patriot of his adopted country, developed a hatred of Jews (whom he

considered to have more than their fair share in safe billets at home) and of communists. Winning the war was everything to him. In the last days he lost his sight, having been gassed near Wervik (on the Franco- Belgian frontier) in October 1918 as the allies finally broke out of the Ypres Salient. During this period of temporary blindness Hitler had his vision and began to hear voices. Hitler ended the Great War as a decorated war hero (he had won the Iron Cross First Class in early 1918) — and convinced that defeat was the result of treachery at home. He was not alone in this: Ludendorff, the German Chief of General Staff in 1918, put much of the blame for defeat on the lack of discipline at home — and he too thought that the Jews had been less than enthusiastic in their efforts for the Fatherland.

In January 1933 Hitler was appointed as the Chancellor of Germany; the man who appointed him was the President, the ancient Hindenburg — who had been brought out of retirement to help save Germany from the threat of Russia in 1914. The 'Czech corporal' as Hindenburg persisted in calling him had achieved a tremendous coup.

Top left: Brooding remnants of the war still exist in Cronaert Wood as evidenced by this German shelter. There are also extensive trench remains in the wood, until recently part of a trench museum.

Above right: In the middle distance Cronaert Chapel Military Cemetery. It was on the road in the foreground that Hitler carried out an act of bravery that was to result in the award of the Iron Cross. He is said to have revisited the spot in 1940.

Right: Nuremberg, 1927 and Hitler takes the salute of his devotees — the Brownshirts — as his rise to power gets underway.

IMPERIAL WAR MUSEUM

54

Ronald Colman died of pneumonia in May 1958 at his ranch in California, at the age of 67. He had worked 40 years in films both in this country and the United States — a veteran of 56 movies. He epitomised the popular concept of an English gentleman and played his most successful roles depicting the gentleman-adventurer. In 1927 he was voted the most popular male star in Hollywood, and continued as such for many years.

2. Ronald Colman, Fighting Film Star

Amongst his best known pictures are *Lost Horizon* and *The Prisoner of Zenda* made in the late 1930's. In the 1940's he starred in the tear-jerker *Random Harvest* opposite Greer Garson, and in 1947 he went on to win a coveted Oscar for his role in *A Double Life*.

It has been said of Ronald Colman that he was the best, most glamorous and most popular movie star that Britain ever gave to the cinema.

What is not so well known about Ronald Colman is that he took part in a real life drama, a famous action of World War One. The scene of the incident in which he was wounded in the ankle can be located fairly easily, for a monument to his old battalion stands by the roadside. It was on the line of the road where 14 Battalion, London Regiment, the London Scottish met the advancing Germans head on — it was the night of Hallowe'en, 31 October — 1 November, 1914. It was the first occasion in which a Territorial infantry unit 'weekend

Left: Ronald Colman and Lilian Gish in the film *The White Sister* (1923). Colman played the part of an Italian army officer.

soldiers' had gone into action against the enemy.

It was the wound to Private Ronald Colman's ankle that caused him to be returned home and had him finally invalided out of the army in May 1915; thus avoiding four years of horrific trench warfare that was to take the lives of 1,542 officers and men of the London Scottish Territorials before it was finally over.

Prior to the outbreak of war in August 1914,

Below: Mobilisation of the Territorials in August 1914. Here the London Scottish march through the streets of London from their headquarters at 59 Buckingham Gate.

Colman was working as a clerk with the British Steamship Company. He had joined the Territorials in 1909 which involved the usual weekend training and annual camp. He left in 1913 but when war fever swept the nation he rejoined his battalion immediately, "More to get away from the office, than because of the fighting spirit which I did not have," he later claimed.

After only a few weeks the London Scottish, after drawing its rifles (which had just been converted to accommodate a different type of ammunition) left its regimental headquarters at Buckingham Gate and sailed across the Channel in *SS Winifred*. They were the first of the Territorial Force infantry battalions to arrive in France.

For the first few weeks Colman's battalion was used to provide working parties in the rear areas and thus became split up. Their duties included guarding prisoners, providing a guard for General Headquarters and the most unpopular duty, personnel for general working parties.

However as the battles spread northwards towards the Channel ports the battalion was brought together again at St Omer. The Regular battalions were being hard pressed by the German hordes. At that point the problem of transportation raised its head — how to move a body of troops with equipment to where the action was taking place as quickly as possible. The answer lay in the requisitioned buses of the London Omnibus Company, complete with their

usual drivers. Thirty four double-decker buses transported the battalion to the town of Ypres, where they arrived in the early hours of 30th October, 1914.

From then on confusion seemed to reign as orders and countermanding orders were given. First they were marched in one direction, then they were sent off in another, then marched back the way they had come. No reasons were given to the men, but the hours spent moving the battalion in various directions was because of the constantly changing situation. With every new German thrust threatening the retiring British line the London Scottish were being re-directed to help prevent a breakthrough. The desperate nature of the situation made it unclear where those valuable troops should be thrown into the line.

In the end the double-deckers were once more called up and the battalion embused and were driven off to St Eloi, where they were sent in to aid elements of General Gough's cavalry division. The division was stretched from the village of Wytschaete to the village of Messines.

As the battalion marched up the road towards Wytschaete, scouts that had been sent forward reported back that the village was under fire from artillery and small arms fire. It became apparent that it would be unwise for them to deploy from there. They therefore moved across fields into a group of trees known as L'Enfer Wood, sheltered to some degree by the ridge that lay in front of them.

Lt Colonel Malcolm, the commanding officer,

Courtesy of the Curator, London Scottish Regimental Museum

gave orders for the battalion to advance up the slope in extended line in artillery formation (wide gaps between the men to minimise the effect of shrapnel shells) to a position on the far side of the ridge, with a windmill to their right. As they came over the crest of the hill the Germans laid an artillery barrage across their path and they began to sustain casualties, these included two majors who were badly wounded.

A shell landed close to Private Ronald Colman flinging him into an abandoned slit trench. Dazed and shaken he tried to stand, only to find that he was unable to place any weight on his leg. His ankle had been shattered by a piece of shrapnel; there and then he decided that there was no point in pressing on with the advance along with the rest of his comrades. For some time he lay close to the road wondering what to do next.

He was beginning to feel the pain as he hauled himself out of the trench and began crawling on all fours back the way he had come. Bullets were zipping through the air all around and it occurred to him that if he was hit by one and killed he would be discovered with his back to the enemy. What would they conclude? It would appear to them that he had been fleeing from the enemy and that just was not the done

Above: Arriving at the town of Ypres by way of London double-decker buses. They were shortly to be thrown into the line to stop the German advance.

Below: A sketch made by a British officer showing the ridge of high ground between the villages of Wytschaete and Messines. The London Scottish went into action on the crest of the hill with the village of Wytschaete on their left.

Wytschaete

Messines

57

Courtesy of the Curator, London Scottish Regimental Museum

Above: This painting by Caton Woodville, a noted war artist of the day, depicts the action during the night of 31 October, 1914, when the London Scottish stopped the massed German infantry on the Messines ridge.

Right: A small detachment of the London Scottish shortly after the action.

IMPERIAL WAR MUSEUM

thing. Reasoning thus, Colman turned around and began to crawl backwards towards the wood from where the battalion had begun its attack.

For him it was the end of military service, for his shattered ankle was slow to heal. Six months later he was discharged as medically unfit. Ronald Colman had crawled off the battlefield and limped away into the limelight to become the heart-throb of millions.

Meanwhile the London Scottish dug in under intense fire on the forward slopes. This was accomplished in time to meet a German attack launched soon after 9 pm. All along that part of the front, under the light of a full moon, German troops surged forward with loud cheers and brass bands playing — they presented an easy target. However, the men were experiencing difficulties with their rifles which had been so recently modified. It had not been considered necessary to test fire them, now the men, presented with a target of massed infantry, discovered that the magazines frequently failed to feed rounds into the breech correctly. This meant that they had to place every round into the breech by hand.

For the most part the attackers were recent recruits of less than three months, and no doubt needed the encouragement. The dense masses closed with the Territorials and hand to hand fighting took place. On this occasion the Germans were beaten back, but shortly afterward the German artillery began shelling the position, heralding another attack.

A nearby set of buildings named 'Huns Farm'

and the windmill were ablaze giving needed illumination to the German night attack. Faced by overwhelming numbers the London Scottish were driven back off the ridge and retreated over the ground previously covered by Private Colman. The Germans were too exhausted and disorganised to exploit their advantage and carry on their attack.

In the confusion of battle the Territorial battalion had become scattered. It was not until the following day, on 2 November, that they were gathered together again at the little village of La Clytte, which is situated to the north of Kemmel, where a roll call was taken. It was found that 394 failed to answer.

Lt Colonel Malcolm, received a communication from the commander-in-chief Sir John French:

"I wish you and your splendid regiment to accept my warmest congratulations and thanks for the fine work you did on Saturday. You have given a glorious lead and example to all Territorial troops fighting in France."

Above: Memorial to the London Scottish stands just outside Messines on the road to Wytschaete.

Left: A studio portrait of Colman who was to become the Hollywood heart-throb of thousands of women.

Below: Roll-call of the Battalion revealed that around 400 men men were missing — either killed or wounded. Colman was missing from the roll-call, he was in a field hospital with a shattered ankle.

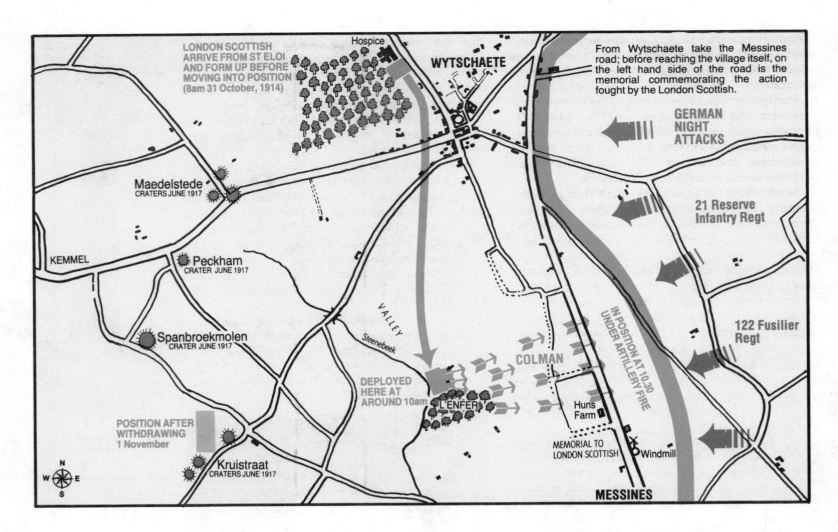

LONDON SCOTTISH ARRIVE FROM ST ELOI AND FORM UP BEFORE MOVING INTO POSITION (8am 31 October, 1914)

Hospice

WYTSCHAETE

From Wytschaete take the Messines road; before reaching the village itself, on the left hand side of the road is the memorial commemorating the action fought by the London Scottish.

GERMAN NIGHT ATTACKS

Maedelstede
CRATERS JUNE 1917

21 Reserve Infantry Regt

KEMMEL

Peckham
CRATER JUNE 1917

VALLEY

Steenebeek

122 Fusilier Regt

Spanbroekmolen
CRATER JUNE 1917

IN POSITION AT 10.30 UNDER ARTILLERY FIRE

DEPLOYED HERE AT AROUND 10am

COLMAN

L'ENFER

Huns Farm

POSITION AFTER WITHDRAWING 1 November

MEMORIAL TO LONDON SCOTTISH

Windmill

Kruistraat
CRATERS JUNE 1917

N W E S

MESSINES

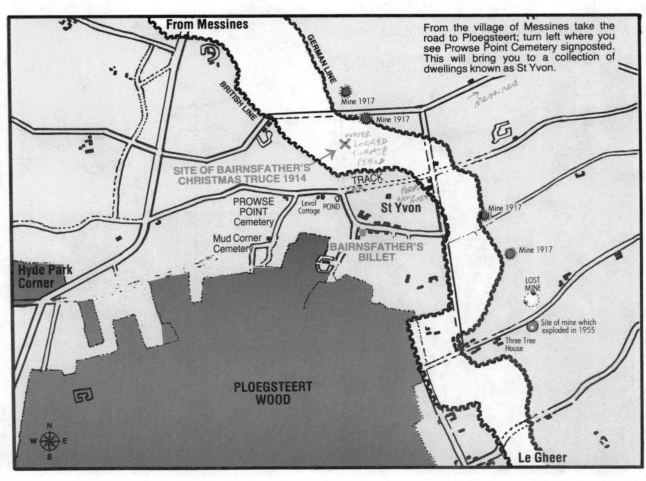

From Messines

GERMAN LINE

BRITISH LINE

Mine 1917

Messines

Mine 1917

From the village of Messines take the road to Ploegsteert; turn left where you see Prowse Point Cemetery signposted. This will bring you to a collection of dwellings known as St Yvon.

WATER LOGGED TURNIP FIELD

SITE OF BAIRNSFATHER'S CHRISTMAS TRUCE 1914

TRACK

Mine 1917

PROWSE POINT Cemetery

Leval Cottage

POND

St Yvon

Mud Corner Cemetery

BAIRNSFATHER'S BILLET

Mine 1917

Hyde Park Corner

LOST MINE

Site of mine which exploded in 1955

Three Tree House

PLOEGSTEERT WOOD

N W E S

Le Gheer

Bruce Bairnsfather has a special place in British regard through his talents as a cartoonist. It was whilst serving in the Front here that he created his two characters that remain instantly recognisable types. Old Bill, the timeworn soldier, skilled in doing the minimum necessary, is perhaps the most famous. He was portrayed as middle-aged, with a huge walrus moustache and a vast nose, supplied with cockney humour and an absolute master of the understatement. His foil was Bert, a gormless youth with the gift of asking the obvious, fresh-faced and with a cigarette always perched precariously on his bottom lip.

3. Bruce Bairnsfather's Christmas Truce

The simple truth of his cartoons struck an instant chord, and were tremendously popular, both at home and with the troops. However as the war went on, and especially after the Somme in 1916, with the realisation of just how serious a business war could be, his popularity amongst the troops diminished.

Before the war Bairnsfather had served in the army; but he decided that soldiering was not for him, and he attempted to take up a career in art. This did not work out either, and when war broke out he was a representative for a firm of electrical engineers. With hostilities he rejoined his regiment (the Warwicks) and was sent out to the 1st Battalion then stationed at Ploegsteert,

Left: Bruce Bairnsfather created this character, 'Old Bill' whilst he was serving as a machine gun officer with 1 Warwicks, on the edge of Ploegsteert Wood in 1914. The cartoon character became a favourite of soldiers and civilians alike.

or 'Plugstreet' as it was dubbed by the British soldiers. He found himself a billet in the small hamlet of St Yvon (or St Yves) a few hundred yards behind the Front Line.

Subsequently wounded, he was transferred

Far left: Bairnsfather's cartoon of himself creating his 'Fragments from France' on the wall of his billet.

Left: Christmas morning, the day of the truce with the Germans. 2 Lieutenant Bruce Bairnsfather stands beside a shell hole in the village of St Yvon.

61

Above: 'A memory of Christmas 1914, "Look at this bloke's buttons, 'Arry. I reckon 'e 'as a maid to dress 'im." ' That was Bairnsfather's caption to his cartoon drawing of the truce.

Right: Walking about in full sight of the enemy during the unofficial cease-fire.

shouting and jocular derision from both sides, our sergeant went along the hedge which ran at right-angles to the two lines of trenches. He was quickly out of sight; but, as we all listened in breathless silence, we soon heard a spasmodic conversation taking place out there in the darkness.

Presently, the sergeant returned. He had with him a few German cigars and cigarettes which he had exchanged for a couple of Manconochie's and a tin of Capstan, which he had taken with him. The seance was over, but it had given just the requisite touch to our Christmas Eve—something a little human and out of the ordinary routine."

The degree to which fraternisation took place seemed to depend entirely on the men in the Front at the time — and the duration of it also varied. In the Plugstreet wood sector, and to the south it was a particularly friendly affair. In some cases local truces were organized, in the main so that the dead of both sides might be given a decent burial. The opportunity was also taken to try and firmly identify the units that were facing each other. In some cases (especially on that part manned by the 1st Hampshires and 1st Somersets) contact seems to have been considerable, with gifts being exchanged — and even rifles. Most of this took place south of Le Gheer at the bottom edge of Plugstreet Wood. Even when the locally

from his regiment at the end of 1916 to duty as an Intelligence officer, the powers that be having realised his potential as a propaganda worker, and he toured extensively, including the United States. The huge success of his wartime work did not follow him into civilian life, and his contribution in that war was never recognised by the award of any decoration. He died in 1959.

Bruce Bairnsfather became involved in the Christmas Truce of 1914 that took part on many sectors of the Western Front. It began for him on Christmas Eve:

"A voice in the darkness shouted in English, with a strong German accent, 'Come over here!' A ripple of mirth swept along our trench, followed by a rude outburst of mouth organs and laughter. Presently, in a lull, one of our sergeants repeated the request, 'Come over here!'

'You come half-way — I come half-way,' floated out of the darkness.

'Come on, then!' shouted the sergeant. 'I'm coming along the hedge!'

'Ah! but there are two of you,' came back the voice from the other side.

Well anyway, after much suspicious

negotiated truces came to an end (usually at dusk), both sides tried to maintain a 'live and let live' principle. A Bavarian soldier sent a message to the 1st Somersets:

"Dear Camarades, I beg to inform you that it is forbidden us to go out to you but we will remain your camarades. If we shall be forced to fire we will fire too high. Please tell us if you are English or Irishmen. Offering you some cigars I remain yours truly camarade."

This reference to the Irish would only have confirmed higher commands concern: they took fright at reports that the Germans had tried to disaffect two Irish regiments. The truce petered out more or less quickly, and measures were taken the following year to try and prevent a recurrence, generally successfully. In any case the mood had changed; Sergeant-Major Ernest Shepherd wrote in his diary on Christmas 1915:

"(I) consider that the exchange of greetings by our troops and the enemy last Xmas was a wrong action. There should not (and cannot) be any goodwill between our troops and the despicable enemy troops opposing us. How could I, or any other, justify my action in exchanging greetings with the same reptiles who with their devilish gas killed — or tortured to death — so many of my comrades on Hill 60 on May 1st and 5th, and killed my dearest chum only three weeks ago. I hoped to be in the trenches today, so that if the hounds came out, I could exact a little compensation for what I have suffered."

Bruce Bairnsfather was serving as machine gun officer to his battalion at the time of the truce.

He noted that during the day both sides came out of their trenches and general fraternisation took place, with much exchanging of schnapps and whisky, uniform buttons and cigarettes. There was even something of a football match,

Above left: British soldier of the Rifle Brigade poses between two German officers during the truce in the Ploegsteert Wood sector.

Above: German and British troops fraternising on Christmas Day.

Below: Bairnsfather's own map of the sector.

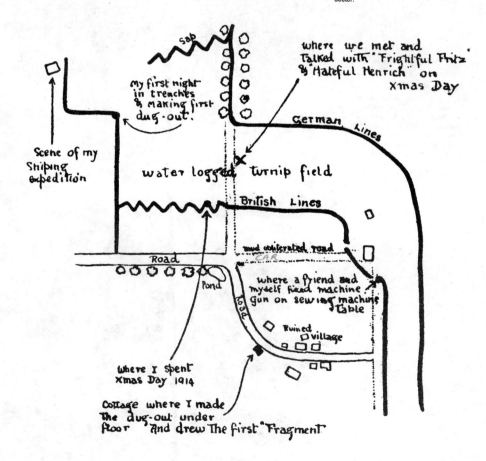

though a turnip field can hardly have been the ideal pitch; as yet it must have been relatively free of shell holes to be possible at all.

One wonders whether Adolf Hitler, whose unit served in the area of Messines Ridge, and who made use of the crypt of Messines church for shelter — a church easily recognisable from the No Man's Land where the truce took place — might not have been a distant and casual onlooker. When Bairnsfather himself returned to the trenches he noted:

"The last I saw of this little affair was a vision of one of my machine gunners, who was a bit of an amateur hairdresser in civil life, cutting the unnaturally long hair of a docile Boche, who was patiently kneeling on the ground whilst the automatic clippers crept up the back of his neck."

Right: The house arrowed stands on the approximate site of the cottage used by Bruce Bairnsfather at the time of the Christmas truce of 1914.

Right: At the position of the car the road bends sharply to the left. The car itself is parked on the rough track ('mud obliterated road', see Bairnsfather's map on previous page) opposite the pond. In the field directly behind the car is where the British front line ran and where, in No Man's Land, Bairnsfather met and talked to the Germans.

Plugstreet Wood is filled with rides and there are a number of bunkers used by the British as headquarters and aid posts under its now leafy shelter. As a small boy I can remember crawling around some of these and finding the remnants of a rum jar; a far greater trophy was the skull of a rat - doubtless the descendant of some trench monster that was the second worse plague (after lice) of the soldier's life. This is a game wood,

and so entry should not be attempted except where, for example, paths exist and are marked for visiting the war grave cemeteries that were established during the war in the heart of the wood.

The wood itself remained in British hands except for a few months in 1918, when the German offensive of April threatened to carry all before it.

Above: Painting of British troops filing through Ploegsteert Wood to take their turn in the trenches.

Left: Hunters Walk, a main thoroughfare through the shattered trees of 'Plug' Wood.

Right: These British soldiers are sheltering behind a concrete bunker in Ploegsteert Wood. Structures such as these still exist in the undergrowth.

IMPERIAL WAR MUSEUM

Below: Ploegsteert Wood Military Cemetery, situated in the middle of the wood. An unusually peaceful setting for the resting place of British soldiers — wilderness surrounding a cultivated lawn.

Winston Churchill, after his effective dismissal from the Admiralty in 1915, served the winter of 1915 - 1916 with the army in France, most of that time with the 6th Royal Scots Fusiliers in the trenches near Ploegsteert Wood. Even then his career had been extraordinarily eventful for a man of 40 — almost as tumultuous as that of his father, Lord Randolph Churchill, the son of the Duke of Marlborough. Randolph had played the resignation threat once too often, and in 1892 he lost his post as Chancellor of the Exchequer and his political career with it. A few years later he died young of a debilitating disease.

4. Winston Churchill, Soldier and Statesman

Winston was educated at Harrow and at Sandhurst and eventually joined 4 Hussars. Already restless, he got permission to work with the Spanish army in 1895 in their campaign against Cuban rebels. He then returned to London in 1896, and continued to make his mark on society and with the powerful establishment. He managed to get into expeditions to all sorts of Queen Victoria's little wars — acting as a soldier-journalist — in the North West frontier in India, in the Sudan (where he took part in a cavalry charge at Omdurman) and a most eventful time in the Boer War. Here he became something of a public hero, and on the crest of popular adulation won his first seat at Oldham.

There followed a highly successful political

TAYLOR LIBRARY

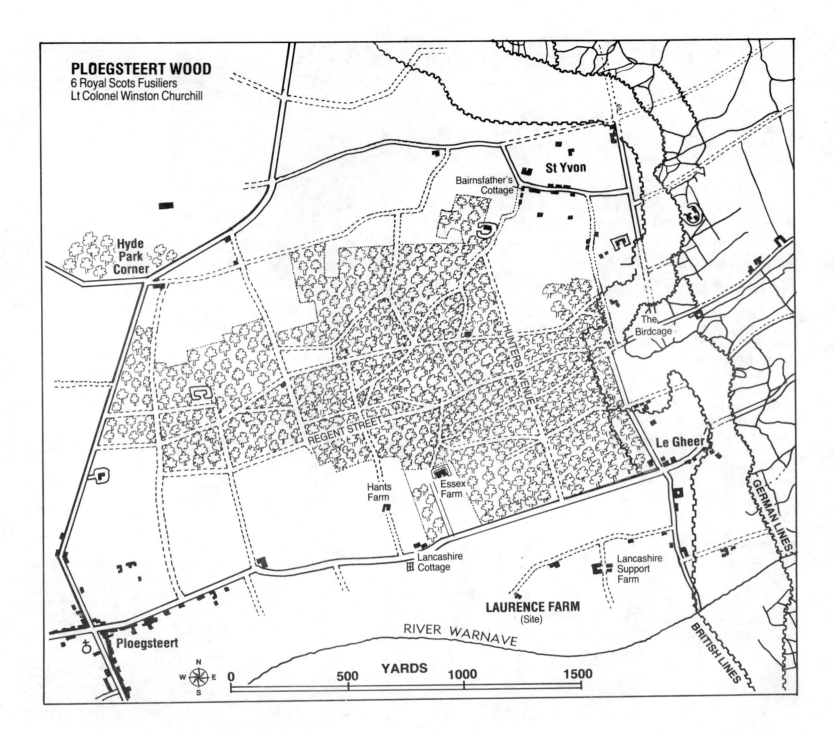

PLOEGSTEERT WOOD
6 Royal Scots Fusiliers
Lt Colonel Winston Churchill

career (having switched sides to the Liberal Party). He was a Minister at 31 and by 1910 had become Home Secretary, where he became notorious by appearing in person at the famous Sidney Street siege. Later that year, as war threatened, Churchill was transferred and became First Lord of the Admiralty. In this position he became a leading advocate of the invasion of Turkey through the Dardanelles, in an attempt to get at the Central Powers through their weakest front. It was an ill planned and resourced expedition; the situation at Gallipoli worsened, and a coalition government was in the process of being formed. Churchill had to go.

Soldiers regard all politicians with caution, and Churchill was no exception to the rule.

Winston used his influence with the Commander in Chief, Sir John French, and together they decided that before he received command of a brigade (an appointment Winston dearly desired) he should first have a period of instruction. Thus as a Major (when he was last in the army he had been a Lieutenant) Churchill arrived eventually at 2 Battalion the Grenadier Guards. The welcome was unpromising; the Colonel said, 'I think I ought to tell you that we were not at all consulted in the matter of your coming to us.' This was followed a few minutes later by the adjutant telling him that his kit had been cut down — to a spare pair of socks and shaving kit. This icy introduction thawed over time, and Churchill left with a good military report.

Left: Winston volunteered his services as a commander in France and was hoping to be given command of a brigade. Here he is seen upon his arrival in France with the British commander in chief, Field Marshal Sir John French. He was posted to the Grenadier Guards to gain experience.

Meanwhile other things had gone wrong: Sir John French had been replaced by Haig, and with French gone all hopes of Churchill commanding a brigade vanished. Instead he was given command of a battalion, 6 Royal Scots Fusiliers, which at the time was situated close by the village of Le Gheer, near Ploegsteert Wood. He did, however, succeed in getting a political friend, Major Sir Archibald Sinclair, as his second in command, who he managed to extract from 2 Life Guards. Sir Archibald was later to become leader of the Liberals in the 30s and served in Churchill's wartime government as Secretary for Air in the Second World War.

To the battalion Churchill brought his infectious enthusiasm — he declared war on lice, he

Below: When Douglas Haig replaced Sir John French, Churchill's hopes of commanding a brigade (four battalions) vanished. Instead, he was given command of one battalion, 6 Royal Scots Fusiliers. He is pictured here with brother officers in the Ploegsteert area where he served from December 1915 to the beginning of May 1916.

By kind permission of the HQ Royal Highland Fusiliers

design, he discarded the glengarry for a French steel helmet, complete in its horizon blue colour, and wore a waterproof which had great quantities of fur to keep him warm through the winter.

He was not popular with other battalion commanders in the sector — in what was generally one of the quietest in the area — by his frequent rifle fire onslaughts on the trenches opposite, complete with called-up artillery support, resulting in the whole sector becoming ablaze with a firefight. On one occasion he had a building shelled from which came the strains of a German band; and the following night had a similar ensemble bought up to his head-quarters; he was delighted when the Germans did not retaliate.

Nothing could detract him from his political inclinations, however; and of course he attracted the famous to his trenches — which was regarded as a mixed blessing by his men. One general was horrified at the vulnerability of his forward headquarters at Laurence Farm, but Churchill assured him that wars were dangerous. Another visitor, the Attorney General F.E. Smith (later Lord Birkenhead) was actually arrested for being in the zone of the armies without a permit.

His military career had a fortunate break in it which allowed him to make his way back to Westminster in the Spring of 1916. Because of 6 and 7 battalions being under strength it was determined to amalgamate them; the Commanding Officer of the 7th had seniority, and so Churchill bowed out. The Parliamentary report on Gallipoli in large measure cleared Churchill of responsibility, and in May 1917 he found himself back in the Government as Minister of Munitions.

tried to get his officers on to their horses more frequently, he took to prowling around the trenches and breastworks, and parades were made a little difficult by his use of cavalry commands. His uniform was entirely of his own

By stopping at Lancashire Cottage cemetery and looking over the back wall in a south easterly direction (the road from Ploegstreet runs east) the observer is looking towards the site of Laurence Farm — about four hundred yards away; and beyond that is Le Gheer and the support and front lines which Churchill would have known.

Above: A soldier of the Royal Berkshires keeps watch through a periscope in the Ploegsteert sector. The trench seen here seems to be well constructed, but the soldier's wellington boots indicate that mud and water remain a problem.

Above right: A shattered crows nest once used by British observers in 'Plug' Wood. The picture was taken just after the war.

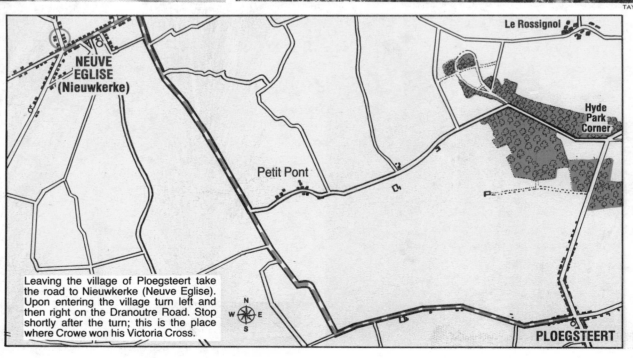

Leaving the village of Ploegsteert take the road to Nieuwkerke (Neuve Eglise). Upon entering the village turn left and then right on the Dranoutre Road. Stop shortly after the turn; this is the place where Crowe won his Victoria Cross.

Failure to break the British-French line in their March 1918 offensive, in the area of the Somme caused the Germans to try further north. Again, the German assault troops experienced initial success as they broke through south of the Ypres Salient in an area held by the Portugese. This was a determined effort by the commander, Ludendorff, to reach the Channel ports. It was known as the battle of the the Lys and was launched in April, 1918.

5. Captain Crowe's Victoria Cross

The 2 Worcesters had observed the Germans streaming past Ploegsteert Wood and across the rolling hills towards them. After some initial engagements with the attackers in which they had caused them some considerable losses, the Worcesters fell back into the village of Neuve Eglise. At 6 pm on 13 April battalion headquarters had been set up in the Mairie (Town Hall). Two platoons from B Company along with Headquarters Company barricaded themselves in the building, using the top floor for a machine gun position. Loopholes were knocked through the walls and the cellar was turned into an aid post for the wounded by the padre Captain Tanner.

Left: Captain John James Crowe. His action in capturing two German machine guns enabled over 100 trapped men to make their escape.

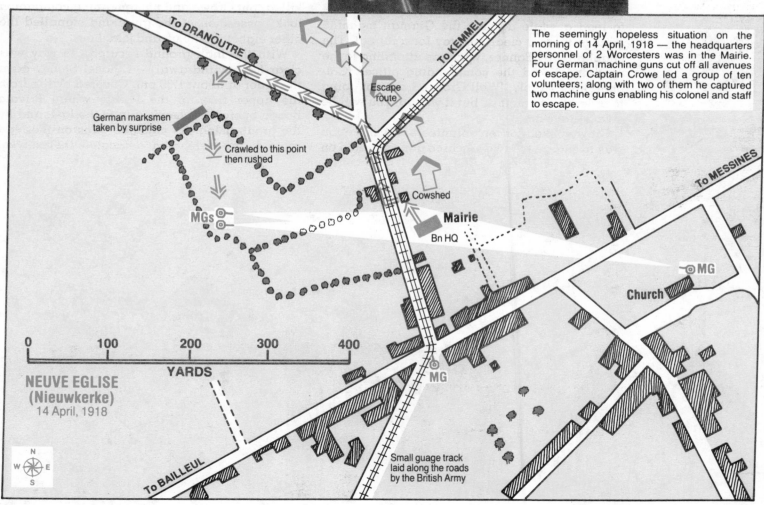

The seemingly hopeless situation on the morning of 14 April, 1918 — the headquarters personnel of 2 Worcesters was in the Mairie. Four German machine guns cut off all avenues of escape. Captain Crowe led a group of ten volunteers; along with two of them he captured two machine guns enabling his colonel and staff to escape.

To DRANOUTRE

To KEMMEL

Escape route

German marksmen taken by surprise

Crawled to this point then rushed

Cowshed

MGs

Mairie

Bn HQ

To MESSINES

MG

Church

0 100 200 300 400

YARDS

NEUVE EGLISE
(Nieuwkerke)
14 April, 1918

MG

N
W E
S

To BAILLEUL

Small guage track laid along the roads by the British Army

As darkness fell all contact was lost with the rest of the battalion and runners sent out to try and make contact failed to return.

There was movement all around the village as German troops infiltrated under the cover of night. Occasional flares put up by the attackers helped the Worcesters to pick out targets and attempts to rush the position were thwarted. Dawn broke on the 14th revealing that they were surrounded and with the light, mortar bombs began crashing into the building — two came through the roof causing casualties. There was no talk of surrender, even when machine guns opened up on the building from three sides — from the church, from the crossroads at the end of the street and from some high ground to the west. Although the defenders were still putting up a spirited defence causing casualties among the enemy, even driving them back for a while, it was clear that it was only a matter of time before they would be overwhelmed.

The situation was desperate as an officer, Second Lieutenant Johnson, volunteered to make a break for it to try and get help. He did not get very far before he was hit and mortally wounded.

Two machine guns set up in a field, on high ground were making any retreat for the trapped Worcesters impossible; they were pouring a continuous stream of fire into the walls of the Mairie. At about 11 am Lieutenant (Acting Captain and Adjutant) John James Crowe volunteered to lead a sortie against the German machine guns to try and clear the way for a retreat. The chaplain, Rev Tanner, who was attending to the wounded heard the commanding officer, Colonel Stoney reply, 'Well Crowe, I am not going to order you to do this, but if you go, you will be a very brave man.'

Crowe asked for ten volunteers, his intention was to charge the two machine guns situated on

rising ground to the west of the Mairie head on. His first move was to break from the building and occupy a nearby cowshed — that was achieved without casualties. He then led his ten volunteers in a dash across the road and once safely there they opened fire from a hedge by the roadside. It became obvious to him that a frontal assault would not be feasible so he decided upon a flank approach.

Leaving eight men by the roadside hedge he took two men with him and crawled down the side of the road to a bend where there was less risk of observation. The three of them turned into the field and began to work their way towards the machine guns. As they reached an intervening hedge they came up behind some German infantry who were busy firing at the Mairie — they were quickly dealt with. Although they could hear the chatter of the guns a short distance ahead of them, because of the slope of the ground, they couldn't see the gun crews. They crawled forward until they could make out the German helmets; obviously the crews had not heard the shooting to their left, so intent were they on raking the Mairie.

Jumping to their feet the three charged the gun crews firing as they went. The Germans were taken completely by suprise and fired a few wild shots in the direction of Crowe and his two men before fleeing leaving their weapons behind. One of the Worcesters was hit and killed, but Crowe and his remaining companion took possession of the guns and signalled the other eight to come up and join them.

With the high ground secured the way was clear for a withdrawal — Colonel Stoney gave the order at about 1.30 pm. Covered by fire from the upper floor of the Mairie where Private Bough operated a Lewis gun to the last, and by the group using the machine guns on the high ground, the defenders extricated themselves.

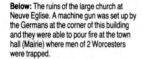

Below: The ruins of the large church at Neuve Eglise. A machine gun was set up by the Germans at the corner of this building and they were able to pour fire at the town hall (Mairie) where men of 2 Worcesters were trapped.

By kind permission of the Regimental Headquarters of The Worcestershire & Sherwood Foresters Regiment

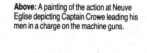

Leaving the ruined building about 100 men and six officers escaped down the road towards Dranoutre — about 30 of them were wounded. Only three were left behind, too seriously wounded to be moved.

Once the exhausted Worcesters had got away then Captain Crowe and his party withdrew, eventually joining up with the others that evening.

Second Army headquarters at Blendecques, was the scene of the presentation of the Victoria Cross to Captain Crowe by King George V, in August. Although he served in France for four years and three months, and was in the thick of the fighting, Captain Crowe came out of it unscathed, although he was blown up twice and buried once. He retired from the regiment in 1920 and became a school attendance officer for Brighton — he died in 1965 at the age of 88.

The action of Captain Crowe is easily followed on the ground today, although the Mairie as it then was has gone, and the buildings in the immediate area have changed. The church used to stand in the middle of a field away from other buildings — these changes have led to some misunderstanding of the action.

The village of Neuve Eglise is a pleasant place to stop for lunch with its large square. A visit to the British cemetery, which is part of the churchyard, helps to tell the story of the place during the Great War.

Above: A painting of the action at Neuve Eglise depicting Captain Crowe leading his men in a charge on the machine guns.

Left: Captain Crowe receives his Victoria Cross from King George V.

IMPERIAL WAR MUSEUM

75

Right: The old Mairie, where the Worcesters were trapped, was on the left hand side of this street.

Right: The German machine guns lay on the crest of the ridge, as viewed from the road in front of the postion where the old Mairie once stood.

Below: The German gunners lay here firing at the Mairie, on the same line as the house to the right. Captain Crowe and his companions approached from the left of the picture.

6. Willy Redmond, Ireland's British Patriot

Major William (Willy) Kearney Redmond, is pictured below marching at the head of a column of Southern Irish troops of 16 Irish Division. Irish Nationalist MP Willy Redmond, jailed in the past for his vociferous opposition to British rule in Ireland, nevertheless felt it his duty to exhort his fellow Irishmen to join the forces of the British Empire at the time of its greatest trial. His brother John, who was the leader of the Irish Nationalist Party was, like Willy, in no doubt as to the overwhelming opinion of the Irish people with regard to the Allied cause. "This," he said, "was the opinion which thousands of Irish soldiers have sealed with their blood by dying in the cause of the liberty of Ireland and of the world."

His brother added his own words:

'In the name of God, we who are about to die...'

BCPL

Left: Major William (Willy) Redmond at the head of a column of southern Irish troops. Differences with the British authorities were put to one side as he threw everything into the common cause — defeat of Germany and her allies.

On Easter Monday, 28 April, 1916 the streets of Dublin's fair city erupted in fire and violence as a band of fervent Irish Nationalists staged an armed uprising against British rule. Several buildings were seized by the Republicans, among them Liberty Hall in Beresford Place and the General Post Office on the corner of Sackville and Henry Streets. By the time that the rising had been quelled by the British Army on 1 May, one of the finest areas of the city had come to resemble some of the shell torn streets of France and Belgium. It was as if the war had stretched across to Ireland, a state of affairs which Mr John Redmond MP, leader of the Irish Nationalist Party, denounced in no uncertain terms at a parliamentary session: "Will the house allow me to say just one sentence? I think it scarcely necessary for my part, but perhaps I ought to give expression on behalf of all my colleagues of the Nationalist Party here, and, as I believe, the overwhelming majority of people of Ireland, to the feeling of devastation and horror with which we have regarded these proceedings." His comments were all the more significant since his brother, William Redmond, also an MP, was then commanding a company of 6 Royal Irish Regiment in Flanders.

IMPERIAL WAR MUSEUM

Above: Locre is only recognisable by the board indicating the name attached to the heap of rubble. Note the ex London bus.

Locre was in a reserve area, about four to five miles from the Front Line. After mid 1915 this area had become relatively quiet, and many units of Kitchener's Army came here to be introduced to the rigours of trench warfare. By 1917 it was transformed into a bustling centre in preparation for the Messines offensive, scheduled for June.

A major wartime feature of the village was the Hospice. This is often refered to in the literature of World War One, and the nuns remained there until 1918, when the building was destroyed in the German advance in April of that year. The building in fact used to be further to the east. The nuns in particular became friendly with the officers of the 16 Irish Division, who were stationed here prior to the great Messines offensive of 1917. Especial regard was shown to Major William Redmond, MP.

Willy Redmond MP was one of Ireland's most famous nationalists; on a number of occasions he had been imprisoned for his outspoken opposition to the British and he was a key spokesman for the cause of Home Rule. However, when the war broke out he, along with his equally prominent brother John, came down firmly on the side of the justice of Britain's cause. Burgoyne noted in his diary a report from

a friend of the impact of one of Redmond's famous Parliamentary speeches. This friend happened to be in the House of Commons and seated close to the German Ambassador when Redmond made his speech saying that, 'we could leave the defence of Ireland to the Irish.' The German Ambassador turned white, and leaving immediately, had to be supported into his carriage, the shock of this news had so great a physical effect on him.

This shock is easily understood when it is realised that Ireland was on the verge of civil war when hostilities broke out in August 1914, and the last thing that the Germans might have expected was support from the Irish Nationalists for the British war effort. They not only supported the war, but the Redmonds worked actively and with some success to produce southern Irish divisions to take their place on the battlefield. Willy, although in his fifties became a captain and company commander (perhaps the oldest serving on the Front) in the 6th Royal Irish Regiment. Before the battle of the Somme he had been promoted to Major and put, somewhat reluctantly, on the divisional staff. However when the battle of Messines was launched in June 1917 he insisted on rejoining his regiment — the division fighting alongside

Above: Mr John Redmond, MP, leader of the Irish Nationalist Party, condemned the armed uprising against British rule that took place in Dublin in April, 1916.

their political foes, the Ulster Division. Before this happened he made a deeply impressive speech in the Commons in March 1917:

"In the name of God, we here who are about to die, perhaps, ask you to do that which largely induced us to leave our homes — and enable us when we meet Canadians or Australians and New Zealanders side by side in the common cause and the common field to say to them, Our country, just as yours, has self-government within the Empire."

Attempts were made to try and keep him out of the actual fighting, but as zero hour approached he insisted on being with his beloved battalion the 6 Royal Irish Regiment, which had moved into position in the line just west of 'Whitesheet Village'. Their objective would be in the vicinity of 'Petit Bois' — 'Red Chateau' and 'Unamed Wood' — afterwards named 'Inniskilling Wood' in honour of that regiment.

Major Redmond was reluctantly given permission by his battalion commander to go over with the attack, but only as far as the first objective. As he hurried across the intervening ground in the wake of the explosions of the huge mines, he was hit first in the hand and then again in the leg. The wounds in themselves were not serious, but at the age of 54, shock set in. Stretcher bearers from the rival 36 Ulster Division picked him up and took him to 16 Irish Collecting Post, situated near Kemmel. From there he was moved to Locre and the Hospice Casualty Clearing Station where he died.

His grave became a source of pilgrimage to Roman Catholics placed as it was by the nuns in the grounds of the Hospice. The present building, almost identical to the old one which was destroyed and was rebuilt a few hundred yards further up the road towards Locre. After the war, Redmond's remains were transferred to the newly created British cemetery across the road from the site of the Hospice and about a quarter of a mile away. However, at the request of his family his remains were once again moved a short distance from the cemetery and placed between two elm trees.

The Belgian Flemings could identify with Redmond and his aims — for they too felt dominated by a French speaking establishment which ignored their cultural and linguistic grievances. And so his grave remains — a unique tribute.

There was another Irishman that the nuns wished to bury in a place of honour alongside Redmond. Fr Willy Doyle spent much time at the Hospice, acting both as chaplain to the nuns

Below: A deputation from Ireland to the grave of Major Redmond, 21 September, 1917. The Mayor of Wexford is speaking and he is holding a bunch of heather brought over from Ireland. Various dignatories, who included the High Sheriff of Dublin, made speeches at the grave and laid wreaths. Staff officers along with north and south Irish troops were present along with nuns (who cared for the grave). After the war the remains were removed and resited across the road at the new British military cemetery. Then later, at the request of the family, Redmonds remains were removed once again and buried further up the field.

and to various battalions in the 16 Irish Division. He had felt the warmth of their welcome:

"Looking back on the terrible winter we went through (that of 1916 — 1917), I often wonder what I should have done, were it not for the room which the good nuns put at my disposal when I got back from the trenches and which gave me the chance of a decent rest and sleep. I don't suppose we shall ever see the convent again; but the memory of the kindness shown us all, myself especially as if I were a part of the Community (of nuns) will not easily be forgotten."

Doyle was killed at Frezenberg in August 1917 during the great Third Battle of Ypres, but he was not to find his place of honour, for his body was never found — hardly surprising since it seems likely that he took the full blast of a shell.

Locre is a good example of a small Belgian village, still retaining something of the tranquility that must have existed before 1914 so rudely disturbed things. In the churchyard is buried Christopher Fowler, who was a Private in the Honourable Artillery Company. This regiment is particularly old — dating back to the reign of Henry VIII — and had two components: infantry and artillery. It is a Territorial unit, and in 1914 many of its members were recruited from the middle classes. Rushed to France in the early days of the war, the regiment was in the line here on Christmas Day. He wrote home:

"Just our luck, in the trenches on

Above: The special regard for Major Redmond is still indicated by his unusual burial place a short distance from Locre Hospice Military Cemetery.

Left: At the age of 54, Willy Redmond was likely the oldest company commander in the First World War.

On the map: To Poperinge

Locre is about two miles from Kemmel, directly west and can be clearly seen from the top of Mont Kemmel

LOCRE (Loker)

Two men executed by firing squad are buried side by side. Privates Byers and Evans

Cemetery in which Fowler is buried

PRESENT HOSPICE

Site of Hospice destroyed in 1918

Belgian Customs

Grave of Major Redmond

LOCRE HOSPICE CEMETERY

To Kemmel

To Bailleul

FRANCE

Above: Locre (Loker) today, restored to its pre war sleepy existence.

Christmas Eve, Day and also Boxing Day. Cold, it was fearfully cold. At one time there were nine degrees of frost and all the time it was below freezing point. My thoughts were rivetted on you and home. Clearly I could see in the imagination the dining, drawing rooms at home. I could almost hear the songs being sung, it was the eve of Christmas. At 11.30 I could see Ealing Common, white with frost on the ground, a clear moon over head and a party from home going to Acton church. Everything was vividly portrayed by my imagination. How I longed to be with you. Although surrounded by friends and the enemy in front of me, I was awfully lonely, terribly lonely."

And the conditions he was serving in?

"We had a particularly rotten time on the last occasion in the trenches. Although we had only one casualty, we were told we were in for two days and night (sic). It rained unceasingly; waist deep in water and mud. We stuck it well for the two days and nights, and just as we were expecting relief we were told to stick it for another day and night. Oh what a disappointment! Whew, can you imagine it? It was almost like a death sentence ... Fortunately they could not shell us much as the trenches are about fifteen yards apart in some places, and woe betide anyone who so much as puts his hair above the top of the trench. The greatest writer of the day cannot describe the wretchedness of the trenches. Sleep in two feet of water is of course out of the question. We exist for letters only. Personally I would sooner be shelled than sniped at, and I believe most of our chaps would."

Soon after his death on March 1915 his parents received a letter from his commanding officer:

"An attack was made upon the German position, and our company held a position immediately in front. We were subjected to very heavy machine gun fire and your son was unhappily hit in the head. He survived his wounds some hours. As he still lived, as soon as it was dark he was taken away to the hospital where he died, so I do not know whether he ever recovered consciousness, but I do not think he did..."

Only a few yards from Fowler lies a school friend, Philip Ward, a Private in the Liverpool Scottish, who had rushed back from Canada whence he emigrated to serve in the war against the Germans.

It was not only men shot by the Germans who ended their days at Locre; Burgoyne noted the execution of two soldiers there in 1915:

"The week I left for leave (5th February 1915) I hear two of the Royal Scots Fusiliers were shot in Locre for being absent from parade for the trenches. It took three volleys to kill one of them. The men of the firing party are so stupid, they will not understand that the kindest thing that they can do is shoot straight."

To the north of Locre is Scherpenberg, another prominent hill, with a large number of bunkers scattered on its surface. Between there, Locre and Kemmel both sides kept a large number of patrols in No Man's Land created by the German advance of 1918. In this vicinity was a huge model of the German trench system which was the target of the Messines offensive, to which all commanders down to NCOs were brought to see what they had to do on the day.

Above: A safe haven from the German guns — the town of Poperinge, some seven miles from the front line.

(H) PLACES OF SAFETY Poperinge, Vlamertinge

This rather pleasant town was almost always safely in the rear of the lines, and so the soldiers whilst there could relax. It is worth noting that apart from Furnes (Veurne), Poperinge was the only Belgian town to escape occupation at some stage by the German forces in World War I. There were odd occasions when a shell did land there — the nearest part of the line was seven miles away.

In general, though, people had happy memories of it — not least because the leave train for a while left from the railway station at Poperinge. In addition for the officers there were good restaurants — the best known collecting the name Skindles, after a fashionable establishment situated on the Thames, and it operated even after the war for a number of years as a hotel. The name still remains above the door — but it is a private house now.

Next door to it is Talbot House (see the section including Sanctuary Wood page 120) open to the public in the morning and afternoon. It is also possible to stay here — there are no restaurant facilities, but there is a kitchen to make your own meal should the fancy take you. The gardens have been much restored with the aid of a British army unit now stationed at Antwerp and thanks to the work of the most recent caretaker Ivy, and her husband Charles Swan.

Mounting the stairs, the rooms still carry mementoes of the war days, and by some of them there written explanations of their wartime function. On the top floor there is a table with some fascinating photographs, some wartime and some shortly after the war, when a benefactor bought the house and presented it to the Toc H organisation. In the attic is the chapel — beware the extremely steep and narrow stairs! Much of the chapel furnishings date from the war period, and there were literally thousands of men who were confirmed and a substantial number who were baptised here. It is a lovely place to stop and be quiet, in the roof cavity where hops used to be put to dry and

83

Above: Captain Noel Chavasse, VC and Bar, MC, is buried at Brandhoek, between Poperinghe and Vlamertinge. He served in the Royal Army Medical Corps and won his first Victoria Cross on the Somme. He was again awarded the VC for his actions at Wieltje, near Ypres for staying at his post although being wounded and going out under fire to help bring in wounded men. His actions resulted in those around him being also inspired to great acts of courage in rescuing the wounded. He died of his wounds and was buried at Brandhoek New Military Cemetery; his gravestone carries the inscription of two Victoria Crosses.

Right: "Tubby" Clayton greets some guests at Talbot House, a haven from the guns for all ranks.

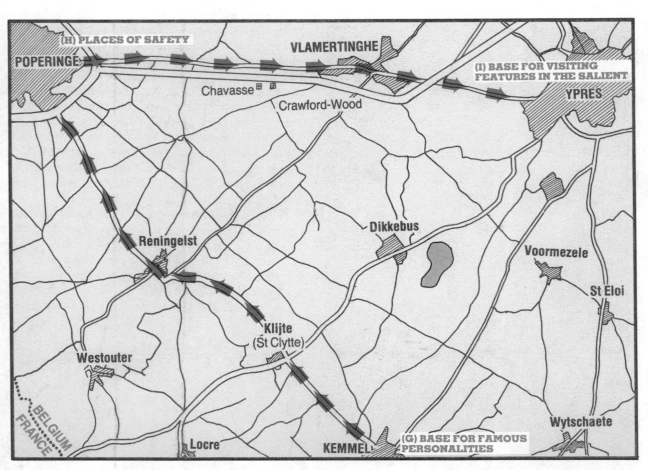

transformed into a place where so many sought comfort. Talbot House came through the war largely undamaged, except for a few shells, one of which burst on the rear of the house and killed one or two men.

Poperinge did suffer a moment of fright, in the German offensive of 1918, and even Talbot House was closed down for a while (it was also known as Everyman's Club, on the grounds that it was open to all ranks — a very unusual state of affairs). But this soon passed, and although a little closer to the line than might be required for comfort, it continued the war as the nearest relatively safe town to Ypres.

are farm-house guest houses in the locality. It offers good restaurants (not cheap, but reasonable) where local specialities may be tried. It boasts an indoor swimming pool if the weather is against you, and for some unaccountable reason you feel the need for exercise. On the other hand there is the National Hop Museum for those who want to look into the mysteries of Stella Artois production. Further details, town maps and so forth are easily obtained from a most helpful Information Office, where good English is spoken.

Poperinge is the centre of the fairly sizeable Belgian brewing industry. In the thirteenth century it had been a prominent cloth city — indeed it was even a member of the economic co-ordinating body known as the Hanseatic League which dominated the Port of London for many years. As Ypres gave the Americans the

For information concerning executed soldiers: SHOT AT DAWN by Julian Putkowski and Julian Sykes. Published by Wharncliffe Publishing, Barnsley.

Left: A prisoner in the condemned cell awaits his fate as dawn approaches.

Below: The main street of Poperinghe at the turn of the century.

Not all was rest and relaxation from the strain and stress of war; for in the New British cemetery that lies within the town's perimeter lies the bodies of several soldiers who were shot in the courtyard of the town hall. This building is in the Grand Place, part of it now housing the Tourist Information Office. Those who were sentenced were held in the small jail, taken from there to the courtyard, enclosed on all sides by the building, and there shot. Executions by the Armed Forces — all three hundred and forty odd of them — provoke almost as much controversy as any other issue in the Great War (there were no executions in the Second).

Like Ypres it too has its fine buildings and square that soldiers from those years would recognise. It also has a traffic system that is a little more confusing, though there is a ring road of sorts so that the centre can be avoided. However, the town is not nearly as big, and even the most timid motorist can eventually find his way around — even if it means doing a couple of circuits in the process.

If you want to stay somewhere which is perhaps not so conscious of the war, Poperinge is the place: it has a number of hotels, and there

IMPERIAL WAR MUSEUM

Right: Heavy traffic on the Ypres — Poperinghe road in 1915. The horses, carts and men on the right of the picture are moving up to the front and on the opposite side of the road the traffic is moving out of the battle area. The centre of the road is kept clear for motorised transport — in this case an ambulance.

Above and right: A welcome sight for troops coming away from Ypres and out of the line, the village of Vlamertinghe. At this point they were almost out of the range of enemy artillery.

word 'diaper' (d'Ieper) so Poperinge gave us the word 'poplin'. With the decline of the cloth trade, the feudal overlords of the region, the abbots of St Omer sought economic prosperity through the hop. Hence when travelling around here now — at least until after the harvest in September, the hop fields and their produce dominate much of the landscape.

There are a couple of cemeteries in the town, but perhaps the more interesting is Poperinge Old Military Cemetery. This is found down a narrow passage, but the cemetery itself covers a large area of grass, with the graves tucked away at the back. This rather strange use of space is explained by the fact that many of the burials (in the grounds of a chateau) were removed after the war — a large number of Frenchmen, and also a large number of civilians, many of whom died as a consequence of the Spanish flu that swept Europe at the end of 1918 and in 1919. All the British burials here date before 1916.

Poperinge came into fleeting prominence in 1940, when it was the pivot on which the British withdrawal to Dunkirk turned in this particular area; whilst the town itself also suffered fairly considerable damage in 1944 during the liberation.

The Salient

Above: Ypres today. The Cloth Hall and St Martin's Cathedral have been lovingly restored. Note the Menin Gate at the upper right hand of the photograph.

Ypres, the tormented city
(I) Base for visiting features in The Salient

This city is known in Flemish as Ieper, so beware potential confusion of sign posts! Actually it is a point worth noting that many of the inhabitants in this area were originally lukewarm in their attitude towards the allies. For many years the Flemish population were regarded as inferiors to the French; officially — on the maps, for example — place names were marked in their French version rather than in the Flemish which reflected the majority of the population.

Many of the chateaux in the area were occupied in the pre-War years by an aristocracy that was largely French speaking — for example Leopold II of Belgium (1865 - 1909) spent much time at the White Chateau between St Eloi and Hollebeke. They entertained themselves by shooting parties in the plentiful copses, many maintained for that purpose, as well as finding themselves conveniently close to the coast and not too far from Paris. Many of the Flemings therefore built up a resentment which is not unlike that found amongst many communities in Europe which find themselves dominated by an unsympathetic establishment — like the Irish in Britain, the Basques in Spain and France, the Hungarians in Roumania and so forth. The

presence of this feeling is perhaps more starkly illustrated in Belgium than elsewhere — not only are there the normal range of political parties — Socialists, Christian Democrats and so on, but there are Flemish and French (or Walloon) sections of the same party.

Ypres is a lovely City. It was effectively utterly destroyed in the holocaust years of the Great War. Father Doyle described it on his way up to the Front in late July 1917:

"In silence, save for the never ceasing roar of the guns and the rumble of the cartwheels, we marched on through the city of the dead, Ypres, not a little anxious, for a shower of shells might come at any minute.Ruin and desolation, desolation and ruin, is the only description I can give of a spot once the pride and glory of Belgium. The hand of war has fallen heavily on the city of Ypres; scarce a stone remains of the glorious Cathedral and the equally famous Cloth Hall; the churches, a dozen of them, are piles of rubbish, gone are the convents, the hospitals and public buildings, and though many of the inhabitants are still there, their bodies lie buried in the ruins of their homes, and the

smell of rotting corpses poisons the air. I have seen strange sights in the last two years, but this was the worst of all. Out again by the opposite gate of this stricken spot (the Menin Gate), which people say was not undeserving of God's chastisement, across the moat and along the road pitted all over with half filled in shell holes. Broken carts and dead horses, with human bodies too if one looked, lie on all sides, but one is too weary to think of anything except how many more miles must be covered."

Churchill for one thought that it should be the site of a great memorial to the War, the area around it being the graveyard of at least a quarter of a million British dead. The Belgians who lived there naturally had other ideas, but did agree to leave the Cloth Hall, the Ramparts and the Menin Gate in a ruined state until the British and Commonwealth Governments came to some decision about a memorial. As time went on only the Menin Gate was left — but these three points even now would be the landmarks with which old soldiers would be most at home.

To start to view Ypres nothing could be better than to arrive in the Grand Place on a summer's evening, find a cafe with seating outside, and take in something of the atmosphere that lingers. To stop that being destroyed by the roar of the internal combustion engine, the best day is probably a Sunday. The view is across an area that used to be one of the most prosperous in the whole of northern Europe in the thirteenth and fourteenth centuries. Ypres was one of the major cities of the north, ranking with London and Paris, and in simple economic (as opposed to political) terms, probably more important. It was the most important of the Flemish towns in the cloth trade, boasted a population of at least thirty thousand in 1300, and was a major commercial centre. However it suffered grievously from plague — in a few months in 1316 it lost two thousand people — and from gross overdependence on one industry: cloth. As the English began to turn from producing just the raw materials to manufacturing, a process that began at the end of the thirteenth century, so Ypres suffered. By 1370 it was only handling 15% of the cloth from its high point sixty years or so earlier. With the establishment of Calais as the home of the Staple (the company that controlled the export of English cloths) Ypres' fate was sealed, especially as politically it did not carry the same power as a city such as Antwerp. The monument to these years of prospserity is the Cloth Hall, in which the cloth was stored having been transported up the waterways, and to which merchants flocked from as far afield as Italy. Ypres disappeared into relative obscurity with the defeat of the Flemish towns by the Duke of Burgundy and the king of France in 1382.

There then followed a long period when Flanders became a plaything of the Great Powers of France, Spain and Austria, under

Below: How the centre of Ypres appeared early in 1915. The towers of the Cloth Hall and Cathedral were zeroed in on by the German gunners and the destruction got underway. British military presence can be discerned in the square.

were prepared for the worst. On the 24th August 1914 the Mayor issued this proclamation:

"Dear Fellow Citizens! Calm ! Calm! If it should happen that the German army should arrive at Ypres, everyone should stay indoors and follow the orders that I posted yesterday. The German commander will be received at the Town Hall by the Burgermaster and Councillors, who will work for your rights. Inhabitants who leave their home or who carry out what may be considered a hostile act risk their own lives as well as those of their fellow citizens.

THE BELGIAN FLAG MUST NOT BE RAISED.
NO BARRICADES!
NO RIOTING!
ONCE MORE, CALM AND PATIENCE!"

whose authority Ypres slipped in and out, generally with indifference as to which foreigner should actually rule. It is to the French that the citizens of Ypres owe the Ramparts; and it is to the great skill of the seventeenth century military engineer Vauban that the British soldier frequently owed his life as he lay in relative safety under the shelter that these great walls offered. This burst of particular excitement took place from about 1650 - 1690; then tranquility returned. Ypres took up its position as being an important market town, the centre to which the rural communities would turn, the ecclesiastical focus of the area, and in due course an important part of the railway system. By 1914 the population had dwindled to about twelve thousand or so — a small fraction of what it had once been.

Then came the war. German cavalry did actually come through Ypres, and the citizens

The Grand Place has been rebuilt to a considerable degree to the situation as it was before the war started. Of course the town is dominated by the Cloth Hall, one of the most impressive memorials to the medieval economy in Europe, and by the early Gothic St Martin's Cathedral.

The Cloth Hall now houses a most helpful tourist information office, from where guides to the Battlefields and to the Town may be obtained in English, as well as large scale ordnance survey type maps. Just next door to this is the entrance (up a flight of stairs) to the Salient Museum. When I first came here in 1968 this was housed in a small chamber in the Tower (it is possible to climb to the top); every year since then the museum has seemed to be improved, with more to be seen and displayed to greater effect. The entrance fee of the equivalent of about fifty pence is well spent, and there is available a number of publications which the more enthusiastic battlefield visitor will find most useful.

In the square it is worth looking at some of the restored houses — built in a style of architecture associated with Spanish/Austrian rule, and which is to be found in towns and cities as far south as Arras. Especially fascinating are the roofs, with their large number of small dormer windows. The local 'quick food' speciality is Frites with Mayonaisse — generally of high quality. For the more extravagantly inclined there are Leonidas chocolates — made with cream and butter they are not for the weight conscious, and although pricey they are far cheaper here than in the UK.

Civilization has arrived in the square in the form of parking charges, but it is perhaps a fair price to pay for the great convenience of parking in Ypres. However, be warned: the people of Ypres seem to enjoy having fairs and festive occasions — especially in September and August — and then not only parking, but even

getting into the city becomes a nightmare. On Saturday there is a market on the square, and if your hotel happens to front on to it you will be invited to remove your vehicle. It is best to ensure that you do this the night before, otherwise you might be boxed in for the rest of the day.

From the square it is logical to walk up to the Menin Gate. There was no structure as such before the war, just a gap in the ramparts. The two lions that used to stand guard have found their way to Australia. The Memorial has lost something by the way in which housing has closed up to it, especially from within the walls of the city; on the other hand it is still an intensly moving structure as name after name, column after column of dead with no known graves are inscribed on seemingly every face of the arch. The Last Post sounded here every evening at 8 pm is probably the most moving ceremony left from the Great War period. The Menin Gate did suffer damage in the Second War, particularly as the Germans were retreating. I know one Belgian who sniped away at the departing occupiers from a position on the Ramparts near the Gate.

An early evening walk that can be highly recommended is a stroll along the Ramparts, which ends at the Lille Gate, although it is worth crossing the road and climbing up the other side to visit the quite beautifully positioned Ramparts Cemetery. For those who are interested in military engineering, the design of the ramparts is fascinating: note particularly how every part of the walls of the ramparts could be covered by artillery and musket fire from another part. Along the walk are small chimney stacks and air inlets for the chambers that were made below and within the walls. There is one small brick structure, which was designed for the storage of ice. During the winter months blocks of ice would be removed from the moat or wherever, and then be placed here so that during the summer months ice might be available.

The Lille Gate is interesting, as it is about the only part of the fourteenth century fortifications that has survived. Under it may be observed the original War Grave signs — the 'Imperial' was dropped in favour of 'Commonwealth' in 1960. On the opposite side of the road is a reconstruction of the oldest house in Ypres, that had survived for centuries until a shell ended that record.

Returning to the square may be done either by walking back inside the ramparts or along Rijselse street. This last gives some fine views of the Cloth Hall and Cathedral towers, as well as some intersting locations: for example Little Toc H, a 'branch' of the Poperinge club, is to be found in what is now a Roman Catholic educational establishment. The Post Office is in a fine building that was reputed to have been

Above: Civilians still throng the town as its destruction gets underway.

owned at one time by the Templers. The walk along the inside of the ramparts used to be a pleasant escape to the past, with all sorts of little streets and passages leading off, and the crumbling walls and chambers of the ramparts exuding history — places, for example, where Staff officers worked, soldiers lived and the

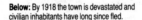

Below: By 1918 the town is devastated and civilian inhabitants have long since fled.

91

Above: Today's view of the Cloth Hall and of Martin's Cathedral — as if the devastation had never happened.

Below: This is an example of the lengths gone to by Belgian post war architects to replace certain buildings that had been totally destroyed. This timbered house had once been the oldest building in Ypres and had suffered total destruction during a heavy German bombardment. The replacement bears but a passing resemblance to the original.

Wipers Times was published. Unfortunately the ramparts have been lovingly restored over the last few years; all traces of shell damage which scarred the outer walls and the eroded inner ones have been removed and replaced by a perfect restoration. Only one small section remained in November 1987 — that associated with the Wipers Times — and even then it was being repaired. Just before the Menin Gate there is one of those delightfully continental urinals — open to all the world.

Heading out of Ypres on the road signposted Poperinge there is another large square in front of the Cathedral. On the corner of this and Elverdinge Street is St George's Memorial Church, and next to it is the building that used to be the school for the war graves gardeners' children, which was built by funds raised by Eton College as a memorial to their war dead. The Church is worth spending time over — it has always been open when I have been there — and contains many memorials of units and regiments that fought here, as well as to individuals. The high point of its year is undoubtedly the Remembrance Day Service on November 11 (still a whole holiday in Belgium and France) when the church is packed to capacity. Leaving the church, continue up Elverdinge Street until you arrive at number 82. This is the regional headquarters of the Commonwealth War Graves Commission, and for those who seek information there are a number of useful publications available. There are the overprinted maps (Michelin 1:250000) which indicates the positions of all the cemeteries; a history of the war graves; information sheets and annual reports (all payable in Belgian francs). For those who are seeking a relative who was killed, they have the registers for both Belgium and France, but please note the advice printed at the end of this booklet.

The Second World War hit Ypres at two very specific stages. The first was in 1940, when it was the scene of an attempted meeting between the allies, Belgium, France and Britain. The King of the Belgians, Leopold III, had effectively taken full control of his armies, and was not particularly interested in the views of his ministers. The French were represented by Weygand, the chief of staff: the King felt that his army could no longer cope with retreats, ruled out a withdrawal to the Yser, and effectively (and probably justifiably) had given up hope. The local French army commander was absent, and thus not able to advise Weygand, and although Weygand did wait for as long as he thought possible, he just missed meeting Gort, the commander of the British troops — someone with whom the King also wished to confer. It was a crucial meeting, this gathering of the 21st May at the Town Hall; it effectively determined the surrender of Belgium.

British troops were to be defending Ypres again in May 1940, but only as a tripping stone to the German forces, part of a perimeter designed to shrink around the evacuation beach-heads near Dunkirk.

Ypres was liberated in September 1944. I can well remember one inhabitant of the town (who lived in Ypres before the Great War) describing the great moment. The people rushed out to greet the soldiers, and naturally spoke to them in English. They were somewhat put out when many of the soldiers looked at them blankly: Ypres had been liberated by soldiers of the Polish division, and the combination of two

Above: One of the realistic displays inside the Salient museum at the Cloth Hall.

foreigners speaking a third language was too much! That night it seemed as though the whole town turned out for the sounding of the Last Post for the first time in well over four years, as the Germans had halted it.

Left: Memorial to the missing — the Menin Gate, in the year after its unveiling in 1927.

Right: From Ypres looking along the Menin Road out into the Salient early on in the war.

Below: The same stretch of road after years of fighting.

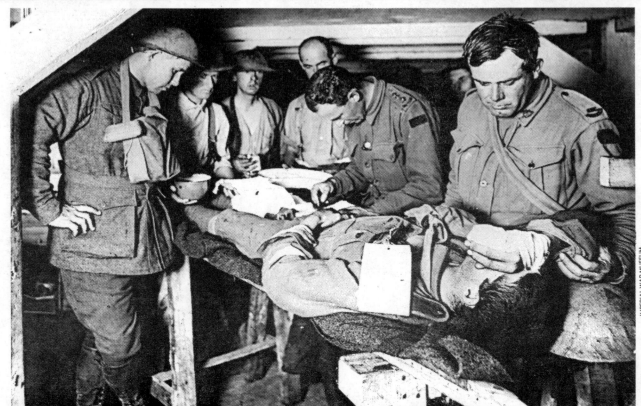

Right: Australian medical personnel attend to a stretcher case at an underground dressing station close to the Menin Road.

Left: Situated close to the aid posts and dressing stations the cemeteries grew as this did outside Ypres.

Below: Before the Belgian scrap metal merchants pounced during the post-war years these rusting hulks stood close to the Menin Road. They had been caught by some accurate artillery fire.

6. TANKS. HELL-FIRE CORNER.

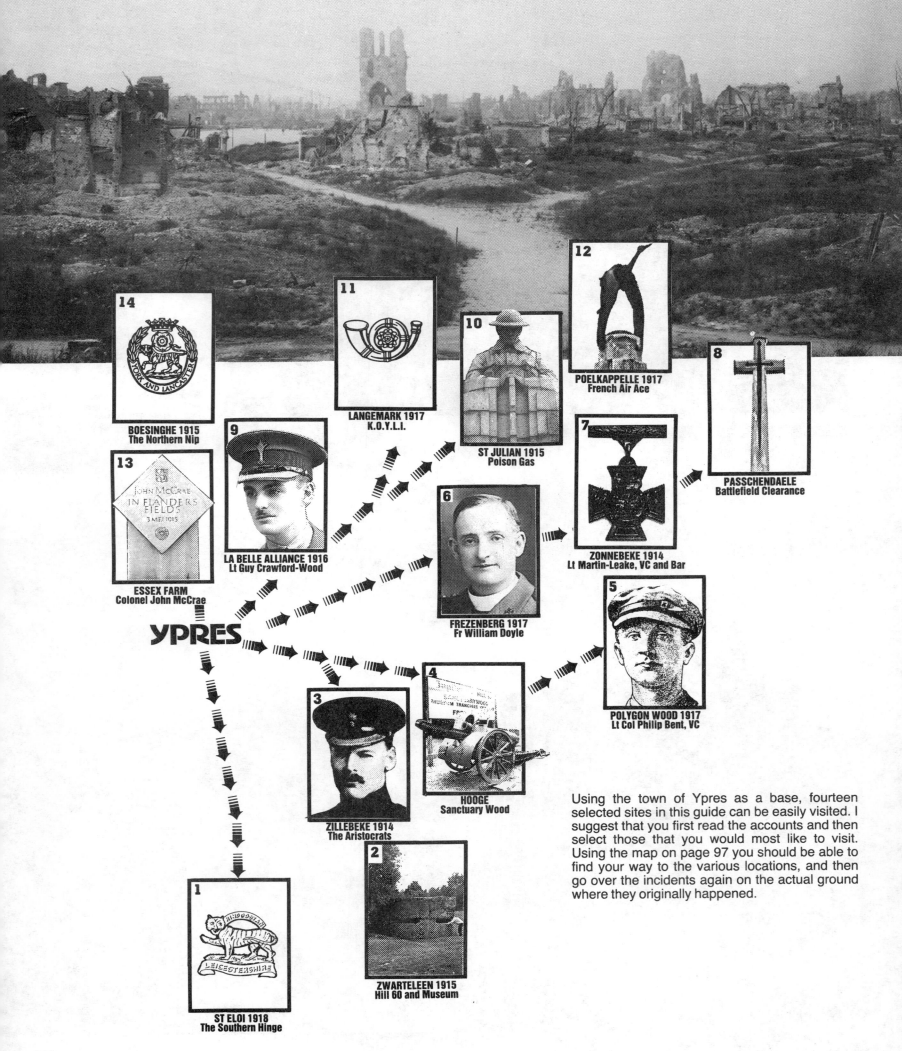

14
BOESINGHE 1915
The Northern Nip

11
LANGEMARK 1917
K.O.Y.L.I.

10
ST JULIAN 1915
Poison Gas

12
POELKAPPELLE 1917
French Air Ace

8
PASSCHENDAELE
Battlefield Clearance

13
ESSEX FARM
Colonel John McCrae

9
LA BELLE ALLIANCE 1916
Lt Guy Crawford-Wood

6
FREZENBERG 1917
Fr William Doyle

7
ZONNEBEKE 1914
Lt Martin-Leake, VC and Bar

5
POLYGON WOOD 1917
Lt Col Philip Bent, VC

YPRES

3
ZILLEBEKE 1914
The Aristocrats

4
HOOGE
Sanctuary Wood

2
ZWARTELEEN 1915
Hill 60 and Museum

1
ST ELOI 1918
The Southern Hinge

Using the town of Ypres as a base, fourteen selected sites in this guide can be easily visited. I suggest that you first read the accounts and then select those that you would most like to visit. Using the map on page 97 you should be able to find your way to the various locations, and then go over the incidents again on the actual ground where they originally happened.

The Ypres Salient was established at the end of the First Battle of Ypres, which lasted from October 19th to November 22nd, 1914, with particularly crucial days on October 31st and November 11th. At the end of this battle there was a bulge in the Anglo-French position, with the centre point being Ypres. The Germans held much of the high ground that dominates the city, and much of the fighting in the area was designed either to remove the Germans from their dominant position or to enable the Germans to consolidate their advantage. There were three other battles that were named after Ypres, but this excludes a multitude of fierce, often large, battles that took place in parts of the Salient. The Second Battle (most famous for the use of gas) lasted from April 22nd to May 25th, 1915. The line established at the end of this battle is the one indicated on the map. With a few minor exceptions, this was how it remained until the Third Battle which lasted from July 31st to November 10th, 1917 and is popularly known as Passchendaele. The Battle of the Lys, April 9th to 29th, 1918, part of Germany's last desperate attempt to end the war in her favour, engulfed in its later stages much of the Salient. The Fourth Battle, in which the British finally broke out of the Salient lasted from September 28th to October 2nd, 1918. The Salient is judged to begin in the region of Boesinghe in the north and to end at St. Eloi in the south, stretching eastwards to various lengths thoughout the war.

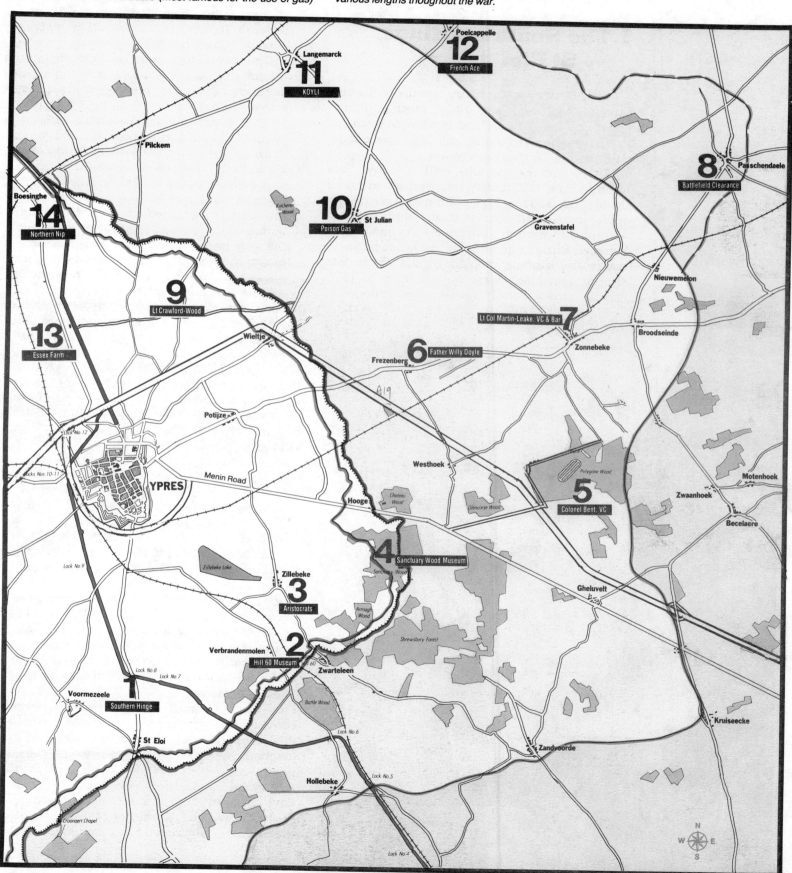

It was from St Eloi that the Ypres Salient proper began, swinging gradually to the east and north, circling the city in an arc that varied in size as both sides launched attacks on each other over the four years of war. Now it is difficult to imagine that this place could have been such a vital spot in not only the First but also the Second World War.

1. The Southern Hinge — St Eloi

In the Great War for many months both sides attempted to hang on to a high piece of ground known as the Mound, and it was the scene of extensive underground mining operations, culminating in the huge mine set off in June 1917; the craters are still visible today. This mine of June 1917 finally removed all traces of the Mound, a 30 foot high prominence created by spoil from local brickmaking, and situated within the triangle of roads. A number of bunkers, British and German may also be seen, inside the triangle created by the roads. But mining operations were not confined to 1917. Private Fraser vividly recalls the Battle of St

Below: Members of the Honourable Artillery Company clean their rifles in a front line trench at St Eloi, April 1915.

Eloi, a fierce battle to hold five sprung British mines, at the end of March and the beginning of April 1916.

"When day broke the sights that met our gaze were so horrible and ghastly that they beggar description. Heads, arms and legs were protruding from the mud at every yard and dear God knows how many bodies the earth swallowed. Thirty bodies at least were showing in the crater, and beneath its clayey waters other victims must be lying killed and drowned."

The Canadians task was to hold the crater positions; but circumstances were incredibly difficult, and the actual position of the line was effectively unknown.

"At 9.30 am prompt the hostile artillery began to speak and by noon it was raging in all its fury. Shrapnel came pouring over the lines in a ceaseless whine, interrupted only by the crumps of 4.3s and 5.9s (types of German shell). From every direction the fire storm was turned upon us. Every gun within range seemed to have cut loose and the very gates of hell let open. Over head bursts then deadly hails of shrapnel were showered into our midst. Heavy shells rocked the earthworks and buried their occupants. Imperials (ie British troops) who had been at Loos and previous battles never experienced such concentrated fire on such a small frontage."

When Fraser and his friends had done a stint in the chaotic shell holes that passed for the Front Line they proceeded a few hundred yards down the road towards Ypres to White Horse Cellar, the site of which is at the extremity of the village, on the right hand side:

"Coming out of the crater the survivors of No. 3 (platoon) retired to White Horse Cellar and its environs, odd stretches of battered trenches connected by shell holes. They took up their positions in the most habitable portions in small groups of two and threes. White Horse Cellar, a cellar in a building in St Eloi, was about the only indication that the village had ever existed. This identical ground had been contested from 1914 till 1918 and is reckoned one of the hot spots of the war. The village is just in the rear of our firing line and in consequence vanished under the influence of artillery fire into thin air early in the war."

Fraser in his account characterises the scene of carnage that was St Eloi in the Great War. Yet this sleepy hamlet, bestriding a series of road junctions, and at the northern edge of Messines ridge, was to play a vital, though much smaller part in the fighting that took place in the crucial days of May 1940, as the British army struggled to withdraw intact to the coast. The area along the St Eloi — Warneton road, and to the east of

the Wytschaete ridge was largely defended by 5 Division, which faced a concerted attack by three German divisions. Put simply, a German breakthrough here on 28 May would have served to divide the British Expeditionary Force, and would have ensured that many more did not make it to the escape beaches at Dunkirk. On 28 May the King of the Belgians had felt forced to capitulate — in fact his army had done well to hold out as long as it had.

Like all effective withdrawals, the British retreat was covered by many and numerous counter-attacks; it also revealed how professional the army could be, when troops, exhausted by days of retreating and fighting switched rapidly to the offensive in a great juggling game as desperate attempts were made to plug gaps. For instance, whilst heavy fighting was going on here, Montgomery's division had to move fifty miles, to the north of Ypres, at night, along small narrow lanes and obviously without easily discernible lights

Above: The village of St Eloi in the early months of the war. The Salient began in the south at this point.

Left: Men of the Northumberland Fusiliers, 'Fighting Fifth', after a successful attack on the German trenches, St Eloi, March 1916. They suffered few casualties and captured much 'booty'.

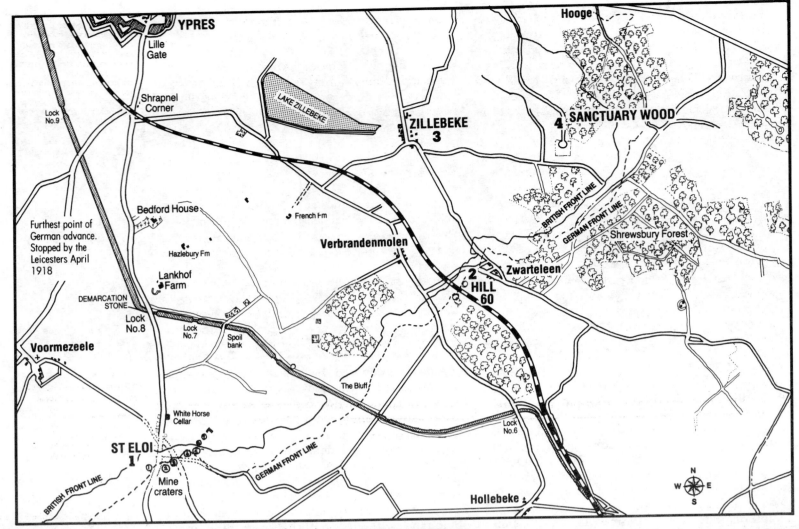

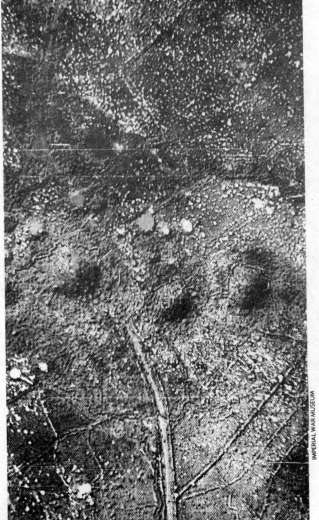

Right: By 1917 all traces of the village of St Eloi had vanished. Heavy fighting and mining activity had devastated the area. The three large craters are the result of British attempts to dislodge the Germans and open up the flank of The Salient. Note the trench lines running around the lip of the craters. Immediately after a mine was blown each side would rush to capture the huge hole left by the explosion, as the lip afforded a height advantage and the crater, cover for dugouts. (See opposite)

(Montgomery had the rear axles painted white, the rear lights illuminating them) and driving literally under a roof of artillery fire, between the British on Mount Kemmel and the Germans to the east. An excellent example of how initiative by battalion commanders and of their reaction to events was shown at St Eloi in those fraught days of May 1940.

The situation in this area was one in which the remnants of two battalions were hanging on to the canal line; if this position fell, it would of course threaten the British units to the south; the Northamptons and 6 Seaforth Highlanders (a Territorial Army unit) had almost ceased to exist. The Seaforths fell back on St Eloi, and were there threatened with being completely overwhelmed by a sea of field grey. At this point the Bren Carriers of the Duke of Cornwall's Light Infantry launched an attack, and achieved complete surprise, leaving, it was claimed, some seventy German dead to their own four casualties.

The cost in manpower was small — but they lost half (ie three) of their vehicles. Transport was at a premium, and so was the ability to be able to make a flexible response to any threat, so this loss was greater than it might seem. However the potentially disastrous gap of early on May 28 had been sealed, and the retreat to Poperinge and the River Yser could continue with a cohesive line in being.

Following the road to Ypres it is possible to view the quietest part (now, at any rate!) of the Salient by taking a right hand turn, undisturbed to a large degree by the hustle and bustle of modern life. There are a number of small and isolated British cemeteries in the area — Chester Farm, Spoil Bank and Hedge Row to name but a few. It is possible to park the car and follow a nature trail with a path along the line of the dried up canal, with large embankments on both sides created by the spoil when the canal was dug.

Along here is another of those bitterly disputed pieces of ground in World War One, the Bluff. Although it is now a Nature Reserve, and therefore covered in undergrowth and trees, it is possible to make out the relics of war, the tortured ground, and the various mine craters created by the Germans in their efforts to dislodge the British from a vital piece of ground that offered observation into the German lines, and would have been yet another thorn in the side of the British if in the hands of the Germans. Congreve comments on this position in a diary entry for the 2 January 1916:

"We are gradually getting the wire thickened up along our front, especially opposite the Bluff. It is very slow work and most nights I go up to egg it on. The Boche snipes a good deal, which makes it harder, but there are surprisingly few casualties."

On April 9 the Germans launched the second of their last ditch offensives, which was known as Ludendorff's Spring Offensive, in Flanders — the Battle of the Lys. The hammer blows rapidly overwhelmed the British defences, and again shrank the Salient, which the British had bled so profusely to extend in the grim Paschendaele offensive of the previous year. To 21 Division, and the men of the Leicestershire regiment, it came as a particularly grievous blow, for they had suffered enormous casualties in the first of these attacks, on the Somme, the previous month. Indeed they had been sent to a quiet sector — the Salient — to recover from the mauling that they had received.

From St Eloi to Ypres the road crosses the Ypres-Commines canal at Lock No. 8; beyond it, on the right, is a nest of British bunkers — perhaps the best examples left on the western Front, known as Lankhof Farm, and a few hundred yards beyond that, also on the right, is the entrance to Bedford House Cemetery. This was the scene of the Tigers endeavour to halt this German onslaught. The attacks halted on the 29 April, and the last throes of the offensive, almost at the gates of Ypres, were foiled here.

Note: Billy Congreve was a regular officer in the Rifle Brigade before the war. He distinguished himself and, when he was killed on the Somme, July 1916, he had already won the DSO and MC to which was added a posthumous VC. For a considereable part of his wartime service he kept a diary which was recently published by Kimber, edited by Terry Norman. Congreve's father, a general during the war, had also won the VC.

AR MUSEUM

Below: This gives us some idea of the size and depth of a crater caused by an underground explosion. This one at St Eloi has been successfully captured by the Germans and turned into a strongpoint in their defence line. Within the relative safety of the hole, the soldiers are free to walk about without fear of being sniped.

The Germans overran the Canal line, and progressed towards Lankhof Farm. These bunkers were never intended as part of a defence line, but rather as shelter for forward medical units, sending casualties on after treatment to the west, so as to avoid the shell trap that the city of Ypres had become; as the Germans advanced it had become a battalion headquarters, and now this too was overwhelmed. The next line of resistance was Bedford House. The present day grandiose drive into the cemetery was that of the original chateau; and there, nestled amongst the ranks of white stones lie the remnants of that building, reinforced by concrete and iron, and which had been turned into a secure stronghold. Here you are standing on the front line of the Leicesters on the desperate day of 28 — 29 April. The seriousness of the situation may be fully appreciated by turning around and seeing just how close Ypres actually is: the Salient was rapidly in danger of becoming a straight line. The fall of Ypres would have been like the fall of Verdun to the French in 1916 — militarily, arguably, insignificant, but with a devestating effect politically and on morale.

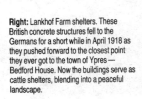

This is a good area to be able to view mine warfare and its results, and to have a cup of coffee in the most recent of a series of cafes that has occupied a position adjacent to the Hill. The cafe is named after Queen Victoria's Rifles, and besides being able to take refreshment it has an extensive, if primitive museum. It is unusual in that you are able to touch the exhibits — those old wooden propellors for example, as well as the more mundane (and deadly) instruments of war. It is a sobering experience to see how man's ingenuity can be tested in trying to devise more effective means to eliminate other human beings; but even more sobering are the three dimensional pictures that may be viewed through stereoscopes.

2. Hill 60 and Museum — Zwarteleen

Hill 60 itself has been left as an unrecovered battle area (other than to make it safe) with perhaps thousands of men entombed under its surface, now given over to sheep which serve to keep the grass down. It was an artificial hill, created from the spoil from a railway cutting; and again its value lay in the dominant position it held over the salient.

The esteem both sides held for this rise in the ground was shown by a concerted British attack in April 1915, followed by a ferocious German counter attack. Congreve noted on April 18:

"The Hill 60 attack was quite a success. We exploded mines along the top of the Hill and our infantry got up there without any losses. They were heavily counter-attacked and at present it is a regular hornet's nest up there. The German heavy artillery are giving us an awful time up there.......Most of our trouble is caused by their bombers who work wonderfully well with the infantry.

"I like the way the Corps referred to it as 'a small operation' — it's rather developing into a bigger one. Evidently the Germans set great store by the Hill. Our fellows now

Above: Looking from the British trenches towards Hill 60. When this was taken the Germans were firmly entrenched on top of the mound. Although there is no sign of life, thousands of soldiers are manning the trenches and keeping their heads down.

up there say the reason they do so is obvious, as one can see all the ground into Ypres and all the roads.

"The men who are lucky enough to come back say it is the worst fighting in the war. I believe that to date we have lost about sixty officers and seventeen hundred other ranks in five days on a place about the size of the centre part of Trafalgar Square."

Congreve was right: the attack had caused the Germans severe disquiet. Why was it that the Germans had not resisted when the attack first went in? The answer lay in a new horror weapon

that was to be launched upon the Western Front — gas. The Times History of the War reported of the attack that:

"In the midst of this inferno could be seen German soldiers, some in their shirt-sleeves and without weapons, falling over one another in their struggle to escape into the communication trenches, others in their terror forcing their way through their comrades at the bayonet's point."

When the Germans were toying with the use of gas, they placed hundreds of canisters on Hill 60 to use against the British. When the British mine

TRENCH 38

RAILWAY BRIDGE AND CUTTING

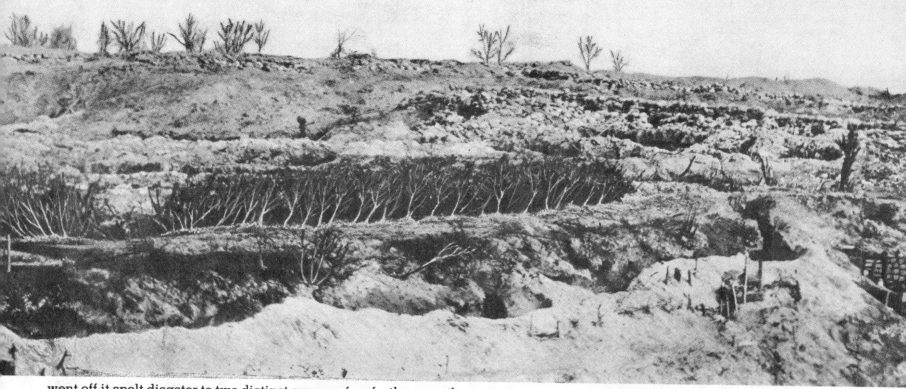

went off it spelt disaster to two distinct groups of Germans.

Firstly, and most immediately, those in the front line who, not at all convinced of the security of these new dealers of death, literally went into hysterical panic when the mine went off, fearful of being killed by their own awful gas; and secondly the German High Command who felt sure that the canisters must be discovered and that the allies, warned, would be able to take counter measures against gas, and thus eliminate any benefits from its use

further north, not to mention bringing in reinforcements.

In fact the canisters, almost miraculously, survived the blast with only a couple of exceptions (and this was seen by the allies as no more than tear gas): whilst it explains the ferocity of the Germans' attempts to dislodge the British over and above the vantage point of the Hill.

The gas attack was launched successfully on 22 April, 1915. Men of 171 Tunnelling Company

Below: This picture is a continuation of the scene above and shows the railway bridge and cutting from where the soil was taken which produced Hill 60.

THE CATERPILLAR

Above: Determined that they were there to stay, the German defenders of the hill produced well constructed trench systems, such as this one at Hill 60.

Below: The explosion of a land-mine beneath an enemy trench — the end result of many months of tunnelling. By these means each side sought to dislodge the other.

reported the effects of the gas which came over in the form of a dirty green cloud. Three former miners from Barnsley named, Davies, Roberts and Billingham were underground at the time in one of the old German mines, and the rest had to give them warning and retire. The Germans had regained the Hill and the tunnellers went to work again.

John Davies wrote to his wife in Barnsley on 17 June 1915:

"The whole place looks grand in summer weather, but the boom of the guns and the constant traffic of horses and men spoils the peacefulness of Belgium. I always tried to lead a good life at home, but I think I shall lead a better one after this, as this war has taught me, and a good many more, a lot that we shall never forget. If anything was to happen to me I should not want you to fret at my loss but rather thank God that I had done my little bit for love and freedom, King and country."

He was killed under Hill 60 on 20 June when the Germans fired a small camouflet explosion that blew in the gallery in which he was working. He is one of the thousands that lie entombed below this heap of rubbish and debris. The *Barnsley Chronicle* published an account of the loss of this man, who with 50 or so other men were recruited from the First Barnsley Pals (13 Battalion York and Lancaster Regiment) when tunnelling operations were seriously begun by the British. To spare the family, one of his friends told them (who passed the news to the paper) that his death was instantaneous and —'he looked as though he was asleep on the stretcher. He has been buried in a beautiful spot with corn flowers growing around his grave...' The reality was, that he had been buried alive or crushed to death, his body was never found, and his name is one of those appearing on the Menin Gate.

The ground now is ravaged, though the remnants of the two craters of 1917 are visible; bunkers and their remains strew the ground,

whilst one was converted from a German to a British bunker and probably saw service in the Second World War. There is also a memorial to the Queen Victoria Rifles. This is one of the relatively few memorials that the Germans took exception to when they occupied Belgium in 1940 because of its reference to the first use of gas by the Germans, and they destroyed it. It was replaced by the present monument.

One of their officers, Second Lieutenant Geoffrey Woolley became the first Territorial to win the Victoria Cross here for his actions in the desperate fighting of April 1915.

Standing on the bridge which crosses the railway line, and looking back towards Ypres one can see a hundred yards or so on the left a confusion of bushes and small trees. This is the site of 'the Dump' which was exactly what it

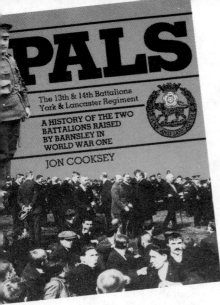

PALS

The 13th & 14th Battalions
York & Lancaster Regiment

A HISTORY OF THE TWO
BATTALIONS RAISED
BY BARNSLEY IN
WORLD WAR ONE

JON COOKSEY

For further reading: *Barnsley Pals* by Jon
Cooksey includes accounts of the tunnelling
activities at Hill 60 in the early days of 1915.
Published by Wharncliffe Publishing Ltd.,
(Book Division), Barnsley.

Below: Dressing the wounded at Larch
Wood in one of the many mining passages.
It was from this point that the mining
activities under Hill 60 began.

means, a dump for gear and equipment needed
in the line. Looking away from Ypres, on the
right hand side in the trees is the site of another
crater (water filled) — this is on private land.

Another view of Hill 60 may be had from Larch
Wood cemetery. If approaching this by car,
beware your suspension and even more getting
stuck in the mud. I have known people require
the assistance of a Belgian tractor driver, and I
was only saved from a similar fate by the fact
that I had a minibus full of more or less willing
pupils to push me out, leaving them to savour
the effects of Flanders mud liberally splashed
on them by the spinning wheels.

In this cemetery is to be found the body of
Anthony Eden's brother, who was killed early on
in the war.

Larch Wood was where the British began their
mineshaft for the Hill 60 and Caterpillar Mines.
Edmund Blunden, in his classic '*Undertones of
War*' described the place towards the end of
1917:

> "*Larch Wood Tunnels were a magnifi-
> cent work. The passages excelled in height
> and width and air supply. At this time they
> were principally in use as a medical
> headquarters, and once inside them it*

*certainly seemed that safety and calm
were assured. But outside people were
being killed from time to time.*

"*A strange scene was to be viewed from
the southward outlets of this tunnel — the
deep old railway cutting past Hill 60. it was
a dark canal now, the banks of which were
shattered and the timbers tossed aside by
cataclysm.*

"*Hill 60 was not noticeable, having been
transformed into a mine crater, but a
bridge beside it still spanned the railway
cutting with a rough red-patched arch.
Water dripped and slipped down the
chaotic banks into the greasy flood
beneath.*"

As travellers after the event perhaps seeking to
understand how men could survive such inhuman conditions, we are of a different breed to
those thousands of pilgrims that came this way
immediately after the war, going over old
battlegrounds. Blunden was one of those who
came back and his comments are sobering to us
who come after.

"*Zillebeke, where a modest road runs up
past what were once called Valley
Cottages to the Hill 60 region (you may see*

many relics there over a cup of tea). At the ordinary little beginning of that road, once, was the most comfortless and deadly little machine gun post I was ever in. It was no longer there, but my friend at that point underwent, as I thought, all the pangs of all who were ever in it or had to trudge past it in fiery and maddening nights. Let me hope that to most, or to all who go that way, such recognitions will not occur; but to such as myself the things that are not in my book (not necessarily of great consequence or easy explanation) are on many of those roads."

The story that follows is one of the events of 1914, and the start point is really the end, a small churchyard in the parish church at Zillebeke. There may be found 32 British graves, the noticeable point being that there are at least five of them with an aristocratic background.

Above: A war artefact that may be examined on the inside by a determined explorer. This British bunker at Hill 60 was built over an existing German one. Each weapon slit would have had a machine gun behind it. One side of the construction has received a direct hit from a shell revealing the reinforcing rods but leaving the bunker very much intact.

Left: The two figures mark the rim of the Hill 60 crater today — compare with the photograph on page 109.

IMPERIAL WAR MUSEUM

Above: The ruined village of Zillebeke.

3. Aristocrats and the First Battle of Ypres — Zillebeke

The significant action that can be seen here took place during the crisis stages of the First Battle of Ypres during the period 31 October to the 6 November 1914. The Germans had finally captured the village of Zandvoorde on the 30th and then continued their advance against the increasingly thinly held British and French positions that blocked the path to Ypres.

The British line ran in this area from the Commines canal (at the point where it makes a sharp westerly turn) along the front of the large wood called later Shrewsbury Forest. The Germans were in strength in the cover of what was to become named Bulgar Wood. By this stage British units had become so small, depleted by the continuing and unrelenting demands made upon them, that here they formed two groups under the command of Bulfin and Cavan — being known as Bulfin's and Cavan's forces. The forced withdrawal from

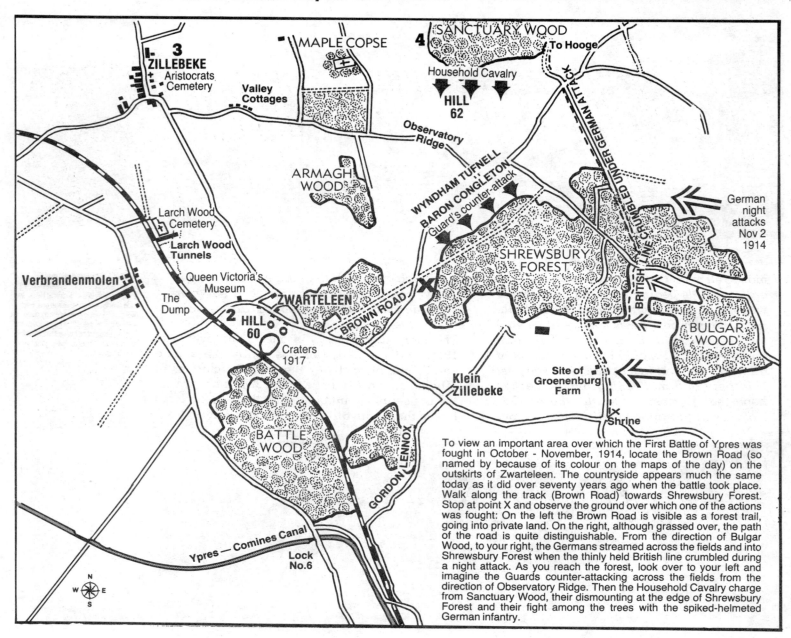

To view an important area over which the First Battle of Ypres was fought in October - November, 1914, locate the Brown Road (so named by because of its colour on the maps of the day) on the outskirts of Zwarteleen. The countryside appears much the same today as it did over seventy years ago when the battle took place. Walk along the track (Brown Road) towards Shrewsbury Forest. Stop at point X and observe the ground over which one of the actions was fought: On the left the Brown Road is visible as a forest trail, going into private land. On the right, although grassed over, the path of the road is quite distinguishable. From the direction of Bulgar Wood, to your right, the Germans streamed across the fields and into Shrewsbury Forest when the thinly held British line crumbled during a night attack. As you reach the forest, look over to your left and imagine the Guards counter-attacking across the fields from the direction of Observatory Ridge. Then the Household Cavalry charge from Sanctuary Wood, their dismounting at the edge of Shrewsbury Forest and their fight among the trees with the spiked-helmeted German infantry.

Lieutenant Henry Bligh Fortescue Parnell, 5th Baron Congleton
2 Battalion Grenadier Guards

He was the first member of the House of Peers to be killed in World War One; he succeeded his father as Baron in 1906. Lieutenant Lord Congleton was the eldest son of Major General Lord Congleton, C.B. and was born 6 September, 1890. He was educated at Eton and New College, Oxford and joined the Grenadier Guards as a University candidate in 1912. He was promoted Lieutenant in March 1913. He was a keen sportsman and traveller and he had hoped to go on an Antarctic expedition, which the war cancelled. He wrote articles on sporting subjects for magazines under the pseudonym, 'Con'. Lord Congleton was mentioned in Sir John French's Despatch of 14 January, 1915, for gallant conduct and skilful handling of his platoon against tremendous odds on 6 November, 1914, thereby saving the British line at that point. He was killed four days later in the action on 10 November, 1914.

Second Lieutenant Baron Alexis De Gunzburg
11 Hussars (Prince Albert's Own)

He received his commission in September, 1914 and became attached to the Royal Horse Guards, 7 Cavalry Brigade, as interpreter. Baron De Gunzburg, who was Russian by birth and educated at Eton, was naturalised in order to enlist in the British Army on the outbreak of war. His regiment went into the thick of the fighting in October 1914. He was killed 6 November and at the time was with the Life Guards. He had been sent along with three other officers to bring up the Royal Horse Guards to support an attack at Zillebeke. They were on foot and had to run across an open field for some 200 yards, when on the way back, he was shot. His mother, Baroness De Gunzburg received a telegram from the King and Queen expressing their sympathy, and adding: "His Majesty has learnt how gallantly Baron De Gunzburg fought with his comrades of the Royal Horse Guards, although his duties as interpreter did not necessitate his presence in the firing line."

Major Lord Bernard Charles Gordon-Lennox
2 Battalion Grenadier Guards

He was the third son of the seventh Duke of Richmond and Gordon, K.G. He was born in London in May 1878 and educated at Eton College and Sandhurst, from which he joined the Grenadier Guards in 1898. He took part in the Boer War and the operations carried out in the Orange Free State, including actions at Poplar Grove and Driefontein, for which he received the Queen's medal with two clasps. From 1904-06 he was seconded for service with the Chinese Regiment at Wei-hai-Wei. He was promoted Captain in 1909 and became the Assistant Military Secretary to the then General Officer Commanding-in-Chief, Northern Command. For his services in the war he was mentioned in the supplement to Sir John French's Despatch 14 January, 1915. He was killed in action at Zillebeke 10 November, 1914. In 1907 Lord Bernard Gordon-Lennox married Evelyn, second daughter of the first Lord Loch, and left two sons.

Lieutenant Colonel Gordon Chesney Wilson, M.V.O.
Commanding The Royal Horse Guards

He was killed in action 6 November, 1914. He was the eldest son of Sir Samuel Wilson, M.P. and was born 3 August, 1865. He joined the Royal Horse Guards from the Militia and reached the rank of captain in 1894. He took part in the Boer War during which he was on the Staff as A.D.C. to Major General Baden-Powell, Commanding the Mafeking Frontier Forces, August 1899 to May 1900. He was also Baden-Powell's A.D.C. after that officer's promotion to Major General, South Africa, May to July 1900. He was present for the defence of Mafeking and was twice mentioned in despatches receiving the Queen's Medal with three clasps. He was promoted Lieutenant Colonel in October 1911. Lieutenant Colonel Wilson married, in 1891, Lady Sarah Isabella Augusta, sixth daughter of the seventh Duke of Marlborough, they had no children.

Captain The Honorable William Reginald Wyndham
Lincolnshire Yeomanry attached 1 Life Guards

He was killed in action 6 November, 1914, being the third son of the second Baron Leconfield. He was born 1876 and was the heir presumptive to his brother, the third Baron Leconfield. Captain Wyndham joined 17 Lancers as Second Lieutenant in March 1896, becoming Lieutenant in 1897 and Captain in July, 1901. He served in the Boer War, 1899-1900, receiving the Queen's medal with three clasps. A riding accident in 1903 caused his retirement from the army and he took a farm in East Africa. After a spell in America he returned home and became well known in Ireland as a racehorse stable owner. He was a member of the Jockey Club, to which he was elected in 1912. With the outbreak of war he made every effort to return to the army and in August 1914 he was promoted to the rank of Captain in the Lincolnshire Yeomanry. He was eventually successful in being attached to 1 Life Guards, where his father and two brothers had served.

Above: Events in November 1914 — the First Battle of Ypres when massed German attacks aimed at Ypres were stopped near Sanctuary Wood and Shrewsbury Forest. (Painted by Caton Woodville, First World War artist.)

Zandvoorde had created problems, maintaining communications through the densely forested area were naturally difficult.

This is one of the few points on the Western Front where it is possible to get a savour of how the ground actually looked when the battle was fought. Apart from changes in the character of the roads, the woods, fields and their boundaries remain the same. It is possible at this stage to show just what an effective instrument of waging war the BEF of 1914 actually was. Units were thrown in at short order, rapid changes of command caused by casualties to officers from the highest to the lowest, exhaustion and hunger, the performance of that most difficult of military manoeuvres, withdrawal whilst in contact with the enemy — none of this threw the British troops into confused turmoil. It is also as well to bear in mind that the director of this state of affairs who managed to nurse the army through this extreme trial was Douglas Haig.

There is a good account available of the actions in the Klein Zillebeke/Hollebeke area in the diaries of 'Ma' Jeffries, who was the second in command of 2 Battalion the Grenadier Guards. The battalion had been in all the major actions of the BEF since it first went into serious action near Mons. Exhausted and harried now for four long months, it faced one of its greatest tests.

On 31 October the British line had become endangered due to difficulties in an area known as the Gheluvelt spur; a general withdrawal took place and due to problems of communication elements of Bulfin's force now found

themselves in danger of being outflanked — indeed the spiked helmets of the German infantry were already swarming around the left flank. Battalions of the Northamptonshire and Sussex regiments held a crucial position from Groenenburg Farm, from there, along the front of Shrewsbury Forest, up to the track that led to Hooge, thus also safeguarding the position of Cavan's force to the south west. However, with communications made extremely difficult in the forest, and with the Germans on their heels, the position tended to crumble, and to be pushed further and further back into the trees of Shrewsbury Forest.

Reinforcements were very few on the ground, but a party of Gordon Highlanders were got together, and the holding battalions were told that help was on its way. In fact, instead of consisting of some two hundred men as had been originally hoped, complete with the apocryphal cooks and bottle washers it came to no more than eighty men. When they heard this force coming, the Northamptons and the Sussex opened fire, giving the Germans the fabled and feared 'magic minute' — fifteen rounds of accurate rifle fire poured out in a minute. Joining with the Gordons, the British line in that sector stormed into a charge. It was a charge almost out of control, and the fury of it pushed the Germans back some half mile.

To be fair to the Germans, they suffered just as much as the British from the fog of war, and of course it was extremely dificult to maintain control over the attacking troops in the close country and the fluid situation. On the 31st the

114

Grenadiers were taken out of the line for a short rest — at Larch Wood.

For a while the line was restored. But there were no reserves of fresh troops and the army had suffered grievously. General Capper commanding 7 Division commented on how bad things were: 'Yes, so bad that there's no Division left, so that I'm a curiosity — a Divisional Commander without a Division.' The Grenadiers were ordered up to make a sweep of the wood to clear the German stragglers and to re-establish the line — the Germans themselves were confused as to what was going on, and the Grenadiers were the more cohesive of the two forces, and therefore able to take control of the situation.

On the 2 November the Germans attacked for the third or fourth time that day under cover of darkness, by the light of a small moon and the burning of some nearby farm buildings. They emerged from the cover of Bulgar Wood; and again confusion arose, as someone shouted a warning that the Northamptons were going to charge. The British stopped firing, and it took the best efforts of Jeffreys and others to get them firing again. The Germans continued their

Below: German method of attack against infantry trained to fire off fifteen aimed shots a minute resulted in heavy casualties.

Above: The result of massed attacks employed by the Germans during the First Battle of Ypres.

Above: Lt Carleton Wyndham Tufnell

the Household Cavalry, at that time in reserve in Sanctuary Wood. Like something out of a western, they galloped up, dismounted and carried out an infantry attack, which saved the situation but it cost them the loss of the commanding officer of the Royal Horse Guards (Colonel Wilson) as well as Lieut Wyndham, both of whom are now buried at Zillebeke.

Jeffreys reported that 'poor Tufnell was shot through the throat and died soon afterwards. He was a first rate officer and is a great loss.' They were to remain holding this position until the 11 November; on the previous day they had suffered particularly badly.

The line was just forward of the Brown Road (the remnants of which are clearly visible today) which got its name from the fact that as it was a metalled road, it was coloured brown on the maps. As this was an easily identifiable spot on the map, and as the position had been held for a few days, the German artillery zeroed in and began to take its toll, especially as the flank nearest the canal had been turned. Amongst the casualties were 'poor Bernard Lennox' and also 'Congleton (a first rate boy)'. Lennox had been aware of how lucky he had been — in the last entry in his diary on 4 November he wrote after hearing of the death of a friend, 'I suppose one gets inured to seeing all one's best friends taken away from one and can only think one is lucky enough to be here oneself — for the present.'

From here the battalion moved off to a wood near Hooge Chateau — to find themselves almost immediately thrown into another vital battle, in the last death throes of First Ypres as both armies halted, overcome by exhaustion and by the need to fight Winter.

advance, though there was a ripple effect as their ranks sustained heavy casualties. Above the rifle fire there was the steady beating of a drum urging the attackers on — and despite the heavy fire being put down, Jeffreys noted that the drummer did not fall, even though he did not take cover behind trees as his fellows did — probably because no one thought to shoot at him.

The Germans were not to be put off the prize of the strategic objective of outflanking the allied lines. Again they pressed on, this time near the canal and railway line, where they threatened to break through on the junction between the Irish Guards and units of the French army. Under pressure the line began to disintegrate and the Grenadiers rushed up a platoon under the command of Lieut the Baron Congleton and machine gun section under Lieut Tufnell. Jeffreys reported that they were the only troops that the battalion had in reserve and went on to comment that they 'did splendid work'.

Meanwhile a call for assistance was made to

Right: Field of German dead; a combined defence by French and British troops against continual attacks resulted in the deaths of over 20,000 Germans during the four weeks of intense fighting, in October - November 1914.

Just south of the Menin Road stands Sanctuary Wood, and beyond that a Canadian Memorial, from which it is possible to view the wood, Observatory Ridge, Maple Copse, Tower Hamlets amongst other points of vital importance during the battles around the besieged city of Ypres. They are not easily connected by road; and of course nature has repaired the ravages of mankind to an almost unimaginable degree to those who fought here.

4. Sanctuary Wood and Museum — Hooge

The approach to Sanctuary Wood, from the Menin Road near the village of Hooge, is along a road now known as Canada Lane; after half a kilometre or so a museum and cafe are to be found on the right hand side. The museum is probably the oldest in the Salient area, and in the possession of the same family; it also has a cafe, and the management is quite happy for visitors to eat their sandwices in the cafe section whilst they enjoy a coffee or beer.

There follows an interesting and varied

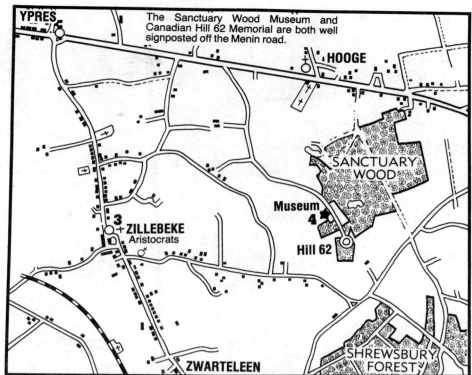

The Sanctuary Wood Museum and Canadian Hill 62 Memorial are both well signposted off the Menin road.

Below: An artillery piece stands guard outside Sanctuary Wood Museum.

117

This page: The exhibition room and some of the items and photographs on display in the Trench museum near Sanctuary Wood.

exhibits room, with some superb examples of early war years' headgear and the same type of gory and unsentimental stereographic photographs that may be seen near Hill 60. In a further room there is a display of weaponry, some of which has nothing to do with World War I, as well as a range of uniforms. An unfortunate omission is adequate labelling of the items. What labelling there is, at best, is limited, but at least an impression is gained.

Through the rear of the building and into the wood is a trench system which is original — or at least is based on original trench sites, complete with tunnel shelters, corrugated iron supports and for most of the year mud. The more intrepid explorer requires a torch and a pair of wellingtons. The more unusual of the exhibits for me are the old (and presumably original) German grave stones that are to be found alongside one of the paths.

With a bit of peering and straining it is possible to get a view back to Ypres from the edge of the museum grounds, and also to appreciate the difficulty experienced by troops coming up to the trenches under observation from the Germans. It is quite easy to spend an hour or two here, and is an essential part of any visit to the Salient. The museum is open every day, and seemingly at all hours — I have been there with a group as late as 6pm, and visited it in the depths of December.

Coming out of the museum, on the opposite side of the road, is the great mass of Sanctuary Wood, where 'Bulfin's force' — one of those bodies of men that were formed by putting all sorts of different regiments together into a temporary unit in the confused days of October 1914 — was in action. Bulfin used the wood as a point at which to hold his reserves, on occasion to send men back to rest, and in the confusion of the battles going on, as a point at which men who were lost or were stragglers could be gathered and in due course re-deployed.

It is private property now, but inside there are the signs of ravaged ground, some concrete fortifications, and along the eastern edge, evidence of mine warfare in 1915, the craters remaining.

In May 1915 during the sweeping German attacks of Second Ypres they came up to the eastern edge of Sanctuary Wood and it was no longer a place of relative safety, but effectively was in the front line area.

Next to the museum is the Sanctuary Wood cemetery. Outside it is a private memorial to 2/Lt Keith Rae; he was killed in a front line trench near the Hooge Crater in July 1915, defending the position against a new German horror weapon, the flamethrower, and was never seen again. The family erected this memorial originally in the grounds of the rebuilt Hooge Chateau, but it was moved at the request of the owner to Sanctuary Wood in the seventies

IMPERIAL WAR MUSEUM

Above: Sanctuary Wood British trench, no longer a place of sanctuary as it originally was in October 1914, when it was used as a regrouping area for stragglers during the confused fighting of that period. In subsequent fighting the wood was devastated.

Left: Today, part of a preserved trench at Hill 62, Sanctuary Wood Museum.

119

— I suspect the reason being that he felt no longer able to guarantee its security as his own life was moving to an end.

The cemetery itself falls into two parts — that nearest the road, which was created after the war and used as a concentration cemetery, and that at the rear, which was made at the time. Amongst others buried here are a German airman, and standing on his own, Gilbert Talbot. He was another casualty of that fighting around Hooge in July/August 1915. He was brother of army chaplain Neville Talbot, a friend of Congreve's. Gilbert's name was to be immortalised in a unique way. Neville Talbot worked with another chaplain, Tubby Clayton, who had conceived the idea of opening an All Ranks (in itself highly unusual) club in Poperinge. Tubby determined to call it Talbot House, in honour of Neville but Neville himself preferred to think of it as a memorial to Gilbert; and so was born Toc H — to become in the dismal post-war years a lamp of hope to distressed ex-servicemen.

Proceeding to the top of the road, from Sanctuary Wood museum, we come to one of the numerous Canadian battlefield memorials that are scattered along the Western Front. Designed as an observation point, the memorial is centred on a great plinth, until a few years ago the designers failed to achieve that purpose, because they surrounded the place with hedges and low, densely packed trees. Whilst beautiful to look at, it made observation difficult. Now these are all cleared and it is possible to see over important areas of ground, though the visual impact of the memorial has been somewhat altered!

This is not Hill 62, by the way, nor is it Mount Sorrel, which is off to the south west. The memorial is on the approximate site of Top Tor tunnels. But that is a minor point. Mount Sorrel sounds as though the name had existed in Belgium for years; in fact it is the name of a small (though now rapidly expanding, due to a Rolls Royce works) village in Leicestershire. The prominence was given the name during the time that a Territorial battalion of the Leicesters was serving in the area in 1915.

From the memorial there are good views across to Tower Hamlets and the Gheluvelt spur beyond, to Shrewsbury Forest and to the right Maple Copse, Armagh Wood and the fighting of 1916, which this memorial in particular commemorates.

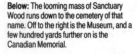

Below: The looming mass of Sanctuary Wood runs down to the cemetery of that name. Off to the right is the Museum, and a few hundred yards further on is the Canadian Memorial.

WESTERN FRONT ASSOCIATION

Polygon Wood has now returned to the peace and quiet of pre-war days, and has escaped the menace of progress by a narrow squeak as motorway traffic roars past. Inside the wood, now a nature reserve, there are some signs of conflict, mainly in the form of the occasional concrete blockhouse or MEBUS as they were sometimes known. The word comes from the initial letters of the technical construction devices that went into the German pillbox and blockhouse concepts. Dominating all is the Butte de Polygon used before the war, amongst other things, by the Belgian Army as a range. It is a sobering thought about the devestation caused that this rather insignificant mound was described by the official historian cartographers as the most prominent feature within the Salient. It is surmounted by a memorial to the Australian 5 Division, which in turn looks down on a simple but effective memorial to the New Zealand missing.

Left: Lt Colonel Philip Eric Bent was born in Halifax, Nova Scotia. He enlisted in the Royal Scots at the outbreak of war and shortly afterwards was commissioned in the Leicestershire Regiment. After a while with the Bedfordshire Regiment he returned to the Leicesters in the Autumn of 1916. The following year he was awarded the DSO. Then on 1 October, 1917, after a heavy German attack he rallied various units in a spirited counter-attack which was successful. He was shot in the head and his body was never found despite searches made by his men. His name is carved on the Tyne Cot Memorial to the missing.

5. Colonel Bent, VC — Polygon Wood

Prior to the British offensive in the summer and autumn of 1917, known as the Third Battle of Ypres, the Germans had covered the Polygon Wood area with a liberal sprinkling of concrete machinegun posts. It was against those positions that the youngest colonel in the British army led a counter attack and won the Victoria Cross.

Lieutenant Colonel Bent was 26 years old when he brought his battalion, 9 Leicestershire's into the line at Polygon Wood to relieve the Australians. The attack in this region which had begun at the end of September, although hampered by heavy rain, had achieved a measure of success. Now men of 110 Brigade were to make good the Australian gains. All the four battalions which made up the brigade originally consisted of Leicestershire men who volunteered into Kitchener's army, but had since been diluted by fighting on the Somme and at Arras.

The Germans never allowed time for the consolidation of positions gained, and characteristically launched heavy artillery barrages

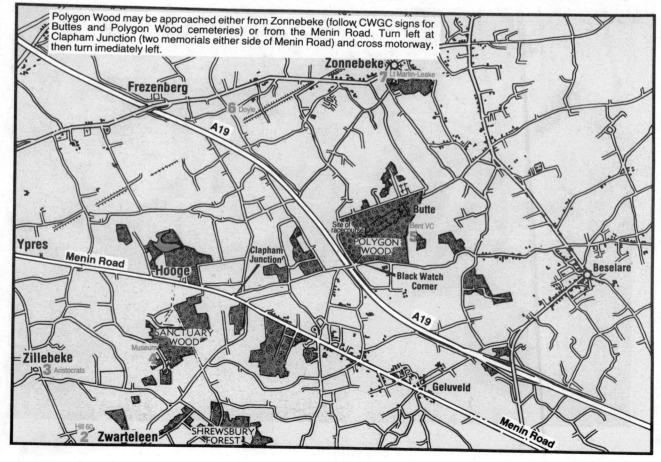

Polygon Wood may be approached either from Zonnebeke (follow CWGC signs for Buttes and Polygon Wood cemeteries) or from the Menin Road. Turn left at Clapham Junction (two memorials either side of Menin Road) and cross motorway, then turn imediately left.

IMPERIAL WAR MUSEUM

Above: Australian troops manning the trenches at Polygon Wood (looking north towards Zonnebeke). Trees and undergrowth had been blasted away leaving short stumps to indicate where a wood once flourished. Shortly after this photograph was taken the Leicesters moved into these trenches to relieve the Australians and the action, as described, took place.

IMPERIAL WAR MUSEUM

Right: Leicesters on their way up to Polygon Wood to relieve the Australians.

and infantry attacks to prevent a position being consolidated and held. David Bacon, a quartermaster's sergeant in Colonel Bent's battalion tells the story graphically as the Leicesters moved up to take over from the Australians. The relief took place on the night of the 30 September:

"The track now narrowed to one of eighteen inches in width, continued via Black Watch corner to Polygon Wood. The night was very dark and the track broken in many places by shell fire, moreover it was exceedingly slippery owing to recent rains and the mud. It was most necessary to keep in touch with the man in front, and that alone was difficult; and the depth and the consistency of the mud was such that if one slipped off the track it often took hours to regain it, while in some few cases men were lost entirely. On arrival at Polygon Wood, which by the way was no longer a wood at all, but a mere mass of mud and shell holes, the 9 Battalion relieved the 32 Australian Infantry Battalion in a line of shell holes near the extreme edge of the wood."

He comments that the relief was achieved without casualties — on reflection an ominous accomplishment. The positions were occupied, which were a series of strong points rather than a line of trenches.

"Away to the left, within the British lines two hundred yards distant, rose a large mound known as Polygon Butte; this had been tunnelled by the enemy to be utilised as dugouts, but the entrance had been blown in prior to his evacuation. A Canadian tunnelling company was already at work opening up and strengthening the works. About 5am we were rudely awakened by a terrific barrage, supplied by the enemy . . . and it is no exaggeration to say that the shells burst as thick as a hailstorm and the din was awful. Tree stumps, mud and everything that happened to be about, was going up in all directions. That he did not, even in the first few minutes, let alone throughout the assault, hit the Headquarters (of the Battalion) position was but short of miraculous, and every moment was awaited as the last. Dawn was breaking, and at 5.15am enemy planes flew low over our Lines, so low in fact that the occupants

Right and above: This aerial photograph of Polygon Wood was taken at the time of the action described in the acount — the racecourse is still clearly discernable from the air despite heavy cratering of the ground. Note the RE8 biplane, which is about to fly over the area held by the Leicesters, and where Colonel Bent won his VC. The photograph was taken by the observer pictured above. The RE8 (nicknamed Harry Tate, after the music hall star) British two-seat reconnaissance and artillery spotting aircraft lacked manoeuvrability and made a prime target for German fighters. Its engine was unreliable and early models tended to go into a spin, requiring many modifications before it was considered safe. Nevertheless, over 4000 RE8's had been built by the end of the war.

could be seen quite plainly, the while they fired drum after drum of machine gun bullets into the troops."

The German infantry assault came a few minutes later, and the situation on the left flank in the area of the Butte became dangerous. Bent personally collected a platoon that he had held in reserve together with various other elements that he could quickly gather up. After issuing orders to his other officers on how they could further consolidate the position, he led his scratch force in a determined charge on the infantry occupying the ground that had just been lost. The attack was successful, thus he prevented his A Company from completely crumbling and was able to establish the line.

"The Colonel led the charge shouting 'Come on the Tigers' (the regimental cap badge). This gallant attempt was, for the moment, entirely successful, though Colonel Bent was shot through the temple whilst leading his men."

The position was held, and reinforcements of the 7 Leicesters arrived from their support position in a much exhausted and disordered condition — fully half of their effectives had been knocked out on the journey up to the front; conditions were so bad. The brigade was

Above and inset: Bunkers then and now in Polygon Wood.

withdrawn from the line on the night of the 2nd. Bent's action in mounting the counter attack and thus regaining important ground, greatly assisted subsequent operations.

"No trace was found, either during the night (ie the 1st) or afterwards, of the body of the Colonel, though thorough searches were made."

Philip Bent, a battalion commander at 26, already the recipient of a DSO, and twice mentioned in dispatches, was awarded a posthumous VC. His name is carved on the Tyne Cot Memorial to the Missing.

This page: The Butte at Polygon Wood at different periods but viewed from the same angle. The large picture above was taken after the action fought by the Leicesters in 1917. The shell torn bodies of more than 100 Germans litter the ground. Then the mound in the early post war years, and on the right, as the Butte is today, amidst densely packed trees.

Above: Pte Jack Horner, 8 Leicesters

Private Jack Horner, serving with the 8 Leicesters, was another who suffered in this battle — this time, though, even before he actually got to the front line:

"My Company, 'A' were moving up in single file in support of the 9 Battalion when from nowhere (I don't remember seeing or hearing any shelling) a piece of shrapnel hit my left forearm. I was knocked flat, and when I came around I was alone with a smashed arm. I gripped my arm above the elbow with my right hand to stop the blood flow, and somehow got my arm lying across my stomach, the blood soaking my tunic. I stumbled on, God knows where, for I don't — through the mud and slime, on this great sea of mud. I didn't know where I was going, or how long I had been stumbling around, for I saw no one, and in all this space no one saw me. I saw a chink of light ...It was a German pillbox, but thank heaven they were British, using the pill box as an advanced dressing station...I asked for water — I can still taste the petrol in that water now. Eventually the ambulances came. I don't remember whether they were horse drawn or motors, but it was the most painful and horrible journey I have ever made in my life; with every lurch and bump the smashed bones were digging into the raw flesh."

After the action on 1 October relief from the front

was not to last long. My grandfather, the *Regimental Quartermaster Sergeant in the 7 Leicestershire's* commented in his diary on 4 October:

"Battalion went back to support an attack this morning at 8.30 am. Foulest place that we have struck. Rain, rain, rain and mud."

It is also worth recalling the difficulties that ration parties faced, bringing the vital food and water that would sustain the troops. From the transport lines at Scottish Wood the carrying parties came. Grandfather recorded:

"October 9th: started out with rations this afternoon and got back at 10am next morning. Immediately had to start getting rations ready for that day."

It had taken some eighteen hours across tortured ground, under fire and through glutinous mud to bring up just one day's rations. It was not untypical of the battlefield we call Passchendaele.

There are two British cemeteries located on the edge of Polygon Wood; the first is a battlefield cemetery, with casualties from throughout the war. To the rear is a gate that now leads nowhere except to an empty field. For a number of years after the war there was a German cemetery here; but to the victors the spoil, and the Germans were required to concentrate all their Salient cemeteries into two, at Langemark and Menen. On the other side of the road is the Buttes Cemetery, with vast arrays of British soldiers with no known grave, most of whom were brought here when the battlefields were cleared in the 1920s.

Above: RQMS A. C. Cave, 7 Leicesters

Below: The Butte New Military Cemetery in the dense mass of Polygon Wood. Note the Australian monument on the Butte. Left centre of the picture is the original battlefield cemetery.

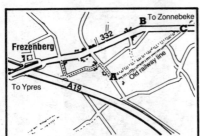

Compare this present day map with the battle map and aerial photograph on the opposite page; the front line on August 1917 when 16 (Irish) Division held and attacked in this area is easily identified today. To assist you in locating points all three have been marked **A B C**. Coming from the town of Ypres on the Zonnebeke road, turn right (about 100 yards) after crossing the new motorway. Take the first left and proceed to a T junction — you are now at the old front line once manned by members of the 16 (Irish) Division, in August 1917. 2nd Royal Dublin Fusiliers were in the trenches either side of the present day junction. Turn right and proceed to where the road cuts across a derelict railway line; this sector was held by the 7th Royal Irish Rifles. A walk along the old railway embankment and the area fought over by the Irish can be easily viewed. A German machine gun post was located on the embankment itself — could you identify that spot using the original battle map?

Far right: A wartime sketch map of the area around Frezenberg showing the British and German positions. The same area photographed from the air showing the German artillery bombardment taking place as described in the text.
Far right below: The 16th (Irish) Division Field Ambulance at Frezenberg.

Right: William Doyle, MC, SJ.

128

Frezenberg is one of those little hamlets straddled along a main road that tend to slip by without being noticed, becoming incorporated into the sub conscious of the next large village. Yet in August 1917 Frezenberg (and the ridge to which it gave its name) was a focal point of an offensive designed to drive the British out of the constraints of the Salient.

6. Father William Doyle — Frezenberg

United at this point were two divisions whose members were implacably hostile to each other — 16 (Irish) Division and 36 (Ulster) Division. Both suffered grievous and enormous casualties as they held the line and attempted to counter attack and fight their way through towards the villages of Zonnebeke and Gravenstafel respectively.

Between 5 and 12 August the two divisions held the lines from which eventually they were to attack, and in the process suffered considerable casualties.

A Roman Catholic padre with 16 Division, Father William Doyle, was killed during the fighting of 1917 in the area of Frezenberg. Officers who were present at the time strongly recommended that the clergyman receive the Victoria Cross posthumously, for his bravery under fire whilst carrying out his duties to the dying. However, it was the padre's clerical superiors who successfully blocked all attempts to confer the nation's highest honour on 'Willie' Doyle.

In his extraordinarily detailed letters home, Father Willie Doyle described some of the events of those days. On 5 August he was at Battalion Headquarters and wrote the following account:

"A strong blockhouse made of concrete and iron rails, a masterpiece of German cleverness. From time to time all during the night the enemy gunners kept firing at our shelter, having the range to a nicety. Scores exploded within a few feet of it, shaking us till our bones rattled; a few went smash against the walls and the roof, and one burst at the entrance nearly blowing us over, but doing no harm thanks to the scientific construction of the passage."

On that occasion he was lucky; the following night he had moved to an Advanced Dressing Station, to be with the doctor working there; a shell burst at the entrance of his old billet, exploding several boxes of verey lights or rockets which had been left at the door. A mass of flame and dense smoke rushed into the dugout, severely burning some and almost suffocating all the officers and men, some fifteen in number, with poisonous fumes before they made their escape.

On 7 August he heard of a party of men caught by a shell, it was around midnight:

"I dashed off in the darkness, this time clutching my helmet as the enemy was firing gas shells. A moment's pause to absolve a couple of dying men, and then I reached the group of smashed and bleeding bodies, most of them still breathing. The first thing I saw almost unnerved me; a young soldier lying on his back, his hands and face a mass of blue phosphorous flame, smoking horribly in the darkness. He was the first victim I had seen of the new gas the Germans are using, a fresh horror in this awful war."

The attack, when it came, on August 16 did not go well; the two divisions had been weakened by the length of time that they had been in the line prior to the offensive moment. The attackers were badly cut up by machine guns in the German strong points known as Vampire, Potsdam, Beck House and Borry Farm. The artillery barrage had not been accurate enough, and the proposal to douse the Germans with gas before hand had been rejected. Even when they achieved positions at or close to their objectives, the Germans reacted strongly and piled over from Zonnebeke in a great counter attack and engulfed the Irishmen.

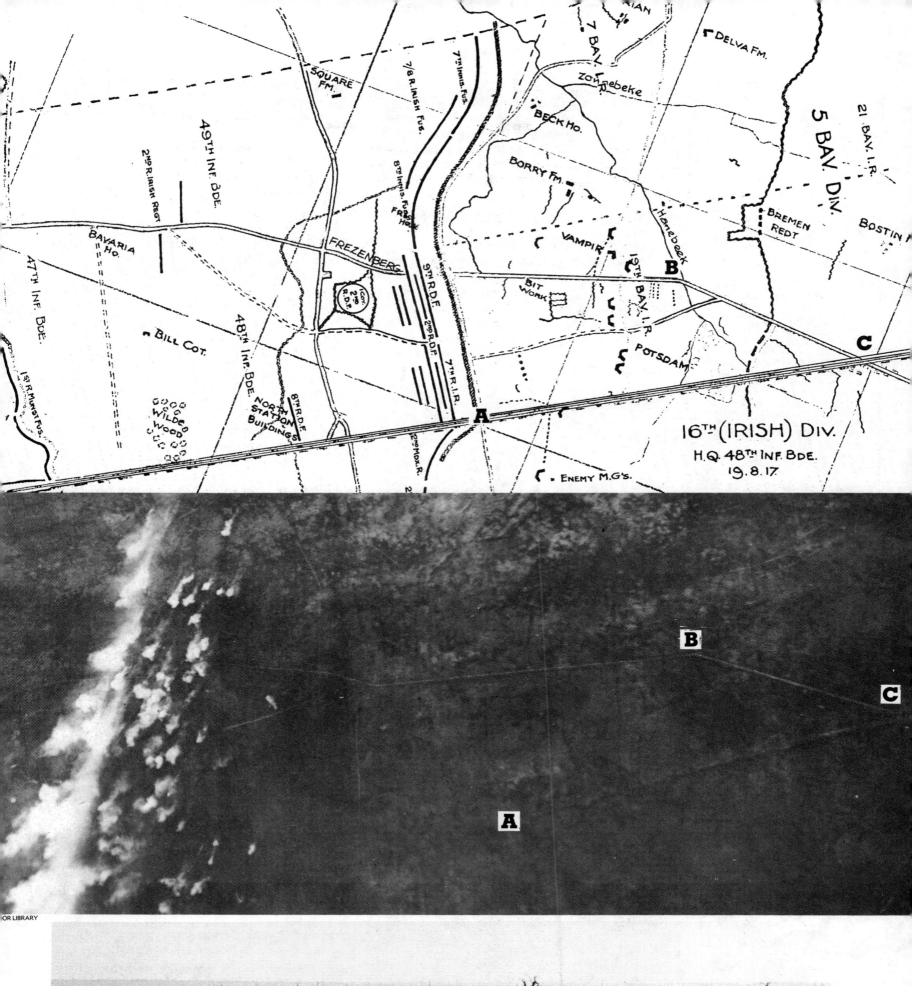

SQUARE FM.
7/8 R.IRISH FUS.
7TH INNIS. FUS.
DELVA FM.
7 BAV.
ZONNEBEKE
BECK HO.
5 BAV. DIV.
21. BAV. I.R.
BOSTIN
49TH INF. BDE.
2ND R.IRISH REGT.
8TH INNIS. FUS.
BORRY FM.
BREMEN REDT
B
VAMPIR
19TH BAV. I.R.
BAVARIA HO.
47TH INF. BDE.
FREZENBERG
1 COY. 2ND R.D.F.
FRE HO.
9TH R.D.F.
BIT WORK
C
48TH INF. BDE.
BILL COT.
2ND R.D.F.
POTSDAM
1ST R.MUNST FUS.
48TH INF. BDE.
7TH R.I.R.
A
WILDEE WOOD
NORTH STATION BUILDINGS
8TH R.D.F.
16TH (IRISH) DIV.
H.Q. 48TH INF. BDE.
19.8.17

2ND MDX. R.
ENEMY M.G's.

B
C
A

OR LIBRARY

IMPERIAL WAR MUSEUM

129

With the greatest reluctance and to preserve the original position, the divisional and corps commanders agreed to a British artillery barrage being put down. Before the battle 16 Division had lost two thousand men; and during the two days that they were in the line they lost another two thousand.

What of Doyle? His last letter home was written on 14 August, but his actions were recorded by one of the best known British war correspondents of the day, Sir Philip Gibbs:

"All through the worst hours an Irish padre went about among the dead and dying giving Absolution to his boys. Once he came back to headquarters, but he would not take a bite of food or stay, though his friends urged him. He went back to the field to minister to those who were glad to see him bending over them in their last agony. Four men were killed by shell fire as he knelt beside them, and he was not touched — not touched until his own turn came. A shell burst close by, and the padre fell dead."

He seems to have been killed close by a bunker, along with two other officers somewhere in the region of the start line for the offensive — where exactly will never be known.

There were others who witnessed his death and their accounts contradict the above report. A soldier in the Ulster Division related:

"I was the right hand Vickers gunner of the Division and was on duty from the moment of the attack until the gun was blown up soon after mid day. Midway through the morning a stretcher party of the Fusiliers (Dublin) passed me carrying the body of an obviously dead officer and they had tears streaming down their cheeks. I naturally asked who the officer was and was told that it was Fr Willie Doyle. 'He's been out in No Man's Land all night and sure there was no need for it; they were all dead anyway.' Gunfire all day was very heavy, and it would appear that the stretcher party never reached its destination."

His body may have been found and buried — but if it was it was not rediscovered later. Descriptions of battlefields make it all quite clear how unsafe were the bodies of those buried on them whilst warfare raged to and fro across the ground.

There is an interesting twist to his story. General Hickie, commanding 16 Division wrote to a friend telling him that the padre had been recommended for a V.C. by his commanding officer, his brigadier and himself. It did not happen: his brother, Charles Doyle, wrote to say that:

"I'm sorry to say that we have learned from a good source that it was the ecclesiastical authorities at the Front that blocked it, on the grounds that Willie went where he should not have gone. As if a priest should not go where dying men may want him! My people are very much annoyed, and Bob is going, or has gone, to London to see Cardinal Bourne (the then Archbishop of Westminster who was also acting as Bishop to the Forces) about it.'

Whilst researching Willie's life I came upon an interesting document: his life had been insured for £500 by his religious superiors for a premium of £25 — they must have found a big hearted insurance company to get such a quotation, given the realities of the conditions in the Front Line.

The two Irish Divisions had fought side by side throughout those summer months of 1917; a show of unity that has not been witnessed, regrettably, since.

Below: Advanced Dressing Station near Tilloy, April 1917. The C of E padre seen here among the dead awaiting burial is Rev Theodore Hardy. He was awarded the Victoria Cross in April 1918 for his work rescuing the wounded, unlike the RC padre Willy Doyle, who's church superiors would not permit the recommendation to take effect.

Zonnebeke is a rather featureless place but it allows one to appreciate the rise that goes to the plateau of Broodseinde Ridge, on which lies the village of Passchendaele, and which name in popular memory encompasses the Third Battle of Ypres. The village of Zonnebeke was completely destroyed by the end of the war — it had already taken a severe pasting in the fighting of late 1914. The Zonnebeke to Moorslede road served as a rough and ready boundary between the French armies and the British Expeditionary Force at the time.

IMPERIAL WAR MUSEUM

Above: An Aid Station to the rear of the front line. Note the pile of scavenged equipment next to the sandbags.

7. Lieutenant Martin-Leake VC and Bar — Zonnebeke

It was in the area between here and the southern edge of Polygon Wood that Arthur Martin-Leake became the first man to win a Bar to his Victoria Cross; there have been only two others since.

He had won the first one in the South African Campaign in February 1902 'when he went out into the firing-line to dress a wounded man under very heavy fire from about forty Boers only one hundred yards off. When he had done all he could for them, he went over to a badly wounded officer, and while trying to place him in a more comfortable position he was shot three times.' He had been severely wounded in the right arm and left thigh.

When he had finished qualifying in London after the war he moved to India and worked in Bengal for the railways. However he had a thirst for involvement in war. When one of the innumerable Balkan crisis of the early part of the century erupted in 1912, Martin-Leake whilst on leave from India, volunteered to serve in a Red Cross unit in the Montenegran Army. At the end of that war in 1913 he returned to India, but on the outbreak of the European war he decided to return as soon as possible to get involved. By fortunate ship-hopping he found himself in Marseilles, and from there to Paris where he offered himself to the Army authorities.

Although perhaps a rather unusual method of joining the army it was not so very unusual for those confused days. He was appointed to the 5 Field Ambulance in the 2 Division in the rank of Lieutenant. His citation for his second Victoria Cross is short and to the point '...is granted a clasp for conspicuous bravery in the present campaign. For most conspicuous bravery and devotion to duty throughout the campaign, especially during the period 29 October to 8 November 1914, near Zonnebeke, in rescuing, whilst exposed to constant fire a large number of the wounded who were lying close to the enemy's trenches.'

As the war progressed, and as more and more men became involved, and acts of heroism were reported all over the battlefield, those who considered men's actions worthy of the highest award had to use more and more fulsome language. Some cynics argued that it was more the literary ability of the recommending officer than the merit of the action that determined who got a VC or not.

Martin-Leake continued to serve until almost the end of the war, although he spent time on a morale boosting mission to the hard pressed Serbs, and visited Italy. He returned to India in due course to his job of Administrative Medical Officer of the Bengal—Nagpur railway, based at Calcutta, and remained unmarried. In retirement he returned to the family house of Marshalls at High Cross near Ware in Hertfordshire, and after a protracted illness from cancer he died just short of eighty in 1953. He is buried in the churchyard there (the only double VC buried in the UK), and a few years ago a plaque was installed and his gravestone refurbished by his old Corps, the Royal Army Medical Corps.

Above: The Victoria Cross, highest decoration for bravery awarded to all ranks in the British Forces. Some claimed that because of the great number of brave acts performed during the Great War, whether a man received the coveted medal or not, depended to some degree, on the writing skills of the recommending officer.

Left: Lt Arthur Martin-Leake, VC and Bar. Note the two small VCs attached to medal ribbon.

131

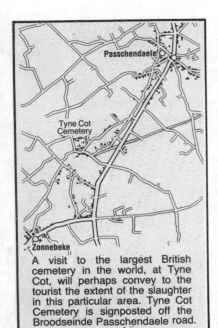

The area over which much of the great Passchendaele Battle was fought, that is to the north and east of Ypres, has now lost most of the scars of the conflict. However, they can still be found — the largely undisturbed ground at Bellewarde, the remnants in Polygon Wood, the occasional bunker, such as the one dug into the side of the road near the New Zealand memorial commemorating their great achievement during the battle — but most, perhaps thankfully — have gone.

8. Battlefield Clearance — Passchendaele

The greatest single memorial to the battle lies in the huge cemetery at Tyne Cot, the biggest British war cemetery in the world. And the nature of the conflict is vividly realised here, for there are some 3,500 named graves, along with almost eight and a half thousand which mark an unknown soldier. Along the majestic curved wall that runs the width of the cemetery are carved just under 35,000 names of men who have no known grave.

It is well sited as a memorial to the battle; Passchendaele, which gave its name to the offensive, is only a mile or so away; from the cemetery the views across the Salient are complete — and it is rumoured that even the sea is visible from here. The cemetery draws its name from a barn which was called Tyne Cottage that was once situated a few yards west of a level crossing (the railway lines have long since disappeared, but the embankment remains — it is a continuation of the same one near or on which Doyle was killed). In the vicinity of the barn were a number of German pillboxes, which were a part of the German Flanders I line. The position was captured by the Australians, and the largest of the blockhouses was turned into a dressing station by 50 Northumbrian Division — always a slightly risky business, as the entrance was facing the wrong way, but given the alternatives such a choice would be inevitable. The cemetery was then established, and after the war thousands were brought here whose bodies were discovered during the great clearing operations. When George V visited Flanders and this particular site he suggested that the cross of sacrifice should be built on top

Above: One of the many German concrete bunkers forming strongpoints between the front line and the village of Passchendaele that had to be overcome by the attacking British.

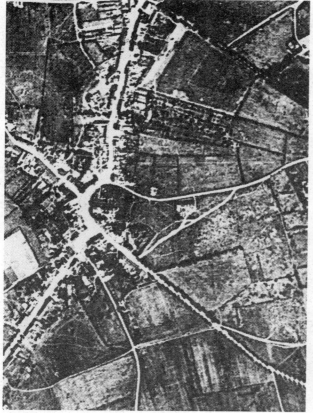 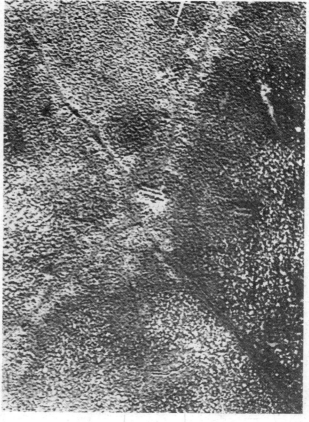

Left: Passchendaele before and after the battle.

Above: The railway line and sidings just south of the village of Passchendaele. This gives some idea of the type of conditions that had to be contended with by both sides.

of that great central blockhouse, and that the original burials of that time should be left as they were, so that now there is a haphazard collection of graves behind the memorial, an indicator of the circumstances of the time.

Those whose names appeared on the walls were the undiscovered who fell in the Salient between August 15, 1917 and the end of the war.

The work of clearing the battlefields took many years — though obviously the most pressing work was carried our quite rapidly. To do this thousands of men from the Chinese Labour Corps — men hired, often from War Lords, to supplement the men working behind the lines, remained to help in the clearance operation. Parts of the battlefield were sold to metal

Right: When the guns had ceased and the hot shrapnel stopped flying the ground began to recover. This photograph taken in 1919 near the village of Passchendaele shows the durability of vegetation which quickly regrew and covered the killing fields. By the shell crater is a concrete bunker and shelters. As there are a number of graves around, it is likely that the post was used for treating casualties.

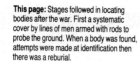
This page: Stages followed in locating bodies after the war. First a systematic cover by lines of men armed with rods to probe the ground. When a body was found, attempts were made at identification then there was a reburial.

merchants and scrap dealers. But the job that the British took most seriously was the clearing of the dead. There were a number of battalions of men that became engaged in the gruesome task of combing the battlefields, registering the dead (and even marking the location where they were found), exhuming them and reburying them in concentration cemeteries such as Tyne Cot. Of course this work had gone on to a degree before the war ended — for example a battlefield clearance of sorts was made on the Somme when the Germans withdrew to the Hindenburg Line in March 1917. The British government even offered a bounty to people who located a British soldier's body and reported the find to the local War Graves Commission. It is something of a sobering thought to realize that bodies are still being found — from a conflict that ended over 70 years ago.

No other place perhaps better illustrates how many more people are making the journey to the battlefields than was the case say twenty years ago; now the grass is beginning to suffer from the tramp of many feet as people come up to this focal point in the Salient for whatever the reason. In the sixties you could reckon to have the place to yourself, along with some gardeners and those remembered; now there

85 A STEEL OBSERVATION POST.

always seems to be some visitor or pilgrim there. The words of Remembrance Sundays the country over are perhaps not so hollow as I once thought: 'We shall remember them...'

A good view of this sector of the battlefield may be had from the Canadian Memorial at Crest Farm, just below the village of Passchendaele. Now that the trees and shrubs have been removed that used to surround it, it is clearly possible to see the almost superhuman task that faced the Canadians as they ploughed their way steadily on to the hugely fortified village at the top of the crest. Even now, when the fields are ploughed, it is possible to visualise the difficulties that must have faced them as they struggled their way through slime, muck and destruction under a torrent of shells and bullets towards what by then was not much more than a discolouration on the face of the earth.

Far left: King George V on a visit to The Salient in May 1922. It was at his suggestion that the Memorial Cross was placed on top of a German bunker. This was done (**Left**) and a stone was left out to show the concrete of the bunker beneath.

Below: Tyne Cot Cemetery today; the largest British cemetery in the world, it also incorporates a hugh memorial to the missing. Bottom right of the picture can be seen traces of the railway embankment which witnessed bitter fighting — and the ground remains unchanged.

WESTERN FRONT ASSOCIATION

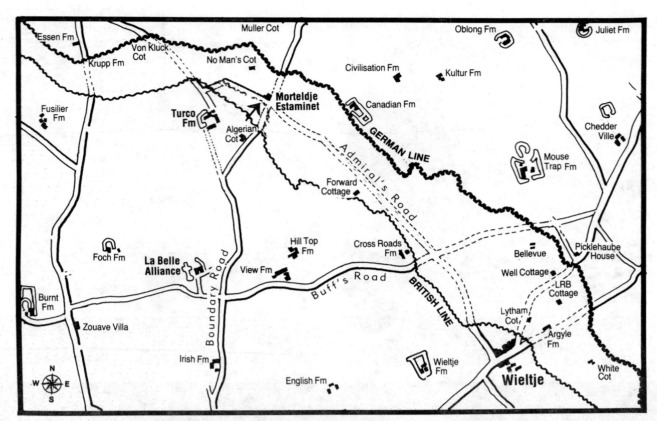

9. Lieutenant Guy Crawford-Wood — La Belle Alliance

This is the story of a raid mainly designed to disrupt German ambitions in the area. The target was Morteldje Estaminet, slightly forward of the German lines.

The Welsh Guards (the most recently formed of the Guards Regiments, being founded in 1915) went up to the line from the Chateau Trois Tours, near Boesinge, where they had been in reserve, on June 28 crossed the Yser Canal, and went down the long communication trench until they came out at La Belle Alliance (the name given to a ruined house.) From there they went up to the front line, just in front of Turco Farm, which was being used as a forward dump for the construction of a new trench forward of it.

Guy Crawford-Wood, a second lieutenant in the Welsh Guards, along with some men from the Prince of Wales Company took over and completed the work which had been started by 2 Scots Guards on the night of June 29 — difficult and unpleasant work.

The trench raid was launched on the night of 1 July, 1916. The original idea was to set out from the trenches about a minute before the artillery barrage came down, but someone was too quick, and the group was immediately spotted by the Germans. In spite of this the German trench was entered reasonably easily; but even when there was no longer any sign of the former occupants, some men lay down and blazed away in front of them with no targets. The engineers, who had accompanied them, then set about their task of blowing up the machine gun positions.

The young officer could easily have lost control of the raiding party. He discovered two men 'having an argument over two wretched Huns, who were screaming and crouching by them with their hands up and yelling Mercy! in a hysterical, panting way. Jones wished to bayonet them, and Harris was hanging on to him and explaining in forcible miner language that they would take the ....'s back as prisoners.'

A machine gun emplacement was found and blown up with four or five lumps of gun cotton. They found the estaminet to be no more than a heap of bricks, and a party of men came over to fortify it. By that stage the Germans had opened up with their artillery, but were aiming at the old British line, unaware of the Welshmen's position. Communication trenches to the old line, dumps and bombing posts all had to be established in the heavily water logged ground. Crawford-Wood volunteered to fetch more wire, whilst those on the estaminet's position were beginning to take casualties, the German gunners having located them. The company was withdrawn at 2am, and men occupying two posts were left to hold the position.

Upon return to the trenches it was discovered that Crawford-Wood had been killed. A fellow officer reported, 'poor little Crawford-Wood has been killed while trying to bring more wire out to me — a recklessly brave boy and a dashing platoon leader. He had brains too.'

Consolidation was always far more difficult than capturing a position; from five hundred yards away near a place called Hill Top Farm, long lines of Welshmen were observed calmly

138

digging in the soft, mashy, pulpy ground, with shrapnel bursting over them and high explosive shells in their very midst. The Germans, determined to remove the outposts, were using field guns and the big trench destroying Minenwerfer, whilst the shallow communications trenches scraped out during the night were already full of water. The Germans launched bombardments all along this part of the British line, and tried to do a cutting out raid of their own.

Lewis guns were sited to cover the estaminet and prevent the enemy from occupying it, and small groups of men held off the Germans and with even more difficultly managed to keep the Lewis guns cleaned. By the night of 2 July the estaminet had been reduced 'to enormous craters ... only able to identify it by a few bricks and a sniper's loophole.' The two front line companies suffered the loss of ninety-six casualties — and 'there were hardly half a dozen men with whole suits.'

The commanding officer of the Welsh Guards was to comment on the death of his officer, 'Crawford-Wood was a great loss. He was a good looking, most gallant and active youngster, and feared nothing in the way of a German or any of their weapons.' He had been wounded three times previously, on the most recent occasion he had been hit by shrapnel in the head, but was back with his battalion by April 1916. To him belongs the dubious distinction of being the only Guards Officer to be killed on what for many other units of the British Army was to be a day filled with casualties — 1st July 1916. He was twenty-two. As a boy at school he had been renowned as a great speaker and writer (he edited and produced a periodical, producing most of the contents himself), but his chief talent lay as an actor. His family was to have more grief, as his younger brother Peter

Above: 2/Lt Guy Crawford-Wood.

was killed in an air accident the following October 1917 whilst serving with the Royal Naval Air Service — whilst as a letter from his father shows his parents almost lost their daughter in a bomb accident (it appears related to munitions production). Guy is buried at Brandhoek Military Cemetery.

The Belle Alliance raid can be quite easily followed on the ground — the farms are there, the small cemetery at La Belle Alliance, and a new building has arisen from the ashes of what was once Mortildje Estaminet. The main threat seems to be the development of a motorway, which at the moment has halted in mid-construction.

Turco Farm

Site of Mortildje Estaminet

Left: The raid area today; Crawford-Wood was killed in the area in front of Turco Farm.

Just north of St Julian stands one of the most imposing memorials within the Ypres Salient, a tall column surmounted by a sorrowing soldier, which commemorates the Canadian action in the vicinity in the last days of April 1915 during the first poison gas attack on the Western Front. The memorial was the result of a competition in Canada to find an architect for their major memorial on the Western Front. This option came second, the first being the colossally impressive pile at Vimy Ridge. Yet I feel this one has the edge on it — perhaps not least because the creator of this memorial served during the war: nothing showy, but something instantly recognisable as expressing sorrow and companionship.

10. Poison Gas — St Julian

The explanation at the base of the statue, that it stands as a memorial to the two thousand Canadians who lost their lives here is misleading. The truth is, that they lost them over a wide frontage of several thousand yards. It was in this particular area that the Canadians fought so vigorously — joined at times by Imperial troops, particularly to the left.

Much of the early action of the Battle, which started on 22 April 1915, was spent in trying to keep contact between the British and French armies — represented at the time by the Canadians and also the Turcos (French troops mainly recruited from Algeria or Morocco) respectively.

From here it is possible to see much of the ground over which the Second Battle of Ypres was fought — to the north west towards Langemark, and to the north towards Poelkappelle, then east all along the Mauser ridge towards Passchendaele. During the course

of the battle the allies were pushed progressively south and west towards Ypres, until by its end on 25 May 1915, to the north and east the German lines were only some three miles or so from the centre of Ypres.

Gas of some sort had been in use from early in the war — but mainly in the form of tear gas. Chlorine gas had not been seen before on the Western Front, and although lethal to some degree its main effect was to cause panic and confusion. The French suffered particularly badly in this regard, especially the colonial troops who suffered very severely from panic caused by the noxious fumes.

Rudimentary gas masks were made — such as dampening cloth in water, and one group of British troops with a former industrial chemist who was an officer among their number, were instructed to urinate on their handkerchiefs or puttees, and hold them against their mouths and noses. This reacted with the chlorine, and served to lessen the effects.

The allies certainly had knowledge that gas was going to be used — on the night of 13 April a German deserter called Jaeger had revealed in some detail the German plans. The reports were forwarded, but higher command thought that the man could well be a 'plant' to distract the allies — how could so humble a soldier be so well informed? When Ferry, the French general involved, wrote up the incident years later, poor Jaeger was arrested and in 1932 sentenced to ten years in jail for desertion and betrayal. The Germans were certainly not proud of the use of the gas — they made no mention of it in their communiques, and indeed blamed the allies for being the first to perpetrate the horror.

In this vicinity there was extremely heavy fighting, which involved the remnants of five Canadian battalions. Gradually giving ground they held the area just to the north and east of St Julian, clinging on to the edge of the ridge. But the end was only a matter of time, especially as details of what exactly was going on were not reaching headquarters, which in any case was in confusion because it was far from clear who exactly was in charge. The last moments of the defenders was recorded by Private Thurgood of 7 Battalion in a newspaper account printed by a Vancouver newspaper in late 1917:

"Our rifles were jammed and the only machine gun that remained had been clogged with mud. Then the enemy broke into the trench further along and started bombing their way towards us. One of our officers ordered us to surrender and we threw up our hands. Though we held our hands aloft and were now unarmed, the cold blooded crew started to wipe us out. Three of our men were bayonetted before an officer arrived and saved the rest of us. Even then our rough captors struck us with their rifle butts and kicked some of our men who were unfortunate enough to be laid out with wounds."

Whatever the ethical points about the first use of this monstrous weapon, gas, it had proved to be an outstanding success for the Germans, only limited by the fact that no real efforts had been made by the German high command to make full use of its potential and back the attack with sufficient reserves to push the initial success to a decisive result.

Above: British soldiers wearing early anti gas hoods. The material of the helmet was impregnated with a chemical and by tucking the hood inside the tunic, it was supposed to be gas proof. This early, ineffectual mask was replaced by a more efficient respirator later.

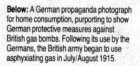

Below: A German propaganda photograph for home consumption, purporting to show German protective measures against British gas bombs. Following its use by the Germans, the British army began to use asphyxiating gas in July/August 1915.

By the opening of the British offensive of 1917 Langemark was well behind German lines. On August 16 men of 7 Kings Own Yorkshire Light Infantry prepared to launch an attack along the right of the railway line into Langemark. Amongst those in that action was a newly commissioned 2/Lt, A.C.H. Robinson, promoted from the ranks soon after the end of the Battle of the Somme the previous year. A good place to view the action of this battle is from Cement House cemetery.

Before the attack began, the commanding officer of the battalion asked his officers if they had any views on the attack and could make suggestion on tactics to be employed. Robinson argued in favour of a concentration of fire on points rather than a barrage in the final stages, and that troops should advance by sections in Indian file. He also had a scheme for dealing with pill boxes which was used to great effect by

his company runner, Private Edwards. The advance went ahead.

A stream, the Steenbeke, was very difficult to cross, the banks having been destroyed months ago and in the unseasonal wet mud already becoming the order of the day. In fact the duckboards used to span the stream broke under the strain. Casualties among the officers was severe. Robinson himself fell over barbed wire and onto an area heavily infected by gas: his clothes ripped by the barbed wire he suffered gas blisters on hands and thighs. All around his fellow officers were falling. On reaching the railway line, instructions were to take a compass bearing to bring the advance north west of Langemark — there was nothing visible above ground by which the place could be recognised.

He knelt on the railway line remnants, and of course the compass malfunctioned, effected by

Below: Men of the Kings Own Yorkshire Light Infantry resting at Wieltje on their way up to the front line for the British offensive in August 1917.

JAMESON

11. Kings Own Yorkshire Light Infantry — Langemark

the remnants of metal in the ground. Moving away a few yards distance he knelt again; a bullet whizzed over him and struck and killed his batman who had followed him up. By this stage he was the only officer left standing with the forward companies — there were 18 officer casualties. Edwards, the company runner won a VC for crawling between two blockhouses and waiting for the metal shutter of one of the machine gun slits to open: then he lobbed in his grenade. When the battalion was withdrawn on the 18th there were only 68 men standing, and four officers — the CO, adjutant, the signals officer, and Robinson. There had originally been over 600 men that went into action. They returned to their support positions at Essex Farm; Robinson was to get the DSO for his action. Private Edwards was to survive the war, and indeed was returned to England to go on morale boosting tours through a number of cities, and talk of his exploits.

Colonel Robinson (a rank he reached during World War II) returned to Langemark on 11 November, 1984 and laid a wreath at 20 (Light) Division memorial in Langemark. At the end of his three day tour, which he thoroughly enjoyed, he died in Dover on his way home to Ashwell in Leicestershire.

Cement House — ie a German bunker — that gives the cemetery its name is now tastefully disguised in the nearby farm, with small trees and covered in a rambling plant you would hardly know it is what it is. At the time of the action described above it had already been captured from the Germans.

The cemetery itself was until very recently one of only a couple in the Salient that still interred newly discovered remains, something that still happens quite regularly. Often bones are uncovered during road works or some major excavation where previously there had been none since the war; sometimes they are uncovered in forestry areas during tree felling. Most of such cases are now removed to a cemetery near Boulogne.

Cement House is now a vast cemetery, and its progressive increase in size can be followed in the register and the subsequent type written additions made to it. It is always worthwhile to look through the registers carefully. In nearly all cases of a VC winner, the details of the citation

are added; and sometimes the relative who is responsible for the entry will add comments about the individual, facts on his background or whatever. There is a particularly poignant one here. Private A.A. Crow of the Essex Regiment was invalided home and out of the army in 1916 in the rank of captain but he could no longer face not sharing the dangers on the Front, or perhaps felt that regardless it was his duty to be there — or perhaps, like so many others, felt alienated by what was going on at Home, the attitudes and the enormous gulf between the Home Front and reality. Whatever his reasons, he rejoined the army, and forbidden to go abroad again as an officer he enlisted in the ranks. His journey ended here. Unfortunately, with a story like this there are so many loose ends one would like to pick up; but there is enough to set the mind to work, and to find another facet of the human character.

Before the war Langemark was the second largest habitation in the Salient area, boasting some seven and a half thousand inhabitants — its nearest rivals, Zonnebeke and Wytschaete having just over three thousand. This small town saw much heavy fighting throughout the war, but particularly (as far as the British were concerned) during 1914 and 1917. It is also distinguished by having the only German cemetery in the Salient, a vast affair, incorporating the bunkers of an old defensive line, and with a huge mass grave of some 25,000 soldiers. German cemeteries characteristically are far more sombre, chilling places than their British counterparts, with modern sculptures, yew hedges, dark forbidding trees and more often than not, an absence of flowers. Here there are no headstones as such — just slabs set in the ground with a list of those buried in the immediate vicinity. It is a Wagnerian and disconcerting experience.

The cemetery has been improved in recent years — car parking, toilets and the registers have been added, as well as a clearing of some of the hedges and the new memorials that stare through you as an entry is made into the main part of the cemetery. In addition great blocks have been erected around the mass grave with the names of those buried there cast in metal on them. Even before entering the cemetery, in a room to the right of the entrance hall, there is an

Above: A view of Langemark from Cement House Cemetery. The ground in the middle distance was inundated, the (now) small Steenbeke having burst its banks due to persistent artillery fire.

Above: Lt Colonel A. C. H. Robinson, DSO, survivor of the action to take Langemark, salutes his fallen comrades at the 20 (Light) Division Memorial. The Colonel died two days later on his way home.

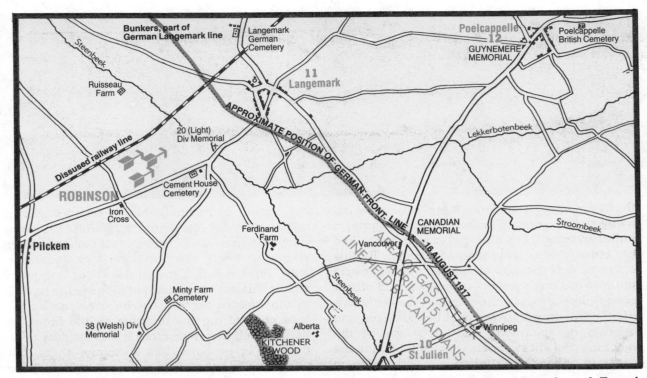

impressive memorial. It is a room lined with oak panels on which are engraved the names of the literally thousands of German students mown down by the British 2 Division. These young men had rushed to join the colours in the first bursts of enthusiasm of August 1914, and barely trained they were thrust into the carnage. The Germans regard this incident as the massacre of the children. In an account published during the war about the First Battle of Ypres, the Germans claimed that the British and French had managed to set up complex, fortified positions before their attack was launched; the truth was far from that, and it was much more a case of field craft skills of concealment, movement and use of ground, as well as a high level of musketry training that ensured that the line was held. The grounds of the cemetery itself were a part of the frenetic fighting that took place at the opening of the Ypres battle.

Above: Stern, sinister figures guard the German cemetery just outside Langemark.

Right: British troops, Royal Garrison Artillery, pose around a German 5.9 artillery piece captured at Langemark. This artillery position received a direct hit by a shell during the action 23 August 1917.

Poelkappelle is a deviation from a normal circuit of the Salient, but driving along it is possible to see the ridge and experience something of that sense of dominance that the Germans must have felt as they looked over the British lines.

12. Under Age Soldier and French Air Ace — Poelkappelle

Stop at Poelkappelle British Cemetery, a large concentration cemetery. Seek out the grave of Private J Condon, Royal Irish Regiment who died on the 24 May, 1915 at the age of fourteen. He is the youngest British casualty of the Salient. It has been difficult to put anything together about Condon — the records of the Irish Regiments are not easily to hand, and his actual age is also difficult to ascertain. Whatever, it would certainly seem that he was not as young as a South African, Ross, who died for the cause a few years later.

It is also difficult to discover how he died; considering that Poelkappelle was well inside German lines at this time, and given that many of the British buried here were concentrated from German cemeteries where they had been originally buried, it seems quite likely that he died whilst a prisoner of the Germans. It is possible, however, to describe the action in which he might well have suffered his fatal wounds.

On the 24 May 1915, as the Second Battle of Ypres was drawing to a close, in the early hours of the morning, the Germans launched a gas and infantry attack on the 2 Battalion the Royal Irish Regiment, occupying trenches in the vicinity of Irish Farm. Despite the best attempts of respirators and sprayers (a liquid sprayed on the gas to neutralise its effect) many men were made casualties by the gas. The Germans managed to capture from another battalion the infamous Shell Trap Farm (renamed by the army Mouse Trap farm, presumably on the grounds that the former name did not do much for morale). The Germans were now able to attack the Irishmen from the side as well as the front; they proceeded to bomb their way down the severely weakened British trenches, but the attack was eventually halted, although the enemy clung on — at least temporarily — to the ground that they had gained. The battalion suffered huge casualties — all the officers bar one who had been in the trenches when the attack began along with 379 NCOs and men. Young Condon, in all probability, was one of those men.

It is common knowledge that many joined the army well under age; there were also many who were killed that served under fictitious names, and the fact is recorded on the grave stone or

Above: The memorial to the French Air Ace, Georges Guynemere in the centre of Poelkappelle.

memorial. Procedures varied, but many of those who were serving under age, and were so discovered were weeded out, often before the battalions left England to begin their overseas service (this was especially true of men of Kitchener's army — many veterans can recall the procedure taking place). Once in France it depended on the circumstances, on the amount of fuss a relative might make, and to a degree on the attitude of the soldier in question. Men were generally not discharged if they were serving under age — rather they were returned to units at home where they might form part of a training battalion or whatever until they became old enough to be sent to the Front.

The crossroads of Poelkappelle is dominated by the scupture of a flying stork, emblem of the squadron, called the Cigognes, which was commanded by Georges Guynemere and which is a memorial to him. He was shot down and

Above: The fourteen year old's grave stone at Poelkappelle British Military Cemetery.

145

killed in this vicinity on 11 September 1917, the victim of a well executed enemy aerial ambush.

Guynemere had 54 'kills' to his credit; but like so many other air aces of the Great War (and the Second, for that matter) the pressure told terribly on him. He fought right through the battle of Verdun, and just prior to the arrival of his squadron in the Flanders region (based at St Pol) he went home on leave to a father who was horrified at his physical appearance. At his father's suggestion to seek an instructor's job, as there must be a limit to human endurance, Guynemere is said to have replied, 'Indeed there is a limit, but it is only there to be excelled. If one has not given everything, one has given nothing.' As time went on he became increasingly paranoid, as well as having to fly machines that were not his own but temporary replacements. A number of sorties without kills led him to feel that people were muttering in the mess behind his back — perhaps he was deliberately avoiding the enemy?

Matters reached such a pitch, with the ace Guynemere unable to sleep, but instead pacing his room; a growing tendency to talk to himself, and other irrational acts that officers were sent to investigate from Paris. It was on the day of their arrival that Guynemere was killed. Like so many air aces he was larger than life, a tendency to being highly strung — certainly not a cold technician as the greatest of the allied air aces, Rene Fonck — but it was these very attributes that brought him, and others like him, so much popular adulation at the time.

Below: Georges Guynemere, French ace and commander of Cigognes (Stork) Squadron. He was finally ambushed in the air, September 1917, and shot down at Poelkappelle. German infantry recovered his body from the wrecked Spad and later reported that he had been shot in the head. However, before he could be buried, an artillery barage removed all trace of him and the wrecked aircraft was blown to bits. At the time of his death he had 54 German aircraft credited to him and was a French national hero.

Above: How the concrete shelters at Essex Farm appeared during the war. The Canal bank has been cut through to allow passage across the water and into the Salient.
Below: Those same shelters over seventy years later. It was here that the wounded received further treatment after being brought out of the line. Those who died from their injuries were buried in the adjacent cemetery.

The drive along the Yser canal is no longer a congenial drive alongside a waterway in an otherwise featureless landscape; for development has arrived on the northern side of Ypres with a vengeance: on the west side it is chiefly housing, on the east there is a steady growth in new industries.

13. Essex Farm — Yser Canal

Having passed under the by-pass, on the right almost immediately there is a British cemetery. This is Essex Farm, snuggled up against the embankment of the canal. The dugouts here were home to many thousands of troops, especially in the days of the great gas attack and the months of Third Ypres. Walking along the track between the cemetery and a new small industrial unit brings you up to the embankment, and looking left there are a series of dug outs remaining. There is nothing very spectacular about them — their survival is more due, I suspect, to the convenient shelter they offered for the farmer's livestock than anything else. But the conditions alongside and inside them helps to fuel the imagination as to conditions during the war; whilst it was near here — or possibly even inside one of the shelters — that John McCrae, a Canadian doctor who was to die in early January 1918 and is buried at Wimereux on the coast, wrote possibly the most well known poem of the war, first published in December 1915:

> "In Flanders fields the poppies blow
> Between the crosses, row on row
> That mark our place; and in the sky
> The larks, still bravely singing, fly
> Scarce heard amid the guns below.
> We are the Dead. Short days ago,
> We lived, felt dawn, saw sunset glow,
> Loved and were loved, and now we lie
> In Flanders fields.

McCrae had been moved to write this poem by the death of a close friend, Lieutenant Alex Helmes who served with the Canadian Artillery and is buried in the neighbouring cemetery. This is also the resting place of a fifteen year old — Rifleman Strudwick of the King's Royal Rifle Corps.

Below: Essex Farm Cemetery as it appeared shortly after the war.

IMPERIAL WAR MUSEUM

This place was more significant than wartime literature tends to indicate; for it lay on the banks of the Yser canal, and through it many troops — French and British — trudged up to the line in the north eastern part of the Salient, not least because there was a bridge crossing here. It is quite easy to pinpoint just where the German, French and British trenches were because of a bend in the Canal and the bridge.

14. The Northern Nip — Boesinge

Where the Salient began in the north, close to the village of Boesinghe, it proved to be a particularly nasty spot for the British troops. It was there that the British held the line on the eastern bank of the Yser Canal; the French continued the allied line on the western bank.

Into that 'hot spot' the West Riding Territorials of 148 Brigade were sent during the night 9 July, 1915. An officer of 1/5 York and Lancaster Regiment (they were from Rotherham, Barnsley and district) Lieutenant Charles Fox, recalled the event:

"When we arrived at the Yser Canal sector our battalion was to go into the line on the extreme left of the British line, where it joined up with the French. We were stuck on the very end of the Salient, on the banks of the Yser. We were in a terrible position — and by far the worst spot was on the extreme left flank, for it meant that the enemy was on the front and the side of you. Which of our four companies would get the worst spot? We decided to toss a coin for it — I lost."

Two days before the Yorkshiremen took over the sector some small gains had been achieved by men of 4 Division — they had advanced a few hundred yards driving the Germans back from their positions. The Germans registered their annoyance by constant sniping from some houses clustered around the east end of Boesinge Bridge. From that position they could enfilade the canal bank for half a mile. Shelling

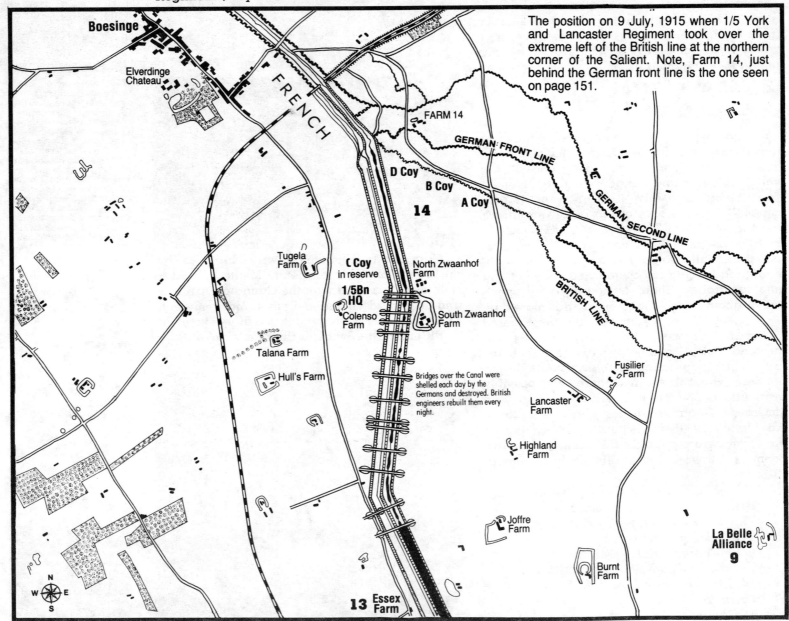

The position on 9 July, 1915 when 1/5 York and Lancaster Regiment took over the extreme left of the British line at the northern corner of the Salient. Note, Farm 14, just behind the German front line is the one seen on page 151.

Above: Charlie Fox's company manned this nip where the Salient began in the north. The Yser Canal was drained in that sector and formed a muddy boundary for the armies of three nations: French on the left bank (trees with foliage) Germans on the right; the start of their front line trench is marked with a cross. The start of the British front line trench is indicated with the white dot. At that point a few yards separated the opposing forces. The barbed wire entanglements placed in the canal bed was to prevent the Germans from getting around the back and turning the British line. Old cans and tins were scattered amidst the wire so as to make a noise should a German patrol attempt to get through at night.

Left: Looking more like pirates and brigands than British soldiers, these 1/5 Territorials from Rotherham managed a smile for the camera as they manned the worst spot in the Salient. Two of them are holding rifle grenades, whilst another catches up on some sleep at the bottom of the trench. They were only a matter of yards from the enemy.

149

Far right: A remarkable photograph taken over the parapet of the British support trench dug into the Yser Canal bank on the extreme left of the line. A communication trench can be seen to the left passing some wooden crosses (graves) and snaking towards the British front line. Beyond the leafless trees (in No Mans Land) can be seen the German front line trench. The ruined building on the German line is Farm 14 (see map).
Far right below: German troops in their more orderly trench, opposite the British.

Below: South Yorkshire Territorials, 1/5 York and Lancaster Regiment in trenches at the northern nip of the Salient. Behind them is the Yser Canal — in front, the might of the German army. Absolute boredom puntuated by sudden death was the lot of the infantryman in World War One.

was continuous during the daytime, the German artillery observers having an excellent view from Pilkem Ridge.

"My first trip into the sector was by night, it had to be, the Germans could see every movement. The nearest bridge crossing the Canal to get to my sector was 500 yards away — and that used to get blown up every day by shellfire. The engineers had to go in every morning to repair it; they were the finest fellows I've seen."

The Boesinge area was possibly the worst part of the whole British front in 1915. Only the presence of the neighbouring French with their

75's and unlimited ammunition made life tolerable. They were more than willing to lay down a barrage to help out; at that time the British artillery were rationed in their use of shells.

"It was an absolutely filthy place there was mud everywhere. I got into this particular trench and waited for daylight. As it grew lighter I stuck my periscope up over the top of the trench and a terrible sight met my eyes — there were piles of dead in front, in the narrow strip of No Mans Land. There had been some heavy fighting in the area and the dead of both

sides could not be buried — the smell of decaying flesh was awful, and there were the flies. The trenches we were occupying once belonged to the Germans and we had to pass through B Company to get to our sector and on the way you had to pass this certain dugout — inside were three dead Germans in sitting positions, they had been caught by gas and had become horribly bloated. In that spot you couldn't walk upright for fear of being observed. Eventually we shoved earth in on top of them to cover them up."

148 Brigade continued to hold that extreme northern part of the Salient for two and a half months.

On the east side of the canal there is a small but moving French memorial to the first gas attack (not far from where North Zwaanhof Farm used to be situated and the French Turcos had their HQ in April 1915). It consists of a Menhir arrangement (if this is not too flippant, perhaps best known as the item of sale of the character Obelix in the well known comic cartoons) and behind it a fifteenth century calvary from the province of Britanny. It was in this vicinity also that the British launched their relatively successful attack on the 31 July, 1917 on the Pilkem Ridge, thus beginning the Third Battle of Ypres.

In Boesinge itself watch out for the 'Klein Bertha' a small German trench mortar that now

151

Right: A demarcation stone at Boesinge; the helmet on top indicates that it was the French who stopped the Germans from advancing further at that point.

sits proudly on the outhouse of a sizeable house on the main street. In the garden of the same building, now hidden from the road, is another one of the demarcation stones indicating the limits of the German advance. By the end of May their line ran along the canal at this point.

An interesting cemetery to stop and visit is that of Bluet Farm, to the west of Boesinge. It consists mainly of Guardsmen, most of whom were killed in the fighting of the 31 July, 1917 and afterwards. It must be one of the very few in the Salient where there are no unknown soldiers buried. It is reported that the 'Unknown Warrior' from the Ypres salient was taken from here — ie he was the only unknown soldier buried in the cemetery. Thus it may be that he now lies at Westminster Abbey; or he may be buried with the other candidates for this honour who were not selected and who now lie buried at St Pol, where the headquarters of the British Army were for some years after the war. There is a gap in the gravestones where a body has been removed. It is a point to ponder that the Unknown Warrior is just that: he could be a soldier, sailor or airman. Sailors served in 63 (Royal Navy) Division, fighting as soldiers and fought with great distinction, notably on the Somme in 1916 and later at Arras.

Right: The Yser Canal today, near the old railway bridge at Boesinge on the old British side of the canal. Opposite, where the concrete drain opens into the canal is where the German trenches began — see page 149 and the white cross.

Below: Outskirts of Boesinge today: the village was destroyed during the war and had to be rebuilt. The building on the left is the old station, built on the site of the original. Marks across the road indicate where the railway line once ran towards the rail bridge (off right) over the Yser.

As the Germans threatened to engulf Belgium completely, it was decided to order the flooding of much of the remaining allied held territory in the north by opening up the sluice gates at Nieuport. This effectively made it impossible for either side to carry out any sort of large scale operation; and it was this flooded area that the remnants of the Belgian army held. The actual section along the coast was held in turn by the Belgians, French and British.

(J) Trench of Death — Dixmude

After the war, the Belgian equivalent of the AA or RAC decided to preserve a notorious section of trench works, just to the north of Dixmude. It is the most extensive trenchwork maintained anywhere in Flanders, although much of the reality is lost by the use of concrete sandbags and so forth. Nevertheless, an impression is given of the complexity of the defence work and the structure of trenches, as well as the evolution of reinforced strong points and bunkers.

The visitor, having paid his entrance fee of about a pound, is also provided with a translation of the guide. Unfortunately it is not altogether clear exactly what was going on, especially as the trenches and prominent points are not marked. But it is clear that this was a highly exposed position, under fire from three sides, and made all the more difficult by the fact that the Germans managed here — and here only — to get across the Yser and set up a position on the left bank.

For four years the Belgians had to wrestle with the difficulties of holding the Germans at this point: supplying their own men in the trench was made difficult enough, because of the part flooded nature of the ground to their rear. Everything had to be brought over plank bridges at night; whilst it is worth sparing a thought for the Germans who had made it across who had to be relieved and supplied by the use of rafts.

The tenacity with which the Belgians held the position is perhaps best revealed right at the end of the trench system, in a secure part of their defence known as the Mouse Trap. By peering through the barbed wire and hedge at the end of the trenchworks, a German bunker can be seen some sixty yards away. If the Germans tried to rush the Belgian defences, they would have to enter by a pit; if they overpowered the defenders

Above: A Belgian soldier keeps watch over the fields that were flooded to stop the Germans outflanking the allied line. All supplies had to be brought over plank bridges to the Belgian outposts.

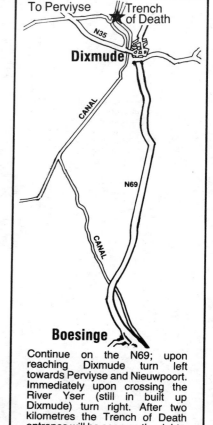

Continue on the N69; upon reaching Dixmude turn left towards Perviyse and Nieuwpoort. Immediately upon crossing the River Yser (still in built up Dixmude) turn right. After two kilometres the Trench of Death entrance will be seen on the right.

Left: A section of the Trench of Death, which was cut along the banks of the Yser Canal, as it appeared during the war.

Below: Entrance to the preserved trench system.

IMPERIAL WAR MUSEUM

here (and presumably in the event of an attack they would have withdrawn) they would have been wide open to murderous fire from the two blockhouses that the Belgians had constructed as their main defence.

Whilst in the Tower (part of the entrance arrangement here) it is a cause for thought to see just how flat and devoid of height the countryside is round about; it is hard to imagine anything much more dreary. A glance at a reasonably large scale map will also show just how dependent this part of Belgium is on an effective drainage system; it would not take much of an artillery bombardment to turn the whole area into a quagmire, over and above what opening the sluices accomplished.

Right: The extreme end of the preserved trench known as the 'Mouse Trap'. On the occasions that the Germans broke into this exposed point the Belgian defenders withdrew into the bunkers (from where this photograph was taken). Thus, from their defensive positions, they were able to pour fire into the Mouse Trap upon the disadvantaged attackers.
Note the demarcation stone indicating the extent of German intrusion onto Belgian territory. It was in that precise area that some of the most bitter fighting of the war between the Belgians and the Germans took place.

154

Above: The German bunker, just 60 yards from the end of the Trench of Death. It was at this point only that the Germans managed to cross the Yser Canal. The fields all around were flooded and the Germans had to supply this outpost across the canal by night. The machine gun post was a thorn in the side for the Belgians manning the banks of the Yser and that is indicated by the artillery damage evident on the concrete.

Left: Inside the bunker, five weapon apertures facing the Trench of Death ensured that maximum fire power was concentrated on the Belgian positions. Imagine the activity in the confined space of this German bunker with, perhaps up to three heavy machine guns clattering away. The bushes seen through the slits mark the end of the trench; the figure is midway between the two positions. Two further weapon openings are situated on the side facing away from the canal, covering what was once flooded fields. The armour plating is still in position along with spyhole shutters. This neglected German bunker is one of the most interesting artefacts of the fighting in this area during World War One.

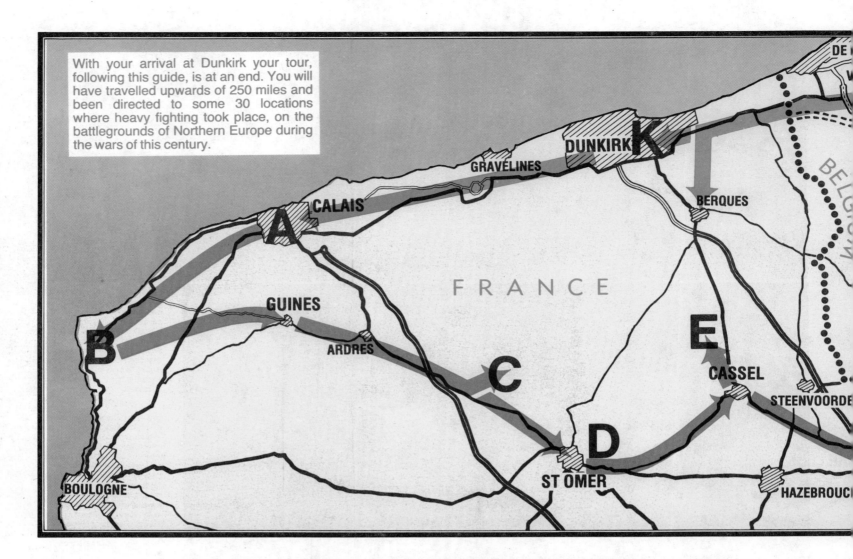

With your arrival at Dunkirk your tour, following this guide, is at an end. You will have travelled upwards of 250 miles and been directed to some 30 locations where heavy fighting took place, on the battlegrounds of Northern Europe during the wars of this century.

(K) Evacuation of the British Expeditionary Force

De Panne is now one of, if not the, major Belgian seaside resort, but it has a certain dignity, and for the traveller passing through for a day or so boasts a number of caravan and camping sites as well as many hotels. It stands on a sandy beach, though the water must be very cold. On the beach the statue of Leopold I (Queen Victoria's Uncle Leopold) the first King of the Belgians is in danger of being overwhelmed by the blocks of retirement flats and hotels that are arising around him.

In World War Two De Panne was Viscount Gort's last headquarters before he was evacuated back to Britain in the last moments of the Dunkirk beachead. Churchill instructed him to return as soon as the forces remaining went to a level normally commanded by a corps commander — he feeling that there was no need to give the Germans a commander-in-chief as a propaganda victory without cause. From De Panne Gort was taken to Bray Dunes and from there he went to Dunkirk. The Royal Engineers constructed makeshift piers (using lorries and planking them over) which enabled thousands of men to be lifted off from Bray and La Panne (the French version of the name).

The major part of the evacuation took place from the eastern harbour at Dunkirk to La Panne, though in the last days most of the evacuation was from the mole at Dunkirk. When Operation Dynamo ended on 4 June, 1940 over 338,000 men had been evacuated.

From ports all over Britain small boats including launches, trawlers, tugs, barges even rowing boats were collected together at Ramsgate. After issuing charts along with instructions and under the watchful eye and discipline of the Royal Navy the civilian volunteers headed across the Channel. During the whole nine days of the operation the usually choppy English Channel stayed calm. A haze hung over the whole area of the evacuation for much of the time making it difficult for the Luftwaffe to pinpoint targets. However, 70 ships of various types and sizes were sunk through bombing or mines.

From 28 May onwards the beaches became more and more crowded until a mass of men

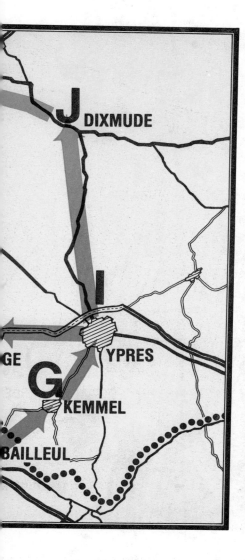

spread over a distance of ten miles of beaches and dunes — the British Expeditionary Force in retreat. As the perimeter shrank, units arrived at the seashore presenting a target that the German pilots could hardly miss. Individual soldiers blazed away with their rifles using up their remaining ammunition, joining in the fire being put up by the ships' guns. As the Germans pressed closer their medium and heavy artillery began to range in on the beaches.

The final phase of the embarkation called for larger ships to get into Dunkirk harbour and clear all stragglers. Complete units of French soldiers were among the last to leave, they had fought a determined rearguard action until their ammunition had become exhausted. The Germans, in their case had failed to discern that those French units had nothing left to fight with and so did not break through for many valuable hours. Belgian and French trawlers packed the last troops aboard and set off to run the gauntlet of dive bombers, E-boats and mines laid by aircraft.

On the crumbling perimeter the Napoleonic forts were being abandoned under the cover of darkness by the French units, who were fighting to the end so that others could get away. Finally, on 4 June, Operation Dynamo came to an end and apart for the occasional shot quiet decended on the shattered town and German advance patrols made their way through the smouldering ruins and litter strewn streets. There were no ships to be seen offshore, apart from wrecks, and the skies were empty of aircraft. Destroyed British equipment, trucks, tanks and guns were everywhere. Corpses drifted with the tide and thousands who had not got away prepared themselves for captivity. Over 3,000 civilians, men, women and children had lost their lives in the bombing and shelling.

Today the town has changed beyond recognition from the hectic days of 1940. Fortifications put up by the Germans during their five years of occupation served them well in 1945 when the First Canadian Army swept along the coastline. It had been decided by Montgomery not to sacrifice time and men capturing Dunkirk from the Germans, which

had been turned into a formidable stronghold. For seven months the well protected German soldiers and sailors sat behind their defences, watched over by a containing force made up mainly of Czech troops. Surrender of the town came with the final collapse of the Third Reich.

Considerable rebuilding has changed the face of the seafront and surrounds. The sandy beaches, where once death rained down on the crowds of men awaiting their turn to wade out to the small boats, are now filled with holiday-makers. Veterans of the evacuation and other visitors make return trips each year to remember those who fell defending the Dunkirk perimeter or who died on the beaches.

A drive along the coast will reveal plenty of remnants of the German defences of the Atlantic Wall — some of them look very impressive objects. Access to the coast is often relatively difficult — mainly because land is devoted to army training areas or nature reserves. Bear a thought if you do stroll along the coast what it must have been like for those thousands of men who had to march the ten miles from La Panne (when that evacuation point became too danger-ous) to Dunkirk.

Coming into Dunkirk there is a French military cemetery signposted off to the right, with a series of notices indicating that most of the land is 'interdit' to the unauthorised. This is

Far left: The packed decks of HMS Vanquisher as it moves away from the West mole.

Below: German troops entering the outskirts of Dunkirk after the main part of the British Expeditionary Force has escaped.

THE TANK MUSEUM

Above: Burnt out fuel tanks at Dunkirk and German soldiers amidst the rubble, walking freely once the remaining defenders had surrendered.

Below: The War Graves Memorial to those with no known grave from the Dunkirk campaign, May to June 1940.

MMONWEALTH WAR GRAVES COMMISSION

the site of Fort Dunes, and it is in this area that Oliver Cromwell's armies achieved European significance by helping the French to defeat the Spanish in 1658. The battle was important not only in that it was perhaps the final nail in the coffin of Spain's European ambitions, but also in that it was probably the most successful English intervention on the continent in the century. The prize was that Dunkirk became an English possession, until Charles II sold it to Louis XIV in 1662, and it ceased to be the harbour of a particularly fierce and effective group of privateers who were known as Dunkirkers, and had done great damage to English shipping.

The battle has some interesting points: victory was achieved by the French army launching an attack on the Spanish centre. Preoccupied, they failed to notice the ebbing tide, and an Anglo-French force, aided by gunfire from Cromwell's fleet used this opening to turn the Spaniards flank. Fighting with the Spanish were the future Charles II and James II; they took to strolling on the beach (before the battle was joined) in an attempt to win over the English commander, Reynolds. The Duke of York (the later James II) actually met up with Reynolds, who wished him well, instructed his men not to fire on the two men, and sent them a gift of wine.

In Dunkirk it is worth visiting the Town Cemetery and memorial to the missing, which commemorates those killed in the 1940 campaign and who have no known grave.

Dunkirk itself has become a vast sprawling port, heavily industrialised and really left me with no inclination to stay longer than was strictly necessary.

1.   Captain Ervine-Andrews, VC

It is worth making a diversion on the way out to Calais, to the old fortified town of Berques and the nearby scene of a VC action. The road out from Dunkirk (the D916) runs alongside a canal; a few kilometres along, on the left hand side of the road, lies the remains of Fort Vallieres, another of these huge, Vauban type constructions, in this case designed as part of a string of fortifications to defend both the port and the French frontier from incursions.

Berques itself is a fascinating, slightly dilapidated town surrounded by formidable bastions and thus confined to a large degree by its own fortifications, which in turn have a complex moat arrangement. Those on the northern side, in fact, became known as the Crown of Hondschoote — needless to say the work of Vauban, although he used here, as he had so often before, the existing medieval fortifications.

Berques was another important point in the defences of Dunkirk, the Germans using Stukas and flamethrowers to gain entrance into the town. It was just outside Berques that Captain Ervine-Andrews became the first army officer to win the VC in the Second World War.

The East Lancs were well on their way to evacuation at Dunkirk when a staff officer came upon them and realised that they were still a fighting unit, albeit without transport. They were instructed to hold a gap in the line along the Berques-Furnes canal. The area that they had to hold was to a large degree flooded — the opening of various sluice gates had served to provide a rudimentary defence. The forward companies had been able to hold off German attacks throughout 31 May, and in the evening they were replaced by A and B companies, B company commanded by Ervine-Andrews.

The defences were based on the various farmsteads dotted about, whose top floors were still above water, and which dominated the nearby ground. However, there was very little protection against German mortars and other attempts to set fire to the buildings, whilst ammunition was in short supply. As the day progressed the situation became more difficult, especially as the Germans gradually infiltrated the position.

As a forward position threatened to fall under the pressure, Ervine-Andrews arrived with a few reinforcements, and climbing onto a burning roof proceeded to pick off seventeen Germans with his rifle. A jammed machine gun having been cleared, these men continued to hold the position as the advancing Germans took shelter in the available (and of course limited) ground cover. The position was held until the late afternoon, when the few remaining men of B company made their way back, often swimming and wading through waterways, to Dunkirk; the battalion reformed on 2 June and were then evacuated back to England.

When Ervine-Andrews received his VC at

Left: Captain Ervine-Andrews, VC of the East Lancaashire Regiment.

161

By kind permission of the 1st Battalion The Queen's Lancashire Regiment

Buckingham Palace on 6 August, 1940 he was greeted at the gates afterwards by another member of his regiment — Spencer Bent, who had won his VC as a drummer in the vicinity of Plugstreet Wood back in December 1914. His old school, Stonyhurst College, a Jesuit Public School, has the distinction of having the first army officer VCs of both the First and Second World Wars.

Casualties of this fighting may be seen in the small communal cemetery at Warhem which is off to the south; it is of interest to me to note how many men of the Second World War are unknown who were killed in this fighting. Why? Did the Germans not take too much interest in British casualties? Hitler for one is known to have been scrupulous in his attitude towards the cemeteries of the war dead, so presumably this would have extended to those of the Second War.

The road from Dunkirk to Calais is largely featureless; however the tiny hamlet of Le Clipon witnessed one of the most unusual forces of the British army in the First World War. Just to the west of Le Clipon a camp was set up which housed 1 Division and a few ancillary units. These were to be used in a projected invasion of the Belgian coast between Ostend and Nieuport, as part of Haig's strategic plan for the Third Battle of Ypres.

They were completely cut off from the outside world — special arrangements were made to ensure that supplies and equipment were brought into the camp without contact being made with anyone in it. Special landing vehicles were built, which would hold an entire brigade with all its equipment, tanks, artillery; the only thing missing were horses. The whole contraption was to be propelled by two monitors, and was some six hundred feet long. The monitor was selected because it was a flat bottomed craft with a shallow draught which had the added advantage of carrying very heavy naval guns.

The sea wall on the invasion site pomised to provide difficulties, as it had an overhang. An exact replica was constructed at Le Clipon, and the problem solved by building a wedge shaped construction that would fit under the overhang. This would be pushed into position by the tanks, and experiments in England showed that this system worked every time. To help with the raising of heavy equipment the female tank would carry a winding gear, follow the other tanks up the wall, and after the situation was stabilised would wind the heavy gear up using a wooden ramp with guides for the wheels of the limbers as well as its own winding cable. It is a point worth reflecting upon that the First World War did come up with many ingenious ideas to make the job of winning the war more practicable than just throwing thousands of men at the barbed wire defences of the enemy.

Gravelines is an interesting place — again a fortified town with bastions, which underlines the military significance of the area in the seventeenth and eighteenth centuries; and

2. Invasion Plans World War One

again Cromwell's army assisted in its capture from the Spanish. It is rather a pretty spot, with character, and might be considered a good place to stop.

It was off the coast here that the progress of the Spanish Armada in 1588 was severely disrupted by the sending in of fireships by the English. Whilst the physical damage might not have been significant it certainly served to dislocate the Spanish fleet.

If the urge remains to look for beach fortifications the best plan is to take the minor road (D119e) to les Hemmes d'Oye and beyond. Walk up any of the minor roads to the beach, and in no time at all bunkers and strong points will be stumbled over: beware — so will rubbish and other undesirable products of human beings in some areas! The control and signalling bunkers are to be found to the rear — notice the rounded nature of these buildings, making them less vulnerable to shells, which might glance off, or at least be deflected when they struck them.

Arrival in Calais is marked by a Union Carbide factory; the road will bring the traveller out close to the ferry ports. Even if you are not travelling by Hovercraft, a visit to its terminal is worthwhile — there is an extensive array of bunkers in the immediate vicinity.

Above: A German bunker, part of coast defences, Second World War vintage, set back several hundred yards from the beach.

Below: British plan to outflank the German line by landing men and tanks by barge during the First World War. It was never put into operation.

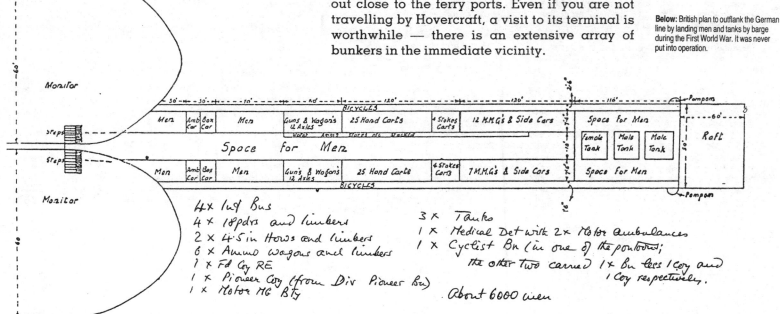

How the Great War arrived in Flanders

In the German war plan, masterminded by General von Schlieffen, it was necessary for the Germans to attack the French through the neutral country of Belgium; the original plan had also involved the invasion of Holland, but that was dropped. By attacking France through the low lying land, with the advanced rail network as an added advantage, the Germans hoped to move speedily in a sweep around the back of Paris and push the French armies in a trap between these advancing armies and the German forces on the Rhine. Speed was essential, before the British could arrive, before winter set in and before the French could recover from the initial shock. With a successful knockout blow achieved the Germans could go on to defeat the slow mobilizing (so it was anticipated) Russians on the Eastern Front.

Things did not work out as planned; the German advance was halted in a counter stroke at the Battle of the Marne (the plan was already badly awry by then), and both sides found themselves in trenches and static. There did seem a solution, however — outflanking.

This stage of the war, from early September onwards, is often misleadingly called the Race for the Sea; its more accurate name would be the Race for the Open Flank. Both sides spent the next two months trying to get around the northernmost edge of the other's army. The British Expeditionary Force was removed from the position it held well to the south on the river Aisne and transferred north to take part in this attempt. Sir John French (the British commander) and his troops were engaged in a fierce struggle that spread from La Bassee northwards. The gap was finally plugged forward of Ypres in some of the most heroic actions that the British army has ever fought. To the north the line was held by the Belgian army, which had ensured its safety by the opening of the dykes. In 1914 an Anglo French force had fought a most successful action in the rises around Ypres and ensured for that town immortality in British history.

The Commonwealth War Graves Commission

Whatever other impression you take away after visiting the battlefields, I expect that the most enduring will be of the tremendous care and concern that the War Graves Commission takes to maintain the beauty and tranquility of the Commonwealth war cemeteries, of which there are hundreds scattered across the battlefields of northern Europe. It is also an organization that I have found to be unfailingly helpful and courteous, and always willing to help where at all possible. The following publications are obtainable from the Commission - a full list and up to date price list may be obtained from the address below - which the visitor using this guide might find helpful:

1. **Michelin Map** 1:200000 overprinted with British cemeteries, an index provided.
2. **The Unending Vigil by Philip Longworth. Published by Leo Cooper. Revised 1985.** A most interesting account of the history and development of the Commission.

The Commission will also help to find the grave or memorial of a relative; however over one million British and Empire servicemen died in the Great War, so do not expect miracles. The following information is vital, though not every piece is as essential as some others. It would help the Commission to know the following:

A. Name (as full as possible — ie all Christian names), rank and number.
B. Regiment and preferably which battalion. Some regiments had tens of battalions, so this will help.
C. Date of death. As near as possible - but even a year is helpful.
D. Place of death - ie France and Flanders, Mesopotamia, Gallipoli - this is always useful.

The Commission will reply, if they have found the person, with as full details as they have available, along with precise details as regards the location of the cemetery or memorial. The address of the Commission is as follows:
COMMONWEALTH WAR GRAVES COMMISSION, 2, MARLOW ROAD, MAIDENHEAD,BERKS S16 7AX. Telephone number: 0628 34221

Advice to Tourers

These various hints are offered as tips that I have found useful over the years that I have been visiting the battlefields. They are by no means fully comprehensive, and are based very much on my own tastes! They are placed in no particular order.

MAPS. I have often been amazed how poorly prepared in this regard British motorists frequently are. We have tried to take especial care in this guide to provide you with good, clear maps, but undoubtedly failings will creep in, despite our best endeavours. Therefore I would strongly recommend that you equip yourselves with at least the first of the following:

1. Institut Geographique National 1: 100000 Numbers 2 and 3
These maps cover the area under discussion in the guide. They can certainly be obtained at the Dover Terminal, and are becoming increasingly available elsewhere. They cost about 20 French Francs, and are often found in good French stationers.

2. The Michelin map Number 53. You may obtain this from the CWGC, details of which are to be found below. This marks on it nearly all British cemeteries (and all the major ones). Omitted quite often are Communal Cemeteries where only a few British soldiers might be buried.

3. You can also obtain a French and Belgian equivalent of our OS maps, but they are expensive: the 1:50000 is about 25 FF and the 1: 25000 is about 40FF. (Please allow for fluctuations in price!). The Belgian equivalent is very hard to come by, but certainly a 1:50000 was obtained by me from the Ypres tourist office last time I was there. They are detailed and useful items, but it can bring the enthusiast close to financial ruin if an attempt is made to cover the whole Western Front. If only from the selfish point of view, thank heavens the Great War was generally so static!

GUIDES. The number of guides that have appeared over recent years, especially on the Great War, has mushroomed; those on the Second War are relatively few. These are ones that I have used:

Before Endeavours Fade by Rose E Coombs, MBE After the Battle Publications. This is a quite outstanding guide to the Battlefields of the First World War, and has taken me (and literally thousands of others) to places that we would never have discovered without her book. Generally speaking her comments are limited to memorials and cemeteries, some anecdotes and a general outline of battles and so forth. She takes you to where things are, and then allows you to follow matters up for yourself. She uses the Michelin 1: 200000 map, which is fine, but rather small scale; and occasionally the very detailed directions go wrong, not least because progress in the shape of roadworks and town development will go on. For even the moderately keen enthusiast, this book is a must. Available in Belgium at the various museums I have mentioned, but also in good bookshops in the UK and obvious sales points such as the National Army Museum and Imperial War Museum. Costs about £8 in Paperback.

Flanders Then and Now by John Giles After the Battle Publications. £16.95. This was originally published in 1970 under the title of the Ypres Salient, Flanders Then and Now but this is a new, revised edition with updated photographs. It is not a full guide, but looks at particular sectors, some of them in considerable detail. It compares photographs taken then with others taken in almost identical spots now, has some reminiscenses and a number of maps, including one or two trench maps. On my third or fourth trip out to Flanders I found it a very useful way of getting something of the feel of that war.

The Battle Book of Ypres by Beatrix Brice. £15. This book has just recently been reprinted, first coming out in 1927. It is a topographical guide to the area around Ypres, taking villages and copses and other important points and explaining some particular event that took place there, often through the eyes of those who partook in it. It tends to make the British blond haired heroes who could do no wrong, but it should be recalled that it was compiled shortly after the end of the war.It is pricey, but again for the keen a very useful part of the library that the really enthusiastic battlefield visitors will need to carry around with them.

Fields of Death: Battle Scenes of the First World War by Peter Slowe and Richard Woods. Published by Robert Hale. £12.95. This deals with all sectors of the British war effort, but has a sizeable chunk on the Ypres area. It deals with particular exploits, referring to accounts often given in autobiographies of men who were there. There are illustrations, and line maps to show you where things are now, so that it is made possible to follow the action. A useful companion to Battlefield touring for the enthusiast.

A new guide to the Battlefields of Northern France and the Low Countries by Michael Glover. Published by Michael Joseph. £14.95. This covers other wars besides the First, and is far more general. In our area he deals with Calais and Dunkirk in 1940, and Ypres in 1914 and 1917. The maps tend not to be all that good, though the AA has provided a 'route card'.

Holt's Battlefield Guides: The Ypres Salient. £1.75. A rudimentary but useful guide (with itineraries and map) around the Battlefield. Obtainable in some of the museums in the Salient area, and I seem to remember also from the Tourist office at Ypres.

There are of course other guides available, for example **The Ypres Salient** which may be obtained in Belgium. I am pleased to say that the excellent little map that accompanies it has recently been brought up to date. The text is made a little tedious by the fact that the it comes in four languages.

All of these guides (with the possible exception of the Glover and of course the locally produced Belgian guide) may be obtained from: **The London Stamp Exchange Ltd, 5 Buckingham Street, The Strand, London, WC2N 6BS, Telephone 01-839-4684.**

MUSEUMS. There are two major national museums which have good displays of Great War material, foremost amongst which is the Imperial War Museum. It also has a vast photographic library, as well as a library of books and deposited tape and manuscript documents relating to wars since the outbreak of the Great War. Whilst these facilities are available for general use, it is necessary to make an appointment. The displays here have improved tremendously in the last few years, and there is a useful bookshop. They also have a programme of film shows. Its address is: Imperial War Museum, Lambeth, London SE1 6HZ Telephone 01-735-8922. The other great museum - one which has done a tremendous amount to fill the gap in public awareness of our military past, is the National Army Museum, Royal Hospital Road, Chelsea. I suggest that a visit here might be accompanied by one to the Royal Hospital, the home of the Chelsea Pensioners. The nearest tube is Sloane Square. This covers all British wars, has an excellent section devoted to the Great War, and also shows the development of the British Army from its earliest beginnings. This is well worth a visit — one of my favourite London museums. Small, but very useful shop and snack facilities are provided.

For those of you well out of the London area there is probably a military museum normally of the regimental variety somewhere relatively close by. Try ringing the closest Army Information Office to you: they probably will not love you, but with luck they should be able to help. There is a 'Guide to Military Museums' by Terence Wise, published by Athena Books of 34, Imperial Crescent, Town Moor, Doncaster S Yorks DN2 5BU at £1.95 for the committed!

ESSENTIALS. Now this is very much my own list, but it is what bitter experience has taught me is the sort of thing that is needed!
1. A corkscrew and bottle opener. If one is going to enjoy wine or beer for the picnic.
2. Toilet Paper. It is a mystery to me why nations that can provide the very best of cuisine so often (but fortunately decreasingly frequently) do not cater for the after effects. Anyway, be prepared is a perfectly sound scout motto.
3. Film. Far more expensive on the continent than in the UK. Slide film is cheaper on the boat in my experience.
4. A breadknife - for the interminable baguettes on the picnics!
5. An icebag or box to keep chilled those beers you might need, soft drinks or whatever. It is amazing to me why cafes in both France and Belgium have a tendency to close when they are most needed — ie at lunchtime.
6. Waterproof, wellingtons or sturdy shoes.
7. A good camera; for the keen you will need a respectable zoom lens and possibly a tripod.

FOOD AND DRINK. You can certainly eat well in both France and Belgium. Really high class establishments are available in St Omer, Cassel, Ypres and Poperinge — and that is only to my knowledge, I am sure there are others. Advice from the Tourist Office is normally pretty dispassionate. My own experience would lead me to suggest the Palace Hotel in Poperinge, and the St Nicholas Hotel in Ypres; the Regina Hotel in Ypres is also, I understand, good. There are innumerable places where you can pick up simple cafe meals in the evening - a good soup, omelette and frites and a beer will probably set you back about £3.50.

Breakfast in many hotels is of the continental variety: ie plenty of bread and jam and coffee. Some will offer you ham and cheese, and the Palace Hotel pities the British by providing a boiled egg! If your stomache can take it, you will have effectively had your lunch by the time you leave the table. As regards lunch, I am a great one for eating it on the hoof, and the most pleasant spot is either in or near a British cemetery in which I can see nothing wrong so long as the most elementary and obvious decencies are observed. Supermarkets will provide all that you require — ham, local cheeses, superb tomatoes and fruit, and whatever you might like to drink. Belgium has a variety of beers, but of course the most prevalent is Stella Artois. Fairly cheap wines are also available, but the place to get these is in France. A word of warning here: French wine is really good value up to about 35FF a bottle — much more than that and the prices begin to compare with the UK. Pates are also good and varied, but again more especially in France. Bread should be obtained from the many bakeries that can be found — there are a couple at least on the Grand Place in Ypres, and one good one at Poperinge. Rolls may be brought here, which make a welcome change from the baguette.

After a hard day touring around, I often find a soothing glass of whisky works wonders - besides a shower, of course. Duty Free is probably the best place to equip yourself for this part of touring if your tastes are so inclined, but spirits are cheaper in the shops than in the UK. Bottled water (not necessary, but nice) is far, far cheaper if bought in the supermarket.

BANKING. It is always useful to have cash, but most hotels will accept Access or Visa, and so will banks when exchanging money. Eurocheque has, of course, made life much easier. Garages generally accept credit cards.

SHOPPING. The best place to get essentials is a supermarket — there is quite a sizeable one in Ypres opposite the Cathedral, and one on the road coming in to Poperinge from Vlamertinge. There are plenty in St Omer. The little 'corner' grocers are found here and there: the two that I often use are close to the Menin Gate in Ypres and close to Talbot House in Poperinge. They are open early and shut late. Monday seems to find a lot of shops closed in Ypres and Poperinge. Cafes often close on one day of the week - this varies. Hotels are often shut on Sundays, so if you plan to arrive on that day ensure that you have booked into a hotel before you arrive. English newspapers are available, (at a price and a day late) from the Presse Shop found on the right hand side of the road when approaching the Menin Gate from the square.

ACCOMMODATION. I have stayed in a number of hotels and one campsite in the Ypres area. I can especially recommend the Palace in Poperinge, but I would also suggest the Regina and St Nicholas in Ypres. Somewhere in the £15 area would cover a single person and breakfast - obviously somewhat less for a shared room. Bathroom and toilet are normally en suite. Less expensive is Talbot House; the rooms are large, but do not have toilet and bathroom facilities in them. Hotels obviously exist in plenty at Calais and Dunkirk. There is accommodation, naturally at St Omer and Cassel, but a pleasant place to stop is De Panne, a big Belgian seaside resort. De Panne also has a long sandy beach, though of course the water does tend to be a little chilly! When visiting the Cap Griz Nez area for the Atlantic Wall, or indeed exploring Calais then the Hotel Normandy, Place de Verdun, Wissant, is ideal (Telephone: 35.90.11.)

The best camp site (the only one?) is situated at Kemmel, Camping Ypra There is a large caravan park and space for tents. There is a restaurant/cafe, as well as a quite extensive camp shop. Showers (paid for by tokens) and clean toilets are a feature of the site. It is well situated for access to the motorway - Dunkirk, for example, is just about an hour away. The telephone number is (057) - 444631. It is signposted off the La Clytte — Kemmel road.

MEDICAL. As for any trip abroad, it is essential to be suitably insured. Many continental countries now insist that you have a First Aid Box in the car — make sure that it is kept filled with the essentials. Trotting across fields might lead you to come into contact with rusty barbed wire or whatever, so I recommend that you ensure that your tetanus booster is up to date.

VEHICLE. Ensure that you are insured against breakdown etc. It is the law in some continental countries that you carry some basic spares, and it is a useful idea in any case (far cheaper in the UK). Have a warning triangle which you can put up in case of breakdown. Petrol is cheaper in the UK, and far cheaper in Belgium than in France. Beware cycle lanes — it can be somewhat unnerving having a bicycle coming at you from the opposite direction; and you must avoid parking actually on them.

WARNINGS. Private property obviously has to be respected. Many are quite willing for you to proceed across their land, but it does not take much to ask, and it saves all sorts of embarrassment if you do!

War Time Relics are quite often HIGHLY DANGEROUS. You should treat everything which is obviously not a shovel or a piece of barbed wire or something obviously not lethal in intent with extreme caution. Souvenirs of your visit are often obtainable at some of the Trench Museums.

As for many rural areas, there are a vast variety of dogs lurking in unsuspecting corners. They are invariably under control, but they make a tremendous racket with their yowling and howling!

TOURIST OFFICES: Ypres — Town Hall, 8900 Ieper, Belgium. Tel. No. 20.26.26.
Poperinge — Town Hall, The Square, 8970 Poperinge, Belgium. Tel. No. 33.40.81.
De Panne — Town Hall, Zeelaan 21. Tel. No. 41.13.02/04.
Belgian National Tourist Office, 38 Dover Street, London W1X 3RB, Tel. No. 01.499.5379.
St Omer — Office du Tourisme, Hotel de Ville, Place du Marechal Foch Tel No 98.40.88.
Calais — Office du Tourisme, 12 Boulevard Clemenceau - also will arrange hotel reservations, given a week or so's notice. Tel No 34.34.22
Dunkirk - Office du Tourisme, Beffroi, Rue Clemenceau Tel No 66.79.21
French Government Tourist Office, 178 Piccadilly, London WIV OAL

General Information

THE BRITISH ARMY was a far different organisation in 1914 from what it is today; the vast majority of its manpower lay in the infantry, and of course there was not the specialised mechanical, transport and technical branches of the army that there are today. Even the Royal Signals was a branch of the Royal Engineers during the war.

The Regiment was the basis of the British Army — both cavalry and infantry. In this account I refer to a number of regiments — the Gordon Highlanders (the Gordons) are an example. By the end of the war some of these regiments had as many as 25 battalions. A battalion had approximately 1,000 men, but this varied very much. A minimum size would be somewhere in the region of 700, except for unusual circumstances such as heavy casualties in a particular action. Reinforcements arrived to a battalion in the form of drafts — as the war progressed they quite often had nothing to do with the territorial association of the regiment.

The Army had different types of battalions during the war — Regular, that is soldiers who took the army as a career; Territorial, that is soldiers who were members of the army as a part time occupation and had some other form of employment; and New Army or Kitchener, that is those who joined for 'three years or the duration' initially on the appeal of Lord Kitchener.

The British Army in France and Flanders, as the north European theatre of operations was called, also had great assistance from the Dominions — the Australians, the Canadians, New Zealanders, South Africans and an Indian Army Corps.

The ranks of the army were largely as they are now — from the private soldier to the lieutenant colonel in a battalion, a brigade commanded by a brigadier (until early in 1918 consisted of four battalions, then it was changed to three), a division commanded by a major general (consisting of three brigades), a corps commanded by a lieutenant general (consisting of a minimum of two divisions, and often a few more), and an army commanded by a general and which had a minimum of two corps. Divisions were moved from corps to corps, but below that level the units were relatively stable.

The Royal Artillery and the Royal Engineers were attached to divisions and brigades; men in the artillery were known as Gunners and the Engineers as Sappers. As the war progressed specialist corps were established — for example the Machine Gun Corps and the Tank Corps.

The Royal Air Force was founded on 1 April 1918, succeeding the Royal Flying Corps. By the end of the war it possessed some 20,000 plus aircraft, compared with the couple of hundred at the beginning of the war. Until 1918 the ranks of the Royal Flying Corps were the same as for the army. Until the arrival of the fighter, most aircraft were used for observation, and the pilot was a non commissioned officer (NCO), with the officer doing the observing as a passenger — rather on the lines of a chauffeur and his gentleman!

TRENCHES are a source of considerable myth, and consequently misunderstanding. There was not just a single line of trenches facing each other from the Channel to the Swiss border as is often stated. The trench itself was a complex structure, with a number of technical terms to describe the fine points of its construction. For instance the front is a parapet, the rear a parados; the familiar zigzag arrangement is a traverse; shelters are dugouts and so on. The trench system was also deep — a front line trench, often thinly held, had a support trench within at the most a couple of hundred yards of its rear, and beyond that was a reserve trench. Connecting all these were a number of communications trenches which went further back to the rear — as far back as was necessary to protect the troops from hostile enemy fire, especially when they were under direct observation. The trench systems were protected by extensive and deep areas of barbed wire — sometimes many yards deep — which served as a most effective obstacle to enemy attack. Conditions in these trenches were variable, but in general pretty bloody; most were dug eight or nine feet into the ground, but in some sectors (for example just south of Ploegsteert Wood) the water table was so high that the trenches were effectively sandbag barricades.

Soldiers could expect to do four days in the front line, four days in support and four days in reserve on a rotation basis (again, according to conditions these periods became variable); but even in reserve they would be expected to work, carrying rations, repairing the wire in the front line and so forth. Every few months, especially after particularly heavy fighting and casualties, a unit would be sent out of the line altogether and move well to the rear to rest and train and carry out a more relaxed routine. The front line system of trenches might, therefore, be several hundred yards deep. Behind this first line of trenches was often a second line, normally not much more than a scratch on the ground and a plan on a map, some three or four miles away. Thus in the fighting on the Somme the Germans had a second line system more or less ready after the first line was captured.

MINE WARFARE began quite early on, and was particularly bloody on some of the French and German sectors. Both sides dug tunnels starting under their own defences, and then placed large quantities of explosives under the enemy front line. When these were blown both sides rushed to occupy the huge hole, a mine crater. Mine warfare was particulary heavy at St Eloi and Hill 60. It was less frequently used as time went on, but perhaps the most effective use of this type of warfare came surprisingly late, in 1917 at Messines Ridge. The visible consequences of these mines remain the most powerful reminders of the Great War — such as at St Eloi, Hill 60, and the various craters along the Messines Ridge, perhaps the largest and best known of which is the Spanbroekmollen or Lone Tree Crater near Wytschaete.

STRONGPOINTS. As the war progressed the Germans especially became adept at constructing reinforced concrete machine gun posts and strongpoints. Increasingly the front line trenches gave way, especially in Flanders, to a series of these connected by trenches, and away from heavily manned front line defences. Later still there was a tendency to go for defence in depth, lightly held front line positions, but deeper defence lines so that the enemy were allowed to exhaust themselves in an advance, and make themselves increasingly disjointed and therefore vulnerable to a counter attack. This was very much the case in the more mobile fighting of 1918.

TRENCH WARFARE also had a routine: Stand To was a custom observed by both sides — maximum presence on the Firing Steps (a ledge which enabled the troops to see over the parapet and thus fire at the enemy) in the hour or so before dawn and at dusk, to guard against a surprise attack. Often fires were banned in the front line, because if spotted it might attract trench mortar fire. The British were especially fearful of the Minenwerfer, a deadly mortar which fired a high explosive projectile extremely accurately. At nightime both sides put men out into No Man's Land, either to repair the wire, to ambush an enemy patrol, to examine the enemy wire or sometimes to carry out a limited raid and grab a prisoner or two from whom information about the state of the enemy on the other side might be obtained. A device that the British developed, the Bangalore Torpedo, was particularly effective at clearing a way through barbed wire. It was basically a pipe filled with explosives, which could be fitted to other ones and thus make a charge of suitable length.

Trench warfare was a complex and technical business; so were attacks — often rushed, but often meticulously planned, with detailed orders, complex artillery fire plans and a lot of thought. They often went very wrong: that is certainly true.

RELIGION In the section on Guise, I refer to a Roman Catholic heresy, Jansenism. Jansen was Bishop of Ypres from 1636 until his death in 1638. His theological viewpoints became known after his death and the publication of a posthumous work. Basically he suggested a more Protestant view of the path to salvation than the Roman Catholic church taught. He stressed the total sufficiency of Christ's death on the cross and mankind's own inadequacy. The teachings were condemned, but not before they had gained considerable support, especially amongst intellectuals, and the movement only really faded away in the nineteenth century. It was particularly strong in Flanders and Holland. The most characteristic symbol was the crucifix with the hands almost vertical above the head — indicating the route to heaven through Christ.

All through Europe it is quite common to come across wayside shrines, sometimes small chapels, sometimes a simple Calvary. These were placed by landowners or parishoners at various points along the road — often at crossroads — so that passers-by might stop and offer a prayer. They are still a common sight, and in the Great War their presence is remembered by frequent references on trench maps to 'crucifix corner'; soldiers in their memoirs often recall that a calvary or shrine had withstood shell fire and the general destruction all around them. Perhaps the most famous of these was the one at Neuve Chapelle, a few miles south of Armentieres.

Religion was a hot political subject in France at the turn of the century. Religious orders were expelled from France, and so many Catholic clergy fled to England, that the normal language in use at Archbishop's House at Westminster Cathedral was French! At the outbreak of World War One the French government tried to stop men in uniform going to mass; but the move was given up when Foch refused to be intimidated. Superior officers were supposed to report transgressors; Foch (then a full General and commanding the Northern Army Group from Cassel) reported himself, but refused to name others in the church on the grounds that he was too busy praying, and it was not his habit to look around in Church. The French government conscripted priests just like any other men — as did the Germans, Austrians and Italians. The late Pope John XXIII was a sergeant in the Italian Army. The British government did not.

The atmosphere of secularism in France was very much present after the war: visitors should note how hardly a village war memorial in France has any Christian symbolism to it — they nearly always portray a soldier in a heroic pose, or some symbol of the French state. The exceptions are the great national French shrines at Verdun and Notre Dame de Lorette, which owe their existence to the local Catholic Bishops of Verdun and Arras respectively.

PLACENAMES are more confusing in this part of the world than most other places. Ypres appears on road signs in Belgium as Ieper and so forth. British usage during the war followed the French — the maps of the times had the French names and this underlines their cultural dominance over the Flemings at the time. The British found these names impossible, and anglicised them any way that they could: Wytschaete became Whitesheet, Godeswaersvelde became God wears velvet; they even parodied them by naming Aid Posts Bandaghem, Mendinghem and Dozinghem in the Poperinge area.

ESTAMINETS AND RELAXATION. When not in the line soldiers tried to find relaxation in the villages behind the lines. Frequently some brave civilians remained behind, and provided a basic food service of egg and chips which supplemented the diet of largely tinned rations. A local estaminet (inn) provided cheap drink, though the beer was almost universally detested as being weak and watered down. The local brew is Stella Artois, and British palates were far from ready for lager in 1914. However Vin Blanc, which became Vin Plonk was popular, and some developed a taste of mixing it with cassis, a syrup not unlike ribena. Whilst in the rear areas it was often possible to take a mass bath, usually in the halved giant barrels of the local brewery. Clean clothes, fumigated and not much else, were collected, but the eggs of the lice soon hatched, and the soldiers were as lousy as they had ever been. Leave varied, but as the war progressed it became more regular, given out on a rather more equitable basis, and for a longer effective period. It could be up to a year, however, and not infrequently longer, between each period of leave, at least for the other ranks.

ACKNOWLEDGEMENTS

I have had much assistance in the production of this Guidebook on the Battlefields of Europe. I first went to the Battlefields in 1968, when I was fourteen, taken by my father. He has accompanied me on most of my many trips since then, and I would like to thank him for his help, advice and not least for helping to correct some of my more transparent howlers in the text. I owe a debt to Rose Coombs and John Giles, whose own guides inspired me (and many others) to tour the ground of France and Flanders with a new interest and from a different perspective. I owe particular thanks to Tony Spagnoly, who has been generous in sharing his knowledge and proffering his vast expertise of the battles that took place 'over there'. The members of the Western Front Association have helped me tremendously in diverse ways: the Chairman and Committee by allowing me to use their photographic material, Trevor Pidgeon (the cartographer) with his assistance on Trench Maps and their interpretation on the occasional tricky point, and the wider membership itself with whom I have travelled on numerous tours and who have shared with me their enthusiasm.

The book has its origins in a suggestion from the Chairman of the Barnsley Chronicle Group, Sir Nicholas Hewitt, who has continued to support the venture despite the interminable length of time that it has taken to produce the finished article. To all the members of the Graphics Department of that newspaper I am particulary grateful; whatever merit readers might find in this guide will be largely due to their work of design and production. Jon Cooksey has helped in the editing and further research required — including making contact with a large number of regimental and war museums both in this country and abroad.

One of the pleasures of this type of touring has been the large number of friendships I have made abroad, and in this particular instance I would like to thank Albert and Tony of the Salient Museum in Ypres and Jacques of the museum on Hill 62 at Sanctuary Wood.

I need, I suppose, to apologise to the significant number of pupils at Ratcliffe who have accompanied me on my Battlefield Tours, as I took them off our planned itinerary to some obscure part covered in this guide to check the odd point or two; and also to my brethren in the community here who endure my, perhaps, eccentric interest.

Finally I acknowledge a debt to two people above all: my great grandfather, whom I never knew, who religiously kept the copies of the War Illustrated throughout the conflict for his serving son, the pages of which enthralled me as a boy; and to my grandfather, who kept a diary of his war service which provided the family connection with that horrendous conflict. Unfortunately he was never to know of the enthusiasm, as he died when I was seven.

I would like to thank the following publishers, museums, individuals and organisations who have been helpful in the production of information, excerpts and illustrative material for this book. Firstly, the Publishers: Hodder and Stoughton, *Flames of Calais* by Airey Neave; The Crowood Press, *A Sergeant-Major's War* by Ernest Shepherd ed B Rossor, 1987; London Stamp Exchange, *A History of the Welsh Guards (1919)* by Dudley Ward, reprinted 1988; Thomas Harmsworth Publishing *The Burgoyne Diaries*, 1985; Collins Publishers, *Undertones of War* by Edmund Blunden, 1928; Sono Nis Press, Victoria B.C. Canada, *The Journal of Private Fraser* ed R. H. Roy, 1985; Buchan and Enright, *A Passionate Prodigality* new edition 1985, William Kimber and Co (part of Thorsons Publishing Group Ltd), *Armageddon Road, a VCs Diary, 1914-1916*, ed. T. Norman 1982; *Massacre on the Road to Dunkirk* by L. Aitken, reprinted 1988; MacMillan London Ltd for *Fifteen Rounds a Minute, The Grenadiers at War 1914* by J. M. Craster.

In Calais I would like to thank: the Calais Tourist Board for their assistance and the Calais Chamber of Commerce for allowing the use of a map based on the one that they produce; Mr David Davies of the Hotel Normandy, Wissant; M. Georges Fauquet of the Calais Historical Society and M. Henri Hidoine and Michel Tahon of the Calais War Museum. In Belgium, Albert Beke of the Salient Museum in the Cloth Hall, Jacques of Sanctuary Wood Museum, Hill 62, the curators of the 'Trench of Death' at Dixmude and Talbot House in Poperinge assisted me by allowing me to photograph exhibits, gave me the use of some of their material, and provided sustenance. Peter Taylor for making available his extensive collection of wartime photographs. Mr E. A. Sollars for the excellent print of the action at Calais in 1940, by Cuneo, that we were able to use for our front cover, and permission to use it from Colonel J. R. Baker, MC, curator of The Royal Green Jackets Museum. The following Regimental Secretaries or Regimental Staff have been most helpful: Mr E. Bartholomew, Education Officer, The Tank Museum; Lt Col (retd) A. M. Gabb OBE, Worcester and Sherwood Foresters; Major D. J. H. Farquaharson, 16/5 Queens Royal Lancers; Mr Alan Morris, London Scottish; Major (retd) W. Shaw MBE, Royal Highland Fusiliers and Capt J. E. Mendoca, 1st Battalion Queen's Lancashire Regiment. Illustrations have been provided from the above and from THCL Books and Raymond Walsh (Ervine Andrews VC); the Commandant, Brigadier Tweedie of Queen Victoria's School, Dunblane (Laurence Farm); Dr Fleischer and the staff of the Bundesarciv, Freiburg, and above all the unfailingly helpful staff of the Department of Photographs at the Imperial War Museum, with especial thanks to Mike Willis for guiding me around the array of photographs, and on more than one occasion pointing me in the right direction. Finally I would like to thank Richard Boyd for translating communications with our German sources.

BIBLIOGRAPHY

Aitken, Leslie, *Massacre on the Road to Dunkirk* (Wm. Kimber, reprinted 1988 by Thorsons Publishing Group Limited)

Bairnsfather, Bruce, *Bullets and Billets* (Grant Richard Ltd., 1916)

Barnet, Corelli, *Marlborough* (Eyre Methuen Ltd., 1974)

Bean, C. E. W., *The AIF in France Vol. IV* (University of Queensland Press, republished 1982)

Belhaven, *The War Diary of the Master of Belhaven* (John Murray, 1924)

Blaxland, Gregory, *Destination Dunkirk* (Military Book Society, 1973)

Blunden, Edmund, *Undertones of War* (Collins, 1928)

Brewer, Gardener & Brodie, edited by, *The Letters and Papers, Foreign and Domestic, of the Reign of Henry VIII 1509-1547* (H.M.S.O.)

The Burgoyne Diaries (Thomas Harmsworth Publishing, 1985)

Chapman, Guy, *A Passionate Prodigality* (Buchan & Enright Publishers, New Edition, 1985)

Cipolla, Carlo M., edited by, *The Fontana Economic History of Europe* Vols I and II, 1972 and 1974 respectively

Cole, Christopher, *McCudden VC* (William Kimber, 1967)

Congreve, edited by Terry Norman, *Armageddon Road, a VC's Diary 1914-1916* (William Kimber, 1982)

Cooksey, Jon, *Pals — The 13th and 14th Battalions York and Lancaster Regiment* (Wharncliffe Publishing, 1986)

Coombs, Rose E. B., *Before Endeavours Fade* (After the Battle Publication, 4th edition, 1983)

Cuich, Myrone N., *Armes Secretes et ourvrages mysterieux de Dunkerque a Cherbourg* (Turcoing 1984)

The Dictionary of National Biography, Various. (OUP)

Ellis, Major L. F., *History of the Second World War; The War in France and Flanders 1939-1940*, (H.M.S.O. 1953)
   History of the Second World War; Victory in the West Vol 8 and 18 (H.M.S.O. 1962, 1968)

Firth, C. H., *Cromwell's Army* (University Paperbacks, 1962)

Fraser, edited by Roy, Reginald H., *The Journal of Private Fraser* (Sono Nis Press, 1985)

Gibbs, Sir Philip, *The War Despatches* (Tandem, 1966)

Giles, John, *The Ypres Salient, Flanders Then and Now* (Picardy Press, New Edition, 1979)

Gillingham, John, *The Wars of the Roses* (Weidenfeld & Nicholson, 1981)

Glover, Michael, *A New Guide to the Battlefields of Northern France and the Low Countries* (Michael Joseph, 1987)

Goodman, Anthony, *The Wars of the Roses* (Routledge & Keegan Paul, 1981)

Hay, Denys, *Europe in the 14th and 15th Centuries* (Longman, 1966)

Horne, Alistair, *To Lose a Battle, France 1940*, (Penguin, 1979)

James, Brigadier E. A., *British Regiments, 1914-1918* (Samson Books Ltd., 1978)

Jeffries, edited by Craster, J. M., *Fifteen Rounds a Minute, The Grenadiers at War* (MacMillan London Ltd., 1976)

Kirby, H. L. and Walsh, R. R., *The Seven VCs of Stoneyhurst College* (THCL Books, 1987)

Longworth, Philip, *The Unending Vigil* (New Edition, 1985)

Lord, Walter, *The Miracle of Dunkirk* (Penguin, 1984)

Macdonald, Lyn, *1914* (Michael Joseph, 1987)

MacWilliams, J. and Steel, R. J., *Gas, the Battle for Ypres, 1915* (Vanwell Publishing Ltd., 1985)

May, Brigadier General E. S., *An Introduction to Military Geography* (Hugh Rees Ltd., 1909)

Maze, Paul, *A Frenchman in Khaki* (William Heineman, 1934)

Neave, Airey, *Flames of Calais* (Hodder and Stoughton, 1972)

Official History of the War, France and Flanders 1914 Vol II, 1915 Vol I and Vol II, 1916 Vol I, 1917 Vol I and Vol II

O'Rahilly, A., *Father William Doyle SJ* (Longman, 1925)

Prescott, John F., *In Flanders Fields. The Story of John McCrae* (Boston Mills Press, 1985)

Prestwich, Michael, *The Three Edwards* (Weidenfeld & Nicholson, 1980)

Pulteney and Rice, *The Immortal Salient* (John Murray, 1925)

Register of the Victoria Cross (This England Books, 1981)

Rice, Beatrix, *The Battle Book of Ypres* (John Murray, 1927)

Rogers, H. C. B., *Battles and Generals of the Civil War* (Sealy Servis & Co., 1968)

Scarisbrick, J. J., *Henry VIII* (Pelican, 1968)

Scouller, *The Armies of Queen Anne* (Oxford, 1966)

Seaton, A., *The Fall of Fortress Europe, 1943-1945* (Batsford Ltd., 1981)

Shelby, L. R., *John Rogers, Tudor Military Engineer* (OUP, 1967)

Shephard, Ernest, edited by Rossor, Bruce, *A Sergeant-Major's War* (Crowood Press, 1987)

Slowe, Peter and Woods, Richard, *Fields of Death, Battle Scenes of the First World War* (Robert Hale, 1986)

Stacey, C. P., *The Canadian Army 1939-1945. An Official Historical Summary* (Ottawa, 1948)

Talbot House, *The Pilgrim's Guide to the Ypres Salient* (1920)

Toland, John, *Adolf Hitler* (Ballantine Books, 1976)

Waley, Daniel, *Later Medieval Europe* (Longman Green & Co., 1964)

Ward, C. H. Dudley, *History of the Welsh Guards* (reprinted by the London Stamp Exchange, 1988)

Warner, Philip, *Passchendale* (Sedgwick & Jackson Ltd., 1987)

INDEX

168